DONNA KOOLER'S

encyclopedia
of
sewing

A LEISURE ARTS PUBLICATION

I

DONNA KOOLER'S

encyclopedia
of
sewing

10 9 8 7 6 5 4 3 2 1

Donna Kooler's Encyclopedia of Sewing
"A Leisure Arts Publication"

Library of Congress Control Number: 2009936437

ISBN 13: 978-1-60140-456-5
ISBN 10: 1-60140-456-5

contributors

produced by

KOOLER
DESIGN
STUDIO
inc.

published by

LEISURE
ARTS

If you have questions or comments
please contact:

LEISURE ARTS CUSTOMER SERVICE
5701 RANCH DRIVE
LITTLE ROCK, AR 72223-9633
www.leisurearts.com

KOOLER DESIGN STUDIO, INC.
399 TAYLOR BLVD., SUITE 104
PLEASANT HILL, CA 94523
www.koolerdesign.com

PRINTED IN CHINA

creative director
DONNA KOOLER

editor in chief
JUDY SWAGER

encyclopedia editor
SUSAN BECK

writers
SUSAN BECK
HISTORY: NICOLE SCALESSA
SHELLEY CARDA

project coordinator
BASHA KOOLER

proofreader
JUDY SWAGER

indexer
SUSAN BECK

book design/production
ASHLEY ROCHA

illustrations
MAURA HOUSTON

support
LINDA GILLUM
MARSHA HINKSON
VIRGINIA HANDLEY-RIVETT

projects designed and made by
SUSAN BECK
SALLEY BOWMAN
SARAH GOODMAN
JO LEICHTE
APRIL OLIVEIRA-WARD
VICKI TRACY

photography/color separations
DIANNE WOODS

photo stylist
BASHA KOOLER

models
CASEY DACANEY
KATY HANKINS
RAYNA PITTER

editor's notes

Even the smallest book needs a team of people to put it together. Writers, editors, illustrators, page designers, proofers, fact checkers…and the list goes on. When the book is an encyclopedia, the list is even longer and it's no exception for *Donna Kooler's Encyclopedia of Sewing*. When Donna asked me to be part of the team that put the encyclopedia together, I knew it would be a challenge, but an exciting and fun one! Having sewn for most of my life, starting at 10 years old, and having worked in the sewing industry for a European sewing machine company for 22 years, I felt that I had more than enough information to share. My goal was to put together an encyclopedia that encouraged and helped beginners, inspired the more experienced stitcher, and offered a reference book for all sewers, no matter what type of stitching they do. What I didn't anticipate was how much it would renew my love of sewing, making me eager to try new things and re-visit favorite techniques. The team members who contributed to this encyclopedia have a wide variety of talents that blended together to create a useful and inspiring resource for sewers everywhere, and I am grateful to each one. I especially want to thank the following:

Linda Lee of The Sewing Workshop—you'll see her garments throughout the pages showing exquisite style and impeccable construction details. Sarah Goodman, who worked by my side to create samples and double-check directions. Vicki Tracy, who offered sewn samples and fun projects with her unique design sense. Donna Lang and Belinda Gibson who generously shared samples from their bodies of work. And, of course, Donna and her daughter Basha Kooler, who had the vision and the organization for creating this encyclopedia.

Susan Beck

acknowledgments

I started this journey in 1999 at the request of Ann Van Wagner Young and Sandra Case of Leisure Arts who persuaded me to produce an encyclopedia for needle-workers. It's hard to believe that now, ten years later, I am completing the fifth encyclopedia in the series; starting with the Encyclopedia of Needlework *then adding* Crochet, Knitting, Quilting *and now* Sewing, *for the unbelievable total of 1280 pages of information. None of these amazing volumes could have been designed, written, photographed and produced without scores of dedicated and talented experts.*

Many thanks to our Editor, Susan Beck, who worked tirelessly to write, edit, and supervise every word, illustration, and image of the 240 pages in this book. Susan's passion for the art of sewing and patience as a teacher provided us with the perfect writer and editor for the Encyclopedia of Sewing. *A special acknowledgment to Basha Kooler who coordinated the entire team, in addition to doing research, art direction, photo styling, chauffeuring, e-mailing, scheduling, and, yes, at times even babysitting to make this book possible. I am very proud to be her mother and am pleased to have the opportunity of working with her. Also my appreciation for a job well done by Ashley Rocha, Nicole Scalessa, Dianne Woods, Judy Swager, Maura Houston, Shelley Carda, and the many project designers who contributed their knowledge, talents, and resources to bring you this beautiful book.*

Just as I took a chance a decade ago to venture into new areas demanding new skills, I hope you will be equally daring when you pick up this encyclopedia and either begin or continue your sewing journey. I hope you will find the material within useful and informative, enticing you to venture down the road to your own creative projects. Nothing has been as rewarding for me as the challenge of creating beauty through needlework. I invite you to join in the ongoing traditions that have allowed us to bring forth beauty from our hands and our imaginations.

Donna Kooler

contents

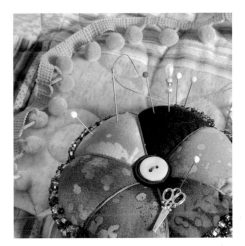

beginnings

INTRODUCTION.............. 9
HISTORY OF SEWING 10

sewing basics

INTRODUCTION.............. 27
TYPES OF SEWING............ 28
SKILL LEVEL................. 30
SEWING SUPPLIES 32
FABULOUS FABRICS........... 36
PATTERNS 40
INTERFACING AND STABILIZERS . 44
PRESSING 47
SEWING ROOMS 52

hand sewing

INTRODUCTION.............. 59
HAND SEWING SUPPLIES....... 60
HAND SEWING TECHNIQUES ... 62

machine sewing

INTRODUCTION.............. 67
MACHINE BASICS 68
EMBROIDERY MACHINES 82
SERGERS 84
SPECIALTY EQUIPMENT 88

construction essentials

INTRODUCTION.............. 91
SEAMS AND SEAM FINISHES ... 92
CONSTRUCTION ESSENTIALS ... 98
CONSTRUCTION TECHNIQUES.. 100
CLOSURES.................. 112
PRACTICE PATTERNS......... 120

custom elements

INTRODUCTION.............. 127
DECORATIVE DETAILS........ 128
EMBELLISHMENTS 142

specialty sewing

INTRODUCTION.............. 163
FLEECE AND FUR............. 164
LEATHER AND PAPER 166
PLASTIC AND SHEERS........ 168
PLAIDS.................... 170
SEWING FOR CHILDREN 171

projects

INTRODUCTION.............. 173
BOHEMIAN BAG 174
SINGING CANARY PILLOW 178
SCRAPPY COTTAGE QUILT...... 182
DEEP POCKET CHEF'S APRON .. 188
GYPSY SHRUG 194
TROPICAL TABLE RUNNER 198
BERRY PIE PINCUSHION 202
BUGS IN THE GARDEN BOOK.. 206
LET IT RAIN YELLOW SLICKER.. 212
SQUARE YOKE BLOUSE........ 216
RUFFLED WEDGE SKIRT 220
GARDEN PARTY LAP QUILT... 224

for your information

HISTORY NOTES................ 230
BIBLIOGRAPHY 230
FURTHER READING 231

RESOURCES 232
GLOSSARY.................. 233
INDEX 236

CONTRIBUTORS 240
FEATURED PATTERNS 240

AT ITS MOST BASIC, sewing is the joining of two pieces of material (usually fabric) with needle and thread. Anyone can do it simply by piercing a threaded needle in and out of the two layers of fabric. It's easy to understand, easy to do, and within a minute or two, you can sew your first piece. But, as with most skills, you can start at the beginning and take it as far as you want. The craft of sewing is interesting because there are literally thousands of ways to do it. You can learn a little in a short time and sew for the rest of your life with a few simple skills; or, you can learn a lot over a long period of time, exploring new techniques, refining your skills, and increasing your competency to the point where you can create almost anything with needle and thread.

Sewers come in all sizes, shapes, genders, and personalities, and they sew for a million different reasons. Some want to save money, some want to make unique clothing that no one else has, and others just feel a need to create. Many love the process of sewing and find it relaxing; some sew because they love the finished project and the fact that they made it. Before sewing became a choice that people made, it did not matter whether you loved the process or the finished project more—you sewed because you had to make clothes to wear and bedding to warm your family. Today, things have changed—people sew because they want to; it makes them feel good. Many times the good feelings continue after you stop sewing. If you made yourself a new dress for an upcoming party, you'll feel great when you wear it knowing that yours is unique and is "just what you had in mind!" If you sew for someone else, you'll smile when you see how much he or she appreciates your handiwork. Even if you make something as incredibly practical as a potholder, you're able to take pride in how well you can provide the necessary items needed for a comfortable existence.

No matter why you are drawn to sewing or how far you refine your skills, you can take delight in the smallest tasks—selecting fabric, cutting out pattern pieces, stitching seams—until they all add up to a finished project you love. So relax, take a deep breath, become immersed in the process, and feel the joy of creating your project.

THE OLD SEWING MACHINE.

"The Old Sewing Machine." *Godey's Lady's Book and Magazine*, January, 1863. Courtesy of The Library Company of Philadelphia.

THE TALE OF SEWING

The origins of sewing predate the weaving of cloth and can be traced as far back as the Paleolithic Age. The craft has evolved from the rudimentary joining of animal skins for warmth to the skillfully crafted clothing and interior embellishments that allow us to live comfortably and stylishly in the twenty-first century. This evolution is directly tied to the industry of man to improve upon the needle, whether made of bone and used by hand or our familiar nickel plated steel that sews the ingenious lock stitch of the sewing machine.

Prior to 1850, plain, practical sewing dominated the average woman's workload. While the wealthy hired seamstresses, most women spent countless hours assembling, mending, and altering garments to extend the life of the fabrics. Housewives by necessity had to be both frugal and creative—making thread and weaving cloth took an immense amount of time, and a garment was not simply a purchase; it was an *investment*. Women often added decorative needlework to clothing and household linens, sometimes as much to conceal multiple alterations or aged fabric

as to create beauty. It was not uncommon for a woman to wear the same dress for over a decade making alterations as needed to meet current trends in fashion.[1] Fortunately fashion trends moved at a leisurely pace. Hard-pressed housewives were able to focus their attention on keeping garments whole, rather than fashionable, even to the extreme of taking apart a garment and turning the fabric to show the wrong side for a season or two, just until the inside and outside became equally faded. Household linens also found their way into the mending basket. Sheets, worn in the middle, were given new life by ripping the sides into strips and sewing them together.[2]

The demand upon women to maintain their families' wardrobes and a comfortable home made needlework an essential skill. Most women learned to sew at a very young age, whether for practical or ornamental purposes. Skills were often bartered among women for tasks such as weaving cloth, pattern making, cutting fabric, sewing, and mending, as no one woman was expected to be an expert in all areas of clothing manufacture. Mending, however, was a required skill for all, occupying much of their time well into the mid-twentieth century.

HANDWRITING ON THE WALL

In the eighteenth and early nineteenth centuries samplers were an integral part of a young girl's early education. They allowed her to showcase recently acquired knowledge of both needlework and the alphabet. A young girl would have completed one, if not two, samplers between the ages of five and nine under the direction of a family member or school instructor.[3] These were often framed and hung on the wall, showing that a young lady's needlework accomplishment was as honored as today's diploma.

Between the years 1800 and 1835 there was an increase in sampler work featuring both fancy and plain needlework in the United States.[4] Wealth, peace, and prosperity allowed a bit of indulgence in the materials and time to devote to a child's artwork. Instead of samplers of darned linen and rudimentary letters for marking linen in a household's inventory, samplers of silken alphabets, gardens, and homes became the albums

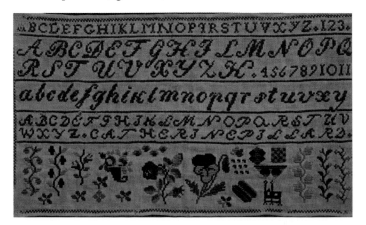

Needlework Sampler, (n.d.). Courtesy of The Library Company of Philadelphia.

in which we see a way of life so distant in time from our own, but so quaintly intimate because of the small hands that produced the images, stitch by careful stitch.

A young lady's education may have also moved from her own home to a school or ladies' seminary during this period. Moravian boarding schools such as the Bethlehem Female Seminary offered a broad curriculum including arithmetic, language, knitting, and plain needlework. In the late eighteenth century some Moravian schools opened their doors to students of all religious denominations, training students in the universal skills of stitchery while expanding their minds and guiding their artistic explorations.[5]

A fine example of plain needlework instruction can be found in the collection of The Library Company of Philadelphia in the form of a "Homework Sampler." The work, artfully mounted on board in the form of a book, was made by a young Emily Bell while attending the Bethlehem Female Seminary in Bethlehem, Pennsylvania, circa 1830. Exhibiting the variety of skills necessary for the proper furnishing of the family wardrobe, the sampler includes examples of buttonhole, hemming, and pintuck stitches.

The curricula of many schools, however, were not as academically diverse, and female "accomplishments" were often the mainstay—focusing on ornamental needlework, etiquette, music, and the arts. As early as 1794, in John Burton's *Lectures on Female Education,* a woman remarks on her nieces spending their time "gadding about," so different from her own youth, remarking that "she had plied her needle for fifty years, with equal pleasure and satisfaction; and that she is grieved to see her young flighty relations sipping their tea for a whole afternoon, in a room hung around by the industry of their Progenitors."[6]

CHILD'S PLAY

Another form of needlework education was achieved through childhood play. A mother's scrap basket provided the means for countless hours of doll dressmaking. Popular periodicals, such as *Godey's Lady's Book* and *Peterson's Magazine,* provided patterns and instruction for outfitting a girl's favorite doll. Using these patterns as a guide, mothers taught their daughters how to draw paper patterns, cut material, and assemble a variety of garments and accessories. In July 1868 *Godey's Lady's Book* devoted their "Work Department" to the "Fashionably Dressed Doll." The knitting patterns for a muff, victorine (scarf), stocking, and boot are provided along with detailed engravings of the undergarments, which could be made from paper patterns provided by request from the "Fashion Editress."[7]

II

Young Ladies Seminary at Bethlehem, Pennsylvania. Tanner, Benjamin, 1775-1848 engraver. Philadelphia: s.n., 1844. Courtesy of The Library Company of Philadelphia.

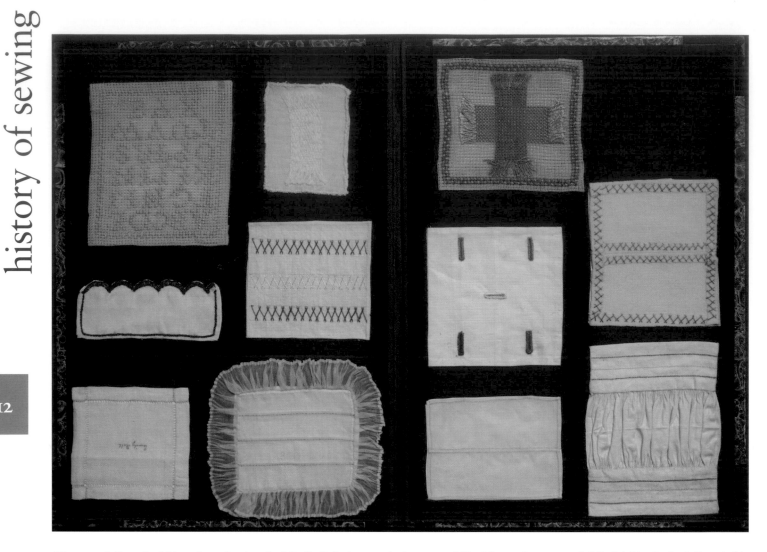

"Homework Sampler." Moravian schoolwork of Emily Bell, (c. 1830s). Courtesy of The Library Company of Philadelphia. Emily Bell probably attended the Bethlehem Female Seminary in Bethlehem, Pennsylvania.

Elementary schools adopted this theory of educational play in the grammar grades as "an excellent preparation for the making of full-size clothing in the upper grades. The seams are not long enough to prove wearisome to the little fingers, the material is easy to procure from the school supplies, and the little dolls' garments are very near to the young mothers' hearts."

This trend in female education experienced a significant reversal in the 1830s when popular women's authors such as Catharine Beecher demanded reform in response to the emerging industrial culture.[8] Her arguments for the teaching of household management are based on the precept that if a parent, sibling, or other relative were to pass away, the remaining eldest female would need to be prepared to step in and take on the duties of the matriarch.[9] Beecher attributed the lack of training for young girls was due to the limited time and patience of mothers to "teach a novice" because "the best housekeepers find it easier and faster to do the work themselves. Daughters of less efficient housekeepers are more likely to gain domestic skills due to the necessity of their labor."[10] In her 1856 book *Treatise on Domestic Economy*, Beecher again beseeches parents and teachers to realize the importance and practicality of making domestic economy a regular part of female education. Whatever their station, young girls were repeatedly encouraged by Beecher, and other authors of the period, to have a basic understanding of plain needlework. This remained true even after the introduction of the sewing machine in the mid-nineteenth century. As late as 1873, Beecher continued to include the same detailed instructions for a variety of plain stitching and the construction of dresses that she provided in her 1856 *Treatise on Domestic Economy.*

Her pleadings gained more relevance as families moved away from the generational household of previous decades to live in urban centers of industry without the advice, training, and support of their mothers, sisters, and grandmothers. Other people relocated to the harsh and remote regions of the uncivilized west, notoriously unpopulated by seamstresses or tailors except possibly in towns with flourishing saloons and dancehalls. In the newly settled regions of the country, women either became fashion designers, milliners, and knock-off experts (thanks to the equally peripatetic nature of *Godey's Lady's Book* and *Peterson's Magazine)*, or they wore the same styles for decades.

The movement to include domestic education in school curricula continued through the end of the nineteenth century and was greatly assisted by legislation such as The Morrill Land Grant Act of 1862, or "An Act Donating Public Lands to the Several States and Territories Which May Provide Colleges for the Benefit of Agriculture and the Mechanic Arts."[11] This provided the impetus needed to introduce formal coursework in domestic science, including needlework, in colleges as well as public elementary and secondary schools.[12]

Despite this systematic training, or perhaps because of it, by the turn of the century ready-made clothing had become more affordable and of higher quality, resulting in a shift from domestic to vocational needlework education. Out in remote territories the sewing machine permitted clothing production to become established under the control of women in small towns. Laura Ingalls Wilder recounts her experiences in such a business in the Dakota Territory of the 1880s, providing men's working clothing for homesteaders and settlers who had not yet acquired wives to make their clothes for them. For the women who had either not acquired skills or who chose to do other things, the local seamstress was a godsend.

Reforming winds, as they so often do, blew across both industry and style at the turn of the nineteenth century. As women became more active outside the home, participating in charitable endeavors and/or entering the work place, they turned their attention to the functionality of clothing, experimenting with and adopting simpler

"Work Department, Fashionably Dressed Doll." *Godey's Lady's Book and Magazine*, July 1868. Courtesy of The Library Company of Philadelphia.

NEEDLECRAFT
The Lines of the Times

7965

7975

7986

7993

7967

Ladies' Shirtwaist

ONE is impressed with the cut of the collar to this blouse, No. 7965, which is given a pretty line with a tuck in each front. The front closing with large buttons and loops that serve to decorate as well, is a "fashion-act." The pattern will prove its worth and increase your willingness to use one again.

silk is easy to launder and most suitable for this model. The pattern is clear and convincing.

The shirtwaist-pattern, No. 7986, is cut in sizes from 36 to 42 inches bust measure. To make the waist in the 36-inch size will require 2¾ yards of 36-inch plain fabric, and ⅝ of a yard of 36-inch figured goods—or 2⅞ yards all one material.

"The Lines of the Times." *Needlecraft* 8 (1917): 24. Courtesy of Nicole Scalessa.

and less form-fitting styles. The popular and easily produced shirtwaist and skirt of the 1890s gave the clothing industry the momentum needed to appeal to the female consumer. This worked to the advantage both of the manufacturer as well as the home seamstress. While the home seamstress found simplified fashions easier to fit and sew than the intricately shaped garments of the earlier part of the century, commercial establishments could

apply assembly line techniques to further streamline clothing production.

In 1913 Butterick Publishing Company, better known for their paper patterns, provided *The Sewing Book Containing Complete Instructions in Sewing and Simple Garment-Making for Children in the Primary and Grammar Grades*. This detailed description of supplies and techniques written by Anne L. Jessup provides a window into the early application of vocational training in the classroom. Students were expected to supply themselves with "thimbles, needles, pins, worsted or thread, emeries, tape-measure, scissors, a needle-book, pincushion, workbag and sewing-apron."[13] Although there is no mention of a sewing machine in the classroom the likelihood of one being available to students is high, as they had become ubiquitous by this time. It was also recommended that the room be equipped with cutting tables and an electric iron.[14] The course was considered completed once the student had fashioned themselves a petticoat, nightgown, undergarments, drawers, trimmings, sleeve protectors, caps, middy blouse, and a neckerchief, in addition to mastering the art of mending.[15]

Child's dress (c.1894), handmade. Private collection.

THE INDUSTRIAL REVOLUTION

The birth of American industrialization is often credited to Samuel Slater, an immigrant from England who in 1790 constructed the first successful American cotton-spinning mill in Providence, Rhode Island.[16] As a protégé of Jebediah Strutt (partner of Richard Arkwright, the inventor of the water-powered spinning machine), Slater had been exposed to all phases of the factory system prior to his arrival in the United States. However, it was not until 1813 that the factory system was applied to all phases of textile manufacture. That year Francis Cabot Lowell and his associates built the first American manufacturing company to process raw cotton into finished cloth.[17] By 1830 hundreds of textile mills were in operation and household fabric production had become limited to rural communities.[18] After the war of 1812 improvements in transportation further fueled the ensuing industrial revolution. The opening of canals provided access to the anthracite region of Pennsylvania in the late 1820s, fostering the emergence of steam-powered mills across New England. Railroad construction followed, facilitating the development of a national market for all manufacturers.

By the mid-nineteenth century nearly all fabric production was by machine. This rapid advancement of the textile industry soon placed American producers in competition with established European firms, sparking a spirit of invention and innovation. As a result, a wide variety of affordable materials emerged in new colors and textures popularizing larger more elaborate wardrobes. Demands were being placed on seamstresses as never seen before.

Beginning in 1851, international industrial fairs became annual events across Europe and the United States, giving manufacturers the opportunity to showcase their new merchandise alongside their competitors. Products exhibited included fabric, needles, dress patterns, and finely spun threads—the convenience and quality of which greatly influenced the invention and eventual popularity of the sewing machine.

In 1876 American women demanded the opportunity to exhibit their own ingenuity and application of new technologies in the 1876 Centennial Exposition. The original space allotted by the Centennial Commission for the use of the Women's Centennial Committee was found to be inadequate.[19] The women requested a building of their own devoted to the arts of female industry. The Commission, for financial reasons, denied this request. Elizabeth Duane Gillespie, granddaughter of Benjamin Franklin, responded with a national fundraising effort that included concerts, art shows, benefits, and bazaars. Many of these activities relied on the profit of needlework sales and other donated items from women across the country. The women successfully raised over $100,000, enabling them to exhibit a wide variety of female achievements that attributed to the progress of the nation.[20] The exhibition building housed paintings, sculptures, and many inventions patented by women. Hannah Suplee exhibited her open-eye easy threading needle, which was used to sew the exposition's hot-air balloons.[21] Demonstrations by women included the operation of sewing and knitting machines, a Jacquard loom, a telegraph office, a cylinder printing press, and a spooling machine. Needlework displays included examples of crochet, knitting, tatting, quilting, and embroidery.[22]

INFUSIONS OF TALENT

The vast waves of immigrants to the United States throughout the nineteenth and early twentieth centuries provided an abundance of cheap labor, both skilled and unskilled in clothing production. Women, who came from lands where sewing machines were as unattainable as golden carriages, had been wielding needles like rapiers since they were tots, and were soon trained in systematic clothing construction. Tailors also arrived or were trained as sewing machine operators when they arrived on shore. Soon there were teeming sweatshops in the major cities, and the children became the impetus for industrial education programs.

The Smith-Hughes Act of 1917 was the first federal effort to finance training for industrial, home economics, and agricultural courses.[23] Further support was provided in 1936 by the George-Deen Act which provided educational opportunities for the teachers of these courses. Massachusetts public schools promoted sewing instruction as a method of encouraging "working-class girls, many with shiftless or employed mothers" to "make their own clothes while gaining skills to make money and the disciplined habits appropriate to good industrial workers."[24] These training programs were so successful that by 1920 it became customary for women to purchase a large portion of their families' wardrobes, both for men and women.[25]

THE HAVES AND THE HAVE-NOTS

This shift from home-constructed clothing to purchased wardrobes was nourished both by the burgeoning economy of the United States and the determination of the immigrants to make their way into the heart of such prosperity. Immigrants quickly adopted the sewing machine as a way to wealth in the new land offering cheap industrious labor for manufacturers and, in turn, cheaper clothing to the marketplace. On March 25, 1911 a horrendous fire started in the Triangle Shirtwaist factory, in New York City. Flames swept through the locked building. All escape routes had been barred to discourage breaks from work without any consideration for safety. Workers tried to wrench open steel shutters and doors, or to pile onto the few working elevators. When fire trucks and firemen arrived the ladders could not reach the upper floors, nor could the water from the fire hoses. One hundred forty-six people—mostly young women—who were unable to escape the-

These sewing notions and tools were common items found in a woman's workbasket during the late nineteenth to early twentieth century. Among them are wooden spools of brightly colored thread; bone, metal, and fabric buttons; serrated tracing wheels, and a bone button hole awl. The stork scissors were particularly popular and often advertised for mail-order in women's publications such as the June 1917 volume of *NeedleCraft Magazine* pictured here. The child's dress and slip (c. 1917) were worn by centenarian Ruth Sanborn King of New Hampshire, author of *Listen to the Crickets: A Memoir on Rural Life in New Hampshire in the Early Twentieth Century*. Artifacts courtesy of Nicole Scalessa. Will Brown, photographer.

building died by suffocation, burns, or by jumping to their deaths. The public mourning and outrage drove humane labor and workplace safety laws into limited, if not general, acceptance. The owners of the building were acquitted of any knowledge that the emergency exits were locked. In 1913 they settled civil lawsuits with munificent payments of $75 to the families of the victims. The appalling working conditions at sweatshops led to the formation of trade unions to protect the working poor, but the immigrants were grateful for any opportunity that permitted advancement beyond the poverty they had left behind. The few strikes that were organized did not completely alleviate the dangerous and abusive conditions under which humans labored. Nevertheless, cultures mingled in such factories, with Jewish, Italian, Irish, and Central European immigrants working side by side.

The earliest sewing machines were put to use by shoe manufacturers and other leather goods industries due to their significant torque to ply through multiple layers of material. Riveting machines were used for even greater reinforcement. Hard-wearing men's work clothing entered industrial production early on, beginning with the manufacture of Civil War uniforms—which can be traced to the standardization of sizing. Men's clothing of all kinds soon followed suit after the war while women's clothing remained primarily a product of the home for decades to come. From the turn of the century until after the World War II, women were divided in their sentiments regarding the sewing of wardrobes. To some it was a necessity, particularly during the years of the Great Depression, but to others it was a burden that was gratefully shifted to clothing manufacturers. This growth in the clothing industry ensured that sewing and tailoring would remain a dependable and lucrative trade.

Heavy winter clothing was also ideally entrusted to commercial enterprises that could more easily lay and cut the wide, thick woolens, add elegant fur trims, and do the additional lining and tailoring required by such garments. This was an area where many small manufacturers found niches that lasted for years, from their owners' arrivals as immigrants in a new land, to third generation descendents who maintain the companies or at least the living memory of the manufacturing business. One such immigrant, Ancell Kanner, left Romania for Canada, where he married and worked as a tailor before coming to the United States in 1904 to establish his own firm. Kanner and Son designed and made coats and suits for men and women, hiring skilled immigrant help from among relatives, in-laws, and new arrivals. The company was renamed simply Kanner Company when, as so often happens, the son discovered new opportunities in the new land. Still, the company continued producing clothing and supporting households until World War II.

During World War II the home sewing machine industry nearly came to a complete halt as factories were converted for war work. In addition, the large number of women entering the work force in support of the war felt earning money to purchase clothing was a better use of their time.[26] Machine manufacturers then began to look toward America's youth to continue the nations sewing tradition. Teenage American girls became a profitable market for sewing machines following the war. The end of paper rationing provided the opportunity for youth publications like *Seventeen* and *American Girl* to include advertisements for machines, patterns, and sewing lessons.[27] The Singer Teen-Age Sewing Course for girls aged twelve to seventeen was frequently advertised through the use of cartoons and dramatic scenarios.[28] The cartoons offered the opportunity to make the perfect dress or maintain a wardrobe worthy of attracting Prince Charming. Advertisements made sewing synonymous with femininity and purveyed the craft as a skill attained by those worthy of becoming a wife and mother. As grown women, sewing provided a creative outlet and a source of thrift, qualities that resonate to the present day.

THE BUSINESS OF LEISURE

The history of American book publishing is closely tied to the commercial and industrial development of the nation. Technological innovations such as papermaking machinery and the cylinder steam press allowed printers to produce quantities of books at affordable prices for a wider audience. Reading as necessity gave way to reading as leisure, and children's literature, fiction, instructional books, magazines, and newspapers came to be preferred over the devotional literature and almanacs that dominated pre-industrial America. By the late nineteenth century, leisure had become an integral part of American middle class culture as technological advances influenced lifestyle. Useful leisure soon became a predominant literary theme for both adults and children. Activity books for young boys included games of skill and lessons in a variety of sciences, while books for girls provided needlework patterns, poems, and fictional tales promoting female domesticity. For young adult and older

A. Kanner and Son production floor, Los Angeles, California, 1933. Courtesy of Barry Kanner.

audiences, anecdotal literature offered moral direction for a variety of circumstances. These sketches often included characters that defeated the odds through industry and moral fortitude. Periodicals promoted useful leisure by incorporating needlework patterns with fashion and home décor advice on pages that were previously dominated by poetry and short stories. Instructional texts, or prescriptive literature, focusing on the home were popular as well. These manuals provided recipes, medical advice, basic needlework instruction, gardening tips, and lessons in economy.

Much of what we know of nineteenth century sewing and mending is from prescriptive literature. Trade cards and catalogs offer additional insight into the materials and tools used to complete those tasks. However, records of the time spent sewing and how it affected the household economy are more difficult to find. Susan Strasser (a historian of American culture) believes this is due to a combination of modesty and devaluation by women of their own influence on the greater national economy.[29] Catharine Beecher promoted hand sewing as a fundamental part of the household economy, even as sewing machines gained popularity. In 1873 she writes, "It is a mistake to suppose that sewing machines lessen the importance of hand-sewing. All the mending of a family, and much of the altering of clothing and house furniture, must be done only by hand."[30] However, the growth of the sewing machine industry in the nineteenth century contradicts Beecher's opinion and indicates sewing machines were a welcome accompaniment in the seemingly endless task of mending. They offered the gift of efficiency in households where women were constantly looking for a means to improve domestic economy. However, it cannot be ignored that with the opportunity for efficiency, more demands would be placed on home seamstresses by their families for larger and more detailed wardrobes. Sewing machines therefore didn't necessarily result in less work for women but, while contributing to greater wealth of time, they actually produced more opportunities for work.

Women remained responsible for outfitting their families through the early twentieth century. Sewing machines, notions, and even correspondence courses in dress-making were advertised under the premise that hand-made goods were superior and less expensive than those found in shops. In October 1916 *Needlecraft* advertised the Women's Institute of Domestic Arts and Sciences home study course in dress-making and millinery. Firsthand accounts of the course provided promotional fodder as one woman proclaimed she had made "prettier dresses—more stylish—better made...and they cost me less than the two I had last season."[31] Home sewing was in steep competition with ready-made clothing in the 1920s and losing ground.

By the 1940s, the pervasiveness of ready-made clothing is evident in the change in language within sewing manuals.

The New Encyclopedia of Sewing in 1949 promoted sewing as an "accessory to economy, a first aid to thrift, a boon to the budget."[32] Fabric was now more durable, affordable, and beautiful than ever before, further supporting this modern view of sewing as a craft of thrift and creativity. In a 1952 guide the author boasts that "women are not only blessed with modern equipment and methods but the improvement of the fabrics with which they work is notable...No longer do mothers have to put in large seams and hems to guard against shrinkage. Our grandmothers were often sorely tried with fabrics that raveled easily, pulled out of shape, puckered, or faded. The array of textiles available to homemakers today is a veritable treasure chest."[33] This was a momentous shift for the industry, as women no longer saw home dressmaking as a necessity. Once domestic sewing was released from drudgery, constructing fashionable clothes was free to be a creative, delightful hobby. The industry took note, changed its advertising strategies, and flourished accordingly.

SEWING FOR CHARITY AND PROFIT

The ideology of domesticity pervaded all forms of literature by the early nineteenth century. Femininity became synonymous with piety, charity, and industry. The moral salvation of the country, as proclaimed from the pulpit to the parlor, was dependent on the virtues of women and their ability to apply those qualities to the domestic sphere. However, many women did not have the luxury of staying in the home. The unprecedented growth of cities due to industrialization and immigration led to inadequacies in housing, sanitation, and employment. The associated poverty, intemperance, and immorality challenged many earlier assumptions about women's roles.

Middle-class women writers became the moral authorities of the industrial age and set standards for organized female benevolence, although public speaking by women to mixed audiences was condemned, and any involvement in issues considered radical or political was to be avoided. Men sometimes served as administrators of women's charities, or women incorporated their organizations, creating legally recognized bodies. The latter step was commonly preferred and required women to manage their fundraising efforts with the utmost propriety. This put money into the hands of women, officially upending the already-threatened tradition that women needed to have financial matters managed for them. The usual methods of fundraising included subscriptions, fairs, and bazaars. Profits fed, clothed, and housed the poor, preserved historic landmarks, built monuments, and supported troops during the Civil War.

Elizabeth Stott and sixteen of her friends founded the Philadelphia Ladies' Depository in 1832.[34] The depository provided distressed gentlewomen a venue for the sale of needlework on a confidential consignment

Women's Permanent Emergency Association. Philadelphia, (c. 1915). Courtesy of The Library Company of Philadelphia.

basis. A small percentage of the profits went to operational expenses, while the remainder was given to the seamstress. This proved an ideal situation for untrained women. Similar depositories emerged in many major cities across the country. Members paid annual dues, as a charitable contribution, ranging from one to five dollars. Members also offered their services as shop managers and bookkeepers. After the Civil War, these organizations became better known as exchanges. Exchanges raised public consciousness regarding the working conditions and exploitation of wage-earning women, particularly those in needlework trades.

When the Civil War broke out, the need for everything from socks to nurses was rapidly evident. Church groups, sewing circles, and similar organizations quickly reestablished themselves as soldiers' aid societies. These societies joined forces under the auspices of the United States Sanitary Commission, one of the organizations with male administrators in which women participated. Town fairs and local benefits initially supplied the funds necessary for clothing, medical supplies, and the training of nurses. When this proved inadequate, major cities held "Sanitary Fairs" incorporating the efforts of many communities. Photographic evidence of aid societies suggests this was

one of the earliest applications of the sewing machine for charitable purposes. These sanitary fairs were among the most prominent charitable endeavors of the nineteenth century, but the century as a whole saw women bring their crafts into the new arena of benevolent enterprise, establishing a tradition that continues to this day.

DEMOCRATIZATION OF FASHION AND HOME DECOR

Nineteenth-century periodicals such as *Godey's Lady's Book, Peterson's Magazine,* and *Demorest's Family Magazine,* reported the fashion trends of both the United States and Europe to their subscribers. These publications provided the knowledge necessary for women to make fashionable garments and ornaments of dress according to seasonal trends. With the introduction of the sewing machine, periodical editors recognized the need for dress patterns, but those provided were often confusing and difficult to make. To prepare a pattern it was necessary to scale it up and resize it for the wearer, then draw it on paper. In 1854 *The Scientific American* provided instruction in the making of tracing paper, likely used for patterns: "A sheet of fine thin white paper dipped into a thick solution of gum arabic and then pressed between two dry sheets, renders the three transparent when dry; it is very useful for tracing purposes as it can either be written or painted upon."[35] Original patterns could also be obtained from professional seamstresses and personalized to fit one's unique figure and taste.

Madame Demorest's Emporium of Fashion and E. Butterick & Company introduced tissue paper patterns scaled to size after the Civil War. William Jennings Demorest was the embodiment of American entrepreneurialism and promoted his wife Ellen as Mme. Demorest. Her Emporium of Fashion became famous for her tinted tissue paper patterns, featuring couture dresses woman could make on their own home sewing machines.[36] Unfortunately, she was unable to patent her tissue patterns before her competitor, a tailor named Ebenezer Butterick did so. Patterns, retailed through dressmakers, merchants, and sewing machine agents, were available on an international scale by the mid 1870s.[37]

At the turn of the twentieth century, patterns could also be purchased from the Woman's Home Companion, Sears, Roebuck and Co., and Vogue.[38] The flexibility of a single pattern to meet the individual taste and figure of the consumer ensured success. Patterns continued to improve and adapt to the changes in needlework expertise, such as the addition of seam allowances in the 1890s.[39] The proliferation of patterns advertised in popular women's magazines and catalogs was mirrored by the publication of detailed manuals of dressmaking for an increasingly less experienced generation of sewers. Beginning in 1928, The Singer Manufacturing Company published a series of pamphlets titled the *Singer Sewing Library*. Volume two of the series, *How to Make Dresses the Modern Singer Way*, encouraged the novice with the promise of a "delightful adventure" comprised of ten simple steps. Step one was choosing a dress with the recommendation to "look through the fashion books. See what is being shown in the smart shops. Decide what the style of your dress shall be. Then buy a pattern as nearly like your ideal dress as you can, or adapt a simple pattern to your needs."[40]

Sewing machines, coupled with the availability of ready-made fabric, threads, and notions enabled women not only to keep up with fashion but also to have the time to ornament dresses with fancywork. "Work Department" articles, and later magazines such as *Needlework,* supplied an endless array of fancywork designs for embellishing garments and home décor. As early as 1830, Lydia Maria Child quoted one of her contemporaries stating "'Everything is so cheap' says the ladies, 'that it is inexcusable not to dress well.'"[41] Fine wardrobes were no longer a distinct privilege of the wealthy, although the ultimate success of the wardrobe still required fine sewing skills.

Trade cards (c. 1870s) (top to bottom): "Wheeler and Wilson's Sewing Machines for Domestic & Manufacturing Purposes, Cash or Easy Terms;" "The Best Thread for Sewing Machines," Willomantic Linen Company; "Making Ends Meet," Singer Manufacturing Company; "What I have Sewed Together Let No One Rip Asunder," Singer Manufacturing Company; "Ye Olden Time," The American Sewing Machine Company; "Gulliver and the Lilliputians," J. & P. Coats Best Six Cord Spool Cotton.

THE LADY'S WORKBASKET

The sewing machine's success was greatly influenced by the concurrent improvement of the notions required for successful sewing. Paper patterns, rustproof pins, stronger threads, and colorfast dyes contributed to the popularity of the home sewing machine. Trade cards became a popular method to promote these products. The use of trade cards for advertising began in the last third of the nineteenth century. Businesses recognized the need for a new form of advertising to distinguish the wide variety of products available to consumers. Trade cards were given to store patrons by retailers or sealed in packaged goods making them the most ubiquitous advertising gimmick of the nineteenth century. In the twentieth century, following the establishment of the women's vote, trade cards took on a new form as men running for political office distributed pin books with beautiful cover illustrations and a portrait of the candidate on the back.

The term "pin money" originally applied to the annual allowance given to women by their husbands or guardians for the annual purchase of pins. Americans relied on expensive English pins until the War of 1812 restricted imports, making supplies scarce.[42] During the war, convicts at the Greenwich Village State Prison in New York City began manufacturing pins under the direction of some English entrepreneurs.[43] They continued production until the end of the war when imports resumed. In 1831 John J. Howe patented the first successful American pin machine to make perfect solid-head pins, bringing their cost down for American consumers.[44] The Howe Manufacturing Company was soon producing about 70,000 pins daily, however packaging was time consuming as workers manually inserted them into paper or cards.[45] In 1843 Howe designed a machine to crimp the paper and insert the pins.[46] Improvements continued in pin manufacture throughout the century, the most useful being the application of nickel plating to combat rust. The earliest nickel plated pins were subject to flaking and required the use of an emery bag to remove rust. Pins soon became an affordable accompaniment to the workbasket, redefining the term "pin money" as supplemental income earned from the sale of needlework in the nineteenth century.

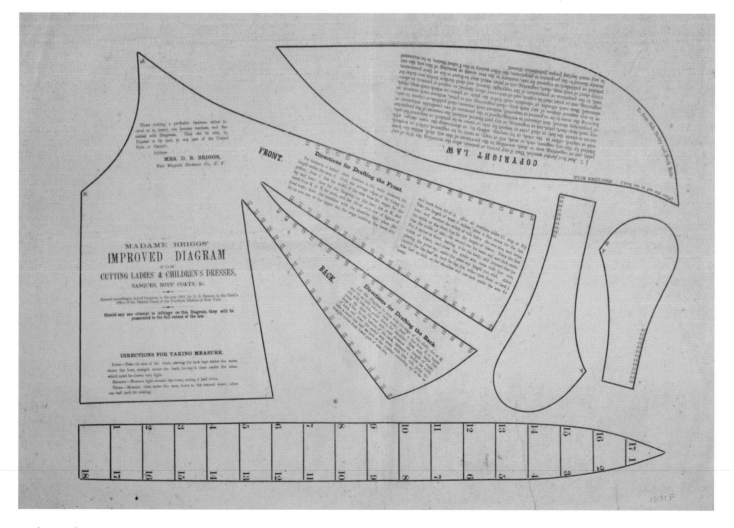

Madame Briggs' Improved Diagram for Cutting Ladies' & Children's Dresses, Basques, Boys' Coats, & [Albany, N.Y.: s.n., 1857]. Courtesy of The Library Company of Philadelphia.

Before 1846 sewing thread was commonly made of three cords with a glazed finish and was inadequate for machine use due to its uneven texture and inadequate strength. American manufacturers strived to produce strong, finely spun threads, equal to the cotton "twist" imported from overseas for both home and mill use. This became an even more lucrative challenge when the need developed for cotton threads that could withstand variant tension controls on a multitude of sewing machine models. The weakness in the thread likely frustrated many early sewing machine owners. In 1872 Horace Greeley wrote that "The demand for machine twist is greater in this country than in any other, since the sewing machine, as a purely American invention, has become so much more generally adopted in both factory and domestic use."[47] In 1866 George Clark was sucessful in developing his famous *Clark's Six Cord Spool Cotton*, advertised as "Our New Thread," or O.N.T., revolutionizing the sewing industry.[48]

Until the mid-nineteenth century, both thread and fabric were colored with ingredients found in nature. The natural resources available to local dyers changed from season to season, and coloring processes varied from dyer to dyer. Fashion trends were directly influenced by local dye industries rather than the dressmakers themselves. Today, textile manufacturers and designers have standard color options, such as the Pantone Color System. Color trends are determined through the use of surveys, or influenced by designers. This flexibility is possible because of the accidental discovery of aniline dye in 1856 by eighteen-year-old William Perkin.[49] Perkin's mauve, the first synthetic dye derived from coal tar, led to an array of brilliant colors. The controlled chemical structure of the dye allowed for the color consistency dyers and textile manufacturers had been working to achieve.

The basic sewing necessities of pins, needles, thread, and fabric have always found a home in the lady's workbasket. Their companion notions, however, have changed, providing an interesting timeline of sewing history. In *The American Woman's Home,* published in 1869, Catharine Beecher provides a detailed description of the contents required for a proper workbasket:

"It is very important to neatness, comfort, and success in sewing, that a lady's work-basket should be properly fitted up. The following articles are needful to the mistress of a family: a large basket to hold work; having it fastened to a smaller basket or box, containing a needle-book in which are needles of every size, both blunts and sharps, with a larger number of those sizes most used; also small and large darning-needles, for woolen, cotton, and silk; two tape needles, large and small; nice scissors for fine work, button-hole scissors; an emery bag; two balls of white and yellow wax; and two thimbles, in case one should be mislaid. When a person

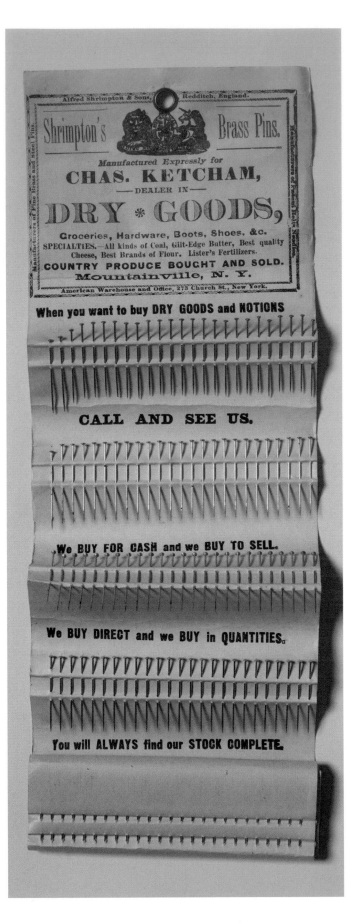

"Shrimpton's Brass Pins Manufactured Expressly for Chas. Ketcham Dealer in Dry Goods." Alfred Shrimpton & Sons, Redditch, England, (c. 1918). Courtesy of Nicole Scalessa.

is troubled with damp fingers, a lump of soft chalk in a paper is useful to rub on the ends of the fingers. Besides this box, keep in the basket common scissors; small shears; a bag containing spools of white and another of colored cotton thread, and another for silks wound on spools or papers; a box or bag for nice buttons, and another for more common ones; a bag containing silk braid, welting cords, and galloon binding. Small rolls of pieces of white and brown linen and cotton are also often needed. A brick pin cushion is a great convenience in sewing and better than screw cushions. It is made by covering half a brick with cloth, putting a cushion on top, and covering it tastefully. It is very useful to hold pins and needles while sewing, and to fasten long seams when basting and sewing."[50]

In 1930 *How to Make Dresses the Modern Singer Way* recommended a sharp pair of scissors at the machine for clipping threads and trimming seams, fasteners, elastic, an iron, and dress form.[51] The 1950s seamstress was expected to have an electric steam iron with a rubber-covered cord, an adjustable dress form, rickrack, pinking shears, snaps, and dressmaker's carbon paper.[52] Today there is an endless array of supplies and resources for the seamstress from hook and loop fastening tape to patterns available for download instantly from the Internet. Whatever you may have in your workbasket, needles, thread, and fabric are the constants which bind one generation to the next enabling "the pride of accomplishment with which says 'I made it myself.'"[53]

THE QUEEN OF INVENTIONS

One of the most arduous tasks for the early American housewife was outfitting her family. In the nineteenth century mechanical innovations gradually emancipated women from hours of utilitarian stitching. Sewing machines, by increasing both production and efficiency, afforded many women leisure time, a previously unknown commodity. Women were experiencing a new freedom of creativity in their sewing that was impossible to foster in years past due to the daily drudgery of the workbasket. This led to the enormous popularity of pattern books, instructional literature, and periodicals relating to needlework that encouraged the embellishment of clothing and articles in the home. In 1860, the sewing machine was proclaimed as the "Queen of Inventions" by *Godey's Ladies Book*. Advertisements and catalog pages proclaimed the time savings of using a sewing machine over sewing by hand.

Expectations were high when *The Scientific American* proclaimed it would create a "social revolution" allowing women to "devote their attention to other things, during the time which used to be taken up with dull seam sewing."[54] And so it did, as ruffles, flounces, and petticoats grew in size and the mechanical marvels of the period liberated the

time needed for such frivolity. Wardrobes became the visible expression of the marriage of technology and leisure.

Elias Howe patented the first practical home sewing machine in 1846.[55] However, it was not until Isaac M. Singer patented his machine under I. M. Singer & Co. in 1851 that they entered the consumer market.[56] The author of an 1852 article in *The Scientific American* reflected on Howe's inability to market his machine saying: "It would have been well for Mr. Howe had he given publicity to his invention at that time, and had it illustrated in our columns. Like every invention of a useful nature, which we have noticed, our inventors took the hint and commenced inventing sewing machines for themselves."[57] The publication had made notice of his machine in 1847 and after many attempts to follow up on his progress could not reach him. In the five years following their initial contact, they had included descriptions of seven more sewing machines in the publication. *The Atlantic Monthly* suggests that Howe's disappearance was due to an attempt to promote the machine in England in the two years following the 1847 article in *The Scientific American*. When Howe returned to the United States, he faced many imitations of his machine, at a time when he himself had little income and his wife had a fatal illness.[58]

Advertisement. Quaker City Sewing Machine (c. 1858). Courtesy of The Library Company of Philadelphia.

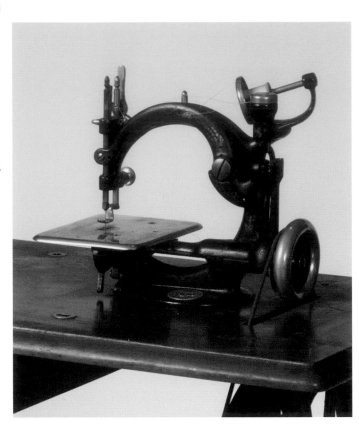

Wilcox and Gibbs Sewing Machine. New York, (c. 1883). Courtesy of Nicole Scalessa. Will Brown, photographer.

The first family sewing machines, made by I. M. Singer & Company and Wheeler and Wilson Manufacturing Company, required a considerable investment at $125, at a time when an agricultural laborer earned about one dollar a day.[59] The novelty of owning one was a privilege of the wealthy in the early 1850s. In an effort to open the market to families of lesser means, the Singer Company introduced a groundbreaking business practice in 1856—the installment plan.[60] Only $5 down was required to take a machine home, with monthly payments of $3 to $5 due thereafter; sales tripled by 1857.[61] Competitors soon followed suit and by the turn of the century the machines were found in nearly every American home. It is estimated that by 1860 Wheeler and Wilson had made 55,000 machines, Singer 40,000, and Grover and Baker 35,000.[62] Sewing machine companies successfully traded on ideas of freedom, family, comfort, and social happiness. By the 1870s more than 200 American sewing machine companies were in business.[63]

The initial success of Singer, followed by Wheeler and Wilson and Grover and Baker, can be attributed to their application of ten essential components not found in earlier machines. These included the lock stitch, an eye-pointed needle, a shuttle for the second thread, continuous thread from spools, a horizontal table, an overhanging arm, continuous feed synchronized with the needle motion, thread tension controls, a presser foot, and the ability to sew in both straight and curved lines.[64]

The success of their sewing machines was not lost on Elias Howe who quickly filed suit in 1850 against Isaac Singer to defend his 1846 patent.[65] A sewing machine feud ensued that ended when Singer lost his battle against Howe in 1854. A judge decided that "the plaintiff's patent is valid, and the defendant's machine is an infringement."[66] Suits against Wheeler and Wilson and Grover and Baker were later settled out of court. On October 10, 1856, it was arranged that the three companies would be licensed under Howe's patent to legally continue manufacturing their machines with a royalty on each machine sold.[67] The parties involved became known as *The Sewing Machine Combination* and not only made Elias Howe a very wealthy man but provided a patent pool for its members to control the industry.[68]

On June 2, 1857 James E. A. Gibbs of Millpoint, Virginia issued a patent for his sewing machine which used a single thread to perform a unique stitch. His "twisted loop-stitch" used only one thread eliminating the need for a bobbin. The stitch was performed with a rotating looper in the shape of a double hook, having its points in reverse directions. This stitch proved stronger than the simple chain stitch that easily unraveled. James Willcox gained license to Gibbs patent on February 18, 1859 and the two men commenced manufacture under the name Willcox and Gibbs Sewing Machine Company. In November of 1863 *The Scientific American* noted the company's unique marketing when describing the shape of the machine "which curiously enough forms a perfect letter "G" the initial of one of the inventors, Gibbs."

Fritz Geugauf, the founder of the Bernina brand, with model 125 in 1945.

"Singer Sewing Machines." *Eighty Years' Progress of the United States.* Hartford, Conn.: published by L. Stebbins, 1867. Courtesy of The Library Company of Philadelphia.

Patent pools, such as *The Combination*, faced dissolution at the end of the nineteenth century when anti-trust laws were established. Consumers were then no longer forced to pay the high prices of name brands as sewing machines became available in department stores and from mail order catalogs. By the early 1900s machines could be purchased for as little as $10.45 with the more elaborate cabinet models selling for around $70.00.[69]

Sewing machine manufacturers introduced working toy, or miniature, machines not long after their full-size counterparts. Model names such as Baby, Junior Miss, and Little Miss were clearly designed for young girls but were marketed equally well to both daughters and mothers alike.[70] These small compact machines were convenient companions on vacations and handy for small mending projects.

By the 1870s manufacturers focused on improving the existing sewing machine technology, such as shuttles, loopers, hooks, and thread guides, for improved stitching and easier operation. In 1887 the oscillating central bobbin hook was invented by American Phillip Diehl, and remains in use today.[71] The first zigzag machine was manufactured in Germany in 1882 by John Kaiser, followed by the first hemstitching machine in Switzerland by Fritz Gegauf, who later founded Bernina. Bernina would also launch the first electric free arm zigzag machine in 1943.[72] Attachments were also a popular area of sewing machine innovation. By 1914 the ruffler, tucker, hemmer, quilter, braider, and edge stitcher were considered a necessity for the home dressmaker.[73]

In 1889 Singer Manufacturing Company introduced the first practical electric sewing machine.[74] Electric sewing machines would not gain widespread appeal in the United States until well into the 1930s, assisted by the establishment of the Rural Electrification Administration. It's estimated only two thirds of the country had electricity in their homes in the 1920s.[75]

Variations on the zigzag stitch were adapted in the twentieth century, providing the means for the wide selection of stitches we've come to expect from today's machines.[76] This is accomplished by allowing the needle assembly to move side to side at the same time it moves up and down. In 1975 Singer introduced the world's first electronic machine, the Athena 2000, followed by the first computer-controlled machine in 2001.[77] Today some machines have the ability to create complex embroidery designs that are programmed by the user from a wide array of digital media devices. Simpler computerized machines offer touch screen displays with on screen assistance. However, this trend has not eliminated the established electric lock-stitch machine found in the majority of American homes. Manual, electric, electronic, or computerized, all sewing machines remain built on the same basic premise of a needle passing a loop of thread through a piece of fabric then being wound by another piece of thread. This simple stroke of genius is what sealed the sewing machine's fate as the "Queen of Inventions."

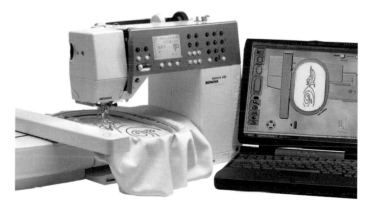

Today's technology offers the home sewer more creative options with his or her sewing machine than ever before.

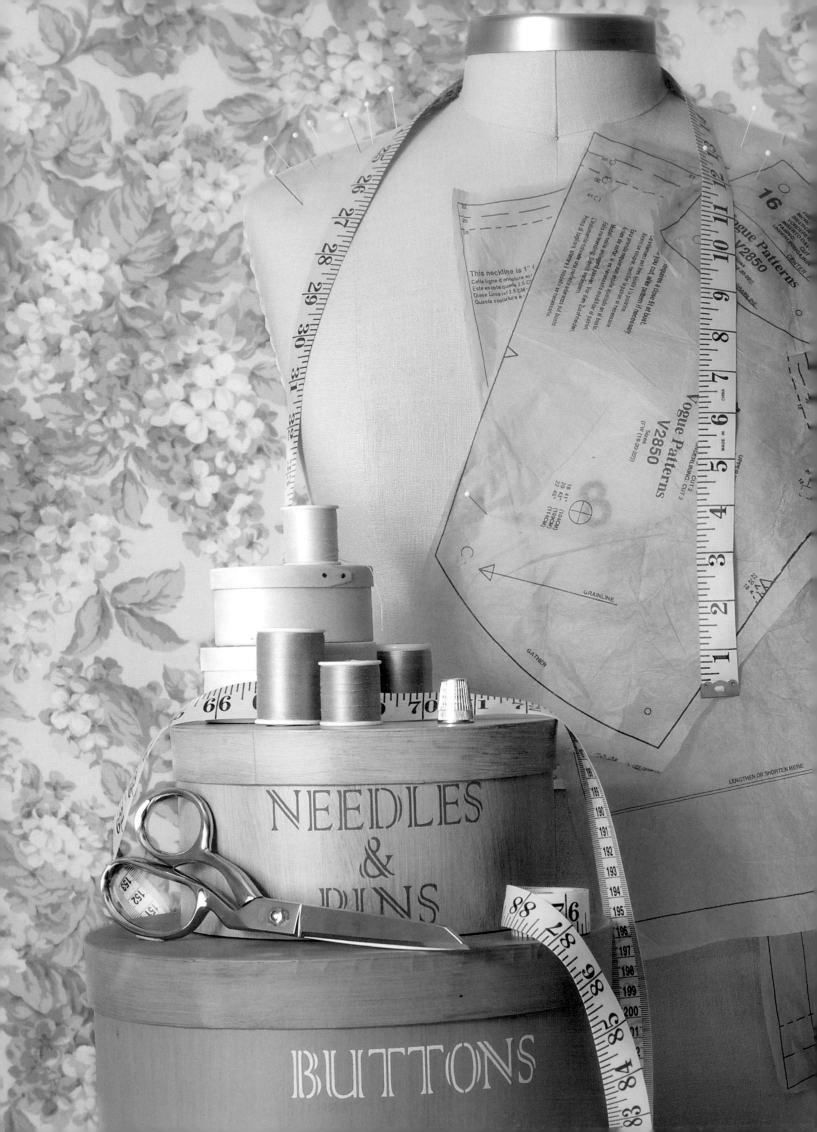

sewing basics

 WHETHER YOU ARE JUST LEARNING TO sew or have practiced your skills over time, some things are the same. The tools you use, the patterns you cut, and the fabrics you sew have many common elements. Understanding these elements makes it easier to get on with the business of sewing, no matter where you are in the learning process.

The dichotomy of sewing is that it is a technical process with creative results. Is it science or art? Is it a right-brain or left-brain activity? Whatever it is, there's more to it than meets the eye. You can take it into almost any direction, depending on your interest, your skill, and your spirit. The following pages delve into the elements of sewing that are essential to successful stitching. Once you are familiar with these, you have a head start on solving the contradiction of precision and freedom.

The sewing world has changed more in the last 25 years than in the entire time since the invention of the sewing machine. New products such as fusible interfacing, rotary cutters, and wash-away markers have completely changed how we sew and how fast we sew. Up-to-the-minute fashion patterns, colorful informative books, and the World Wide Web have put ideas and instructions at our fingertips round-the-clock. Computerized machines, intriguing attachments, and an ever-growing selection of threads have opened creative doors that we didn't even know existed. Because of this, today is the best time to start sewing and the best time to keep sewing.

SEW WHAT?

Sewing is interesting because the items that can be created with fabric, needle, and thread are so numerous and so varied. Many stitchers focus on one type of sewing, such as quilting, and never try their hand at any other type such as fashion or home décor sewing. Others try it all and envision almost anything in fabric! There's no right or wrong way to approach it; it's simply a personal choice or a natural progression as you travel the journey of sewing. As you learn more about sewing, you'll see several types that attract most people. Usually determined by the projects being sewn, the categories all share many common techniques but may also have some specialty skills needed just for that category. Many projects fall into more than one category, so this is not "black and white," and there is no scientific procedure behind the naming of the sewing types. Some categories are easier or harder than others, but within any of these categories you can learn to make a simple basic project and then progress to making more complex and intricate items. The most common categories are:

QUILTING: Quilts range in size from miniature or "doll-size" to king-size bed quilts. Pieced, appliquéd, or made of whole cloth, they are called quilts because they are layered with batting and then quilted, or stitched, through the layers. Other items such as clothing, pillows, and purses can be quilted using some of the same techniques used on bed quilts.

Courtesy of The Sewing Workshop.

FASHION SEWING: The making of garments for women, children, and men, this category may also include fashion accessories such as scarves and purses. The garments may be as simple as a T-shirt or as complex as a hand-tailored suit.

HOME DÉCOR SEWING: Sewing for the home can involve making a variety of fabric items such as throw pillows, bed linens, tablecloths, napkins, quilts, etc.; may also include soft and upholstered furniture.

EMBELLISHING: This category usually doesn't refer to the project itself but what is being done to the project as it is being created. It focuses on surface design such as decorative stitching, thread painting, machine embroidery, or appliqué added to the fabric for almost any type of project, including decorating ready-to-wear garments or other purchased items.

CRAFTING: This broad category encompasses items that don't easily fit into other categories. Often small items such as tote bags, purses, book covers, fiber art pieces, jewelry, etc. fall into this group.

Courtesy of Vicki Tracy.

WHY CAVEMEN DON'T DRIVE

"I can't sew;" "My Mom sews but the sewing 'gene' skipped me;" "I failed Home Ec in school—I just couldn't learn to sew."

These are some of the more common statements made by non-sewers about why they don't sew. People frequently give up easily when learning a new skill. If the results aren't perfect the first time or two, they quit and move on to something else. Typically, the blame is for self, not the project, the teacher, or the choice of materials.

If we look at history, we can find a path of invention, learning, and perseverance that has resulted in most of our modern-day technology and conveniences. Modern cartoons (assuming they are historically accurate) show us that cave dwellers invented the wheel with the same function as a car tire: to roll. Created in the last part of the Stone Age and used over time for a multitude of mechanical applications (water wheel, cogwheel, flywheel, spinning wheel, etc.), the wheel is one of the oldest and most important inventions to the productivity of man. Even though it was created in the time leading up to the Bronze Age, it was thousands of years later, after many versions and transformations, that it came to be used on another important invention: the automobile. It took that long for the technology of the auto to develop and be invented by modern man.

Developing your sewing skills is a little like the progression of the wheel. The first time you sew, you may have success with simple projects, but as you practice and apply what you learn each time, you'll become more proficient and your talent will blossom. So, start slow, build on each skill you learn, and work your way up to driving!

WHAT'S YOUR SKILL LEVEL?

The only reason to care about where your skills lie is to know where to go to be successful and how to move forward in building your skills. It should not be an attempt to judge or grade yourself against some standard of the "Ultimate Sewer." You can sew successfully for years at the most basic level, making hundreds of useful and beautiful items for your friends and family. However, if you have an idea of where you are, you can build on that foundation and add to your skills if you choose.

When deciding what projects you want to sew, your selection can determine your success. If you match the complexity of the project to your skill level, you have a much better chance of completing the item and being happy with the results. In addition, the materials you select can keep the process simple or can add complications that only advanced stitchers can work through. The following chart offers guidelines to help to determine into which level a project falls, so you can decide if it is for you or not. Don't let the chart pigeonhole you into one type or level of sewing, but just know you'll have more success, especially if you are at the beginning of the learning curve, if you take small steps rather than giant leaps into new territory.

SELECTING A FIRST PROJECT

- Try a simple item first such as a pillowcase, apron, knife-edge throw pillow, simple top, vest, or easy skirt. Look for few decorative details and minimal embellishment.
- Select patterns with few pattern pieces; one-piece fronts, no collar, and easy hems are good choices. Save lined projects for after you are comfortable with the basic sewing process.
- Use easy-to-handle fabric such as quilting cotton or medium weight denim—avoid slippery, delicate, or extra thick fabrics.

- Look for patterns labeled "Easy," "Quick," or "Fast."
- Consider the size of the project. Easy-to-handle projects such as pillows, shirts, and purses are good for building skills before moving on to bed quilts and ball gowns.
- Keep your first project relatively plain as you learn about the process of sewing. If you start with a project that requires a tedious job such as gathering yards and yards of ruffles, you may decide you don't like sewing, when it is really the tedium of the task you have selected that you dislike.

SKILL LEVEL

LEVEL	FABRICS	THREADS	PROJECTS	TECHNIQUES	SIZE
Easy	Natural fibers such as cotton and linen, rather than synthetics, which can be slippery and have less body. Mistakes are more obvious on solid fabrics so all-over non-directional prints with no patterns to match are best; no plaids. Woven fabrics rather than knits, so controlling the stretch is not an issue. Fabrics that take a crease well, but don't wrinkle easily such as good quality quilting cottons are easy to handle.	Common fibers such as cotton, polyester, rayon are easy to use at any level.	Fewer pattern pieces, easy fit garment patterns or no-fit projects such as pillows, purses, and scarves. Use simple projects to learn techniques and construction steps before moving on to more difficult items.	Simple versions of almost any sewing machine technique can be sewn but limit the number on early projects. For instance, in addition to simple construction techniques have only one or two embellishments. Decorative Stitching, Raw Edge Appliqué, and Channel Quilting are all easy embellishment techniques.	Tiny items such as miniature quilts are more difficult to handle and control, especially if intricately pieced. Larger projects such as draperies or bed-sized quilts are also difficult to manage just because of sheer size and weight.
Intermediate	All of the above plus: Directional prints and plaids; napped or pile fabrics such as velveteen or corduroy. Knit fabrics such as overlock knits, sweatshirt fleece, sweater knits.	All of the above plus: Metallic thread Monofilament or "invisible" thread.	All of the above plus: Lined jackets, tailored coats, draperies, and slipcovers.	All of the above plus: More complex construction methods and embellishments such as Free-motion Quilting, Thread Painting, and Crazypatch.	Most projects of any size except extremely large.
Advanced	Any type of fabric or material including chiffon, fur, leather, and slippery synthetics.	All of the above.	Any type of project including haute couture, bridal, and men's wear.	Any construction technique and all forms of embellishment.	Any type of project, large or small.

Easy

Intermediate

Advanced

ESSENTIAL SEWING TOOLS: Tape measures, fabric marking tools, scissors and shears, seam rippers, straight pins, pincushions.

SEWING ESSENTIALS

Sewing covers a myriad of different tasks requiring tools and notions to do them effectively and efficiently. Good basic sewing tools will make the job easier and help you avoid mistakes. While new tools and useful gadgets come onto the market every day, there are also a few old favorites that are necessary to start or continue sewing. Make sure you have the following in your sewing toolbox, so you'll be prepared to cut and sew whenever you want.

SCISSORS: Scissors have become specialized for specific cutting situations but two types should cover your basic sewing needs. A pair of bent-handle shears (7" or 8") works for big cutting jobs such as cutting pattern pieces from fabric. The bent handle lets you keep the shears in contact with the cutting surface, and the larger finger holes let you use more fingers for better control. A smaller pair of trimming scissors (4"–5") comes in handy for clipping threads and trimming seam allowances. You may want to have a third pair of scissors designated for cutting paper; use them for cutting apart paper pattern pieces and making templates.

TAPE MEASURE: Fiberglass is better than paper or fabric, as it doesn't stretch out of shape. Many tape measures are ⅝" wide, so you have a quick reference when checking the accuracy of garment seam allowances. If you're into quilting or home dec sewing, look for the extra-long 120" tapes for measuring bed-size quilts and long draperies.

STRAIGHT PINS: Nickel-plated dressmaker's pins are the most common type of straight pin; most sewers prefer pins that have a decorative head such as a glass "bead" or flat "flower" because they are easiest to grasp. Glass-head pins are better than plastic because they can be pressed over without fear of melting.

SEAM RIPPER: Used to "un-sew" mistakes, this tool can also be used to easily remove basting stitches. Look for one with a small point and a sharp inner blade. It should also have a cover, preferably one that can be threaded onto a ribbon necklace, so you can keep it handy, because no matter how much sewing you do, there's always something to "reverse sew" now and again.

PINCUSHION: A convenient place to keep your pins, this can be a soft, fabric one or a magnetic type that makes it easy to pick up pins from the floor and/or tabletop. If using the fabric type, a natural fiber filling such as wool will keep your pins sharper than a synthetic such as polyester.

FABRIC MARKERS: A chalk pencil or fabric marker is great for transferring markings from the pattern to the fabric. Some markers have ink that dissolves with water and others have air-soluble ink that disappears in 24–48 hours. Special pencils are also available for marking almost any type of fabric. Try them all on a variety of projects, and you'll find your favorites. Whatever marker or pencil you choose, do a test to see how well it marks on a particular fabric and how easy it is to remove the marks.

GOOD TO HAVE

The following items are not absolutely necessary but can really help make the job of sewing easier.

ROTARY CUTTER: Similar to a pizza cutter, this tool is indispensible for cutting clean, straight lines. Especially helpful for cutting strips and squares needed for patchwork, it also makes quick work of cutting ruffles, binding, ties, etc. Great for cutting sheer fabrics, this tool should be used with a cutting mat and clear ruler.

ROTARY CUTTING MAT: You'll need a cutting surface to use with the rotary cutter to protect the tabletop. These come in a variety of sizes and most mats have printed grid markings for measuring fabric and aiding in getting straight cuts.

CLEAR RULERS: Available in a variety of sizes and shapes (square, rectangular, triangular, etc.), use these rulers with the rotary cutter and mat to cut straight edges. Made of clear acrylic, the rulers are printed with measurement markings and may include sight lines that make it easy to align fabric edges and patterns when cutting fabric.

APPLIQUÉ SCISSORS: Also called duckbill scissors, this unusual looking tool is great when cutting layers of fabric or lace such as for appliqué or when joining lace to fabric. The flat "bill" helps to avoid cutting the underneath layer when trimming the upper one.

PINKING SHEARS: A pair of scissors with saw-toothed blades that cut fabric, it leaves a zigzag pattern on the edge to help slow the raveling of the cut edge. The name of this tool comes from a carnation-like flower with scalloped edges called "pink."

PATTERN WEIGHTS: Small heavy weights designed to hold paper pattern pieces to fabric, they come in a variety of sizes and shapes and make the pattern-cutting task go faster. They're especially good for delicate fabrics, plastics, and leather that pins may damage.

STILETTO/AWL: Made of metal (often brass), wood, or plastic, this tool is useful for guiding and controlling fabric as it goes under the needle; it's also available as a finger trolley that fits over your index finger.

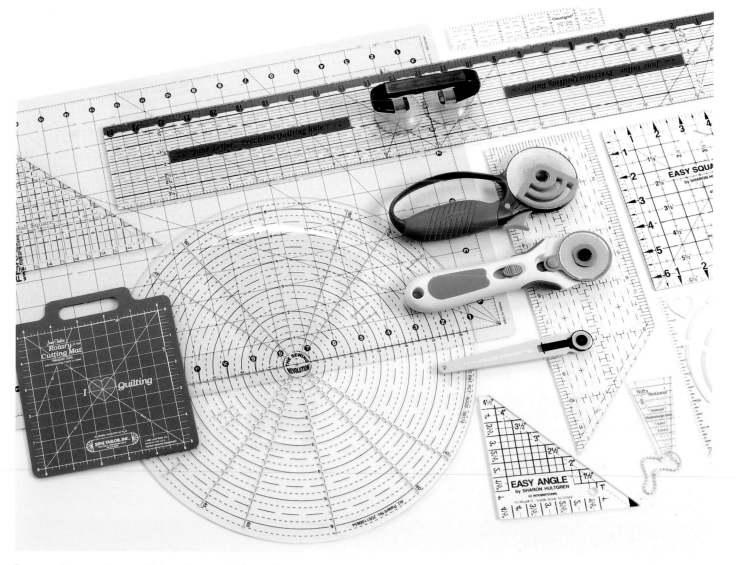

ROTARY CUTTING TOOLS: Mats, cutters, and clear rulers.

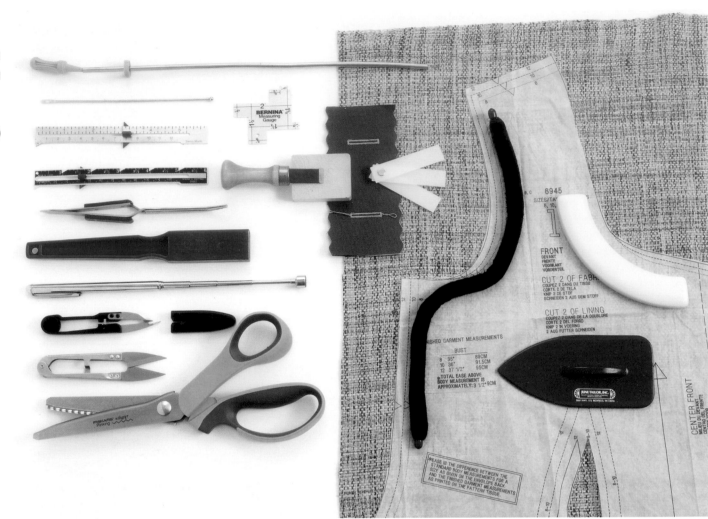

Fast Turn tube turner, bodkin, sewing gauges, buttonhole cutter, reverse action tweezers, compensation plate, magnetic wands, thread snips, pinking shears, and fabric weights.

BUTTONHOLE CUTTER: A beveled cutting edge that fits into the opening of a buttonhole that has been positioned over a block of wood (included with the cutter), the cutter gives a precise cut and eliminates the possibility of cutting through the bar tacks at the ends of the buttonhole.

SEWING GAUGE: This handy small measuring device make it easy to quickly measure markings and seams while sitting at the sewing machine.

THREAD SNIPS: Small spring-operated clippers are used for quick snipping of threads as you sew. Make sure these are sharp all the way to the points for the most effectiveness.

REVERSE ACTION TWEEZERS: These tweezers have a great grip and are closed unless you squeeze the handles to open them—great for threading machine needles and grasping individual threads, hand needles, and other tiny items.

COMPENSATING PLATES OR THICKNESS TOOL: These small, usually plastic, tools allow the presser foot to ride smoothly over the fabric in uneven sewing situations, such as when hemming thick jeans or stitching on the edge of webbing or hook-and-loop tape (Velcro®).

TUBE TURNER OR BODKIN: There are a variety or these available for turning all sizes of tubes to the right side after stitching and for feeding drawstrings and elastic through casings. Try several until you find your favorite.

HOUSEHOLD HELPS

Not all sewing tools are found in the sewing room. There are several items that you may have around the house or can easily purchase for use on your next sewing project.

SOAP: Use a small bar of soap for marking washable fabrics. An emery nail file can be used to sharpen the edge for a fine line marking. Test the soap on scrap fabric before using it on your project.

BATH SCRUNCHIE: Use like sandpaper to smooth the surface of a rotary cutting mat, cleaning fuzz and lint that becomes wedged in the cutting marks.

CHOPSTICK: Use as a turner for nicely turned corners or as a stiletto to guide fabric as it goes under the needle.

PLASTIC ZIPPER BAGS: Snack and sandwich size hold buttons, beads, and small notions. Gallon size and larger are great for organizing supplies, ribbons, even entire projects!

FREEZER PAPER: Good for making templates and pattern pieces for invisible appliqué, the waxy side of the paper will temporarily adhere when pressed to the fabric.

EXAMINATION TABLE PAPER: Sold at medical supply houses, this inexpensive paper comes on large rolls and is good to use as a pattern tracing paper.

DIGITAL CAMERA: Great design tool! Take photos of fabric combinations or quilt block placement as you plan your project and also take photos of completed projects as a record of what you've made.

PILL BOTTLES/FILM CONTAINERS: Put broken, bent, or dull pins and needles in these for easy and safe disposal.

WAX PAPER: Good for altering and making patterns, it's easy to scratch the surface to make markings.

LINT ROLLER: The sticky adhesive is perfect for removing stray threads after ripping out stitches. It's also a great clean-up tool for collecting threads in your sewing area before running the vacuum.

Household items such as plastic zipper bags, bar of soap, chopsticks, digital camera, freezer paper, lint roller, and bath scrunchie can be helpful in your sewing room.

FABULOUS FABRICS

What is it about fabric? Is it the color, the texture, the feel of the fibers that are woven or knit together? What is it about fabric that compels a stitcher to touch, to stroke, to feel each piece? There doesn't seem to be the same intense pull to touch clothing or furniture or other items made of cloth, but the possibility and the promise of what that fabric may become causes a stitcher to stroke and handle yardage. It's part of the process of becoming one with the fabric, trying to determine its future life. Will it be a soft, clingy skirt? Or a bold, textured pillow? Or a fluid, sheer curtain? Many times the only way to know this is to feel the surface of the fabric, letting it drape from your fingers, experiencing the hand of the fabric for yourself.

One touch and many stitchers can identify the raw materials used to create the yardage. The slick feel of polyester, the rough texture of wool, the smooth touch of silk—all are distinctive to an experienced sewer and all have stories to tell about what the fabric may become in a future life. You can always tell a successful stitcher (or even a future one)—he or she listens to fabric and responds with touch.

Most people know more about fabric than they think. After all, it's all around us, in our closets, on our furniture, in our cars. It's impossible to go without touching multiple types of fabric every day. Knowing about fabrics simplifies your sewing because it is important to select fabric suitable for your next sewing project. Fabrics are generally divided into three categories:

NATURAL FIBERS: The fabrics in this category, cotton, linen, wool, hemp, bamboo, and silk are made from plants (cotton, flax, hemp, bamboo) and animals (wool, silk). Natural fibers, often regarded as "status" fabrics, have a distinctive look and feel. They "breathe" and are usually comfortable next to your skin, cool to wear in the summer and warm to wear in the winter. Natural fibers tend to take dyes well but will shrink, fade, and wrinkle fairly easily, so specific care is required.

MAN-MADE: This group of fabrics includes rayon, acrylic, and acetate. They start with natural materials, cellulose or protein but are developed by scientists in a lab. These fabrics generally take dyes well, have good draping qualities, and often have some of the same comfort properties as natural fabrics. Man-made fabrics can imitate the feel and textures of natural fabrics.

SYNTHETICS: Also developed by scientists, these fabrics include polyester, spandex, and nylon. Produced by chemicals and often oil- or petroleum-based, these fabrics are long-wearing, wrinkle-resistant (or wrinkle-free in many cases), and are usually very low-maintenance. These fabrics may not "breathe" well and some do not absorb moisture well, so they feel hot and clammy when worn in warm weather. Microfibers, which are made from polyester, can absorb moisture so are more comfortable to wear than other synthetics.

An assortment of fabrics made from various fibers: silk, cotton, wool, linen, polyester, nylon and hemp.

FABRIC TYPES

FABRIC	CHARACTERISTICS	TYPICAL FIBER	TYPICAL USE
Batik	Refers to resist dying method from Indonesia using wax to create design	Cotton, rayon	Shirts, dresses, quilts
Batiste	Lightweight, fine fabric with a plain weave	Cotton, silk, or synthetic	Blouses, christening gowns, handker-chiefs, lingerie
Boucle	Textured with loops on the surface	Wool, wool blend	Suits, jackets
Broadcloth	Plain weave fabric	Cotton, cotton-polyester blend, wool, silk	Shirts, general all-purpose fabric
Brocade	Jacquard fabric with all-over woven design	Cotton, silk	Jackets, decorator pillows, upholstery
Burlap	Coarse-weave fabric, heavy	Jute, cotton, hemp	Bags, curtains
Calico	Plain weave with printed small-motif all-over design	Cotton	Quilts, shirts, girl's dresses
Canvas or Duck	Heavy, tightly woven, sturdy	Cotton or linen	Upholstery, outdoor furniture, shoes, artist canvas
Cashmere	Knitted or woven, soft, warm	Blend of goat's hair for softness and wool for durability	Tailored suits, knitwear
Challis	Soft fabric that drapes well	Rayon, cotton, wool	Dresses, tops, skirts
Chambray	Plain weave with a colored warp and white weft	Cotton, cotton blend	Shirts, sportswear, pajamas
Chenille	Textured fabric made with chenille yarn that is thick, soft, and fuzzy	Cotton, wool, rayon, acrylic	Bedspreads, throws, jackets
Chiffon	Soft, lightweight, sheer that drapes well	Polyester, silk	Scarves, evening wear
China Silk	Soft, lightweight	Silk	Lining, scarves
Corduroy	Pile fabric cut to have ribs or welts, has a nap that causes the color to look different in each direction	Cotton, polyester, blends	Children's clothing, slacks, jackets
Damask	Similar to brocade with jacquard-weave design	Cotton, linen, blends	Table linens, soft furnishings
Denim	Strong, twill weave with colored warp and white weft. Usually blue but also available in other colors	Cotton	Jackets, jeans, soft furnishings, bags, purses
Doupioni	Luxurious fabric with slubbed surface	Silk, synthetics	Formal wear, home furnishings
Felt	Non-woven fabric from heat, moisture, and pressure	Wool, polyester	Crafts, toys, bags
Flannel	Plain or twill weave, sometimes a brushed surface	Wool, cotton	Suits, sportswear
Flannelette	Has a soft, brushed look with a slight nap on one or both sides. Can be a plain or twill weave	Cotton	Pajamas, children's clothing, quilts, blankets
Fleece	Soft, knit fabric that does not ravel	Cotton, synthetics	Hats, mittens, throws, sweatshirts
Gauze	Sheer, lightweight woven fabric	Cotton, silk, synthetics	Sun dresses, blouses, curtains
Gingham	Lightweight woven check or stripe	Cotton or cotton blend	Children's clothing, blouses
Interlock	Knit fabric, plain colors	Cotton, acrylic, blends	T-shirts, underwear
Lamé	Shiny fabric woven or knitted with metallic thread	Metallic & nylon, synthetics	Evening wear, crafts
Lawn	Lightweight plain weave	Cotton or synthetics	Blouses, children's clothing
Madras	Lightweight plaid fabric from India	Cotton or cotton blend	Shirts, shorts, bags
Organdy	Semi-sheer, crisp fabric	Cotton or cotton blend	Blouses, evening wear
Organza	Sheer, crisp fabric that has a sheen to it	Silk, polyester	Evening wear
Oxford Cloth	Shirting fabric made with a basket weave	Cotton or cotton blend	Shirts
Percale	Smooth, lightweight, plain weave fabric	Cotton, cotton-polyester	Bed linens
Satin	Refers to the weave that results in a sheen	Silk, cotton, synthetics	Bridal wear, lingerie, blouses
Spandex	Knit fabric that stretches in all directions; also known by the Dupont brand name Lycra	Synthetics, also blended with a variety of other fibers	Swimwear, lingerie, sportswear
Taffeta	Shiny, plain weave fabric with a crisp hand; creates a "rustling" sound when worn	Silk, polyester, acetate	Lining, formal wear
Terrycloth	Absorbent fabric with looped pile on one/both sides	Cotton, linen	Towels, bath accessories, beachwear
Ticking	Sturdy, woven, striped fabric	Cotton, blends	Pillow, mattresses, crafts
Tricot	Lightweight knit fabric with stretch on the cross grain but not on the lengthwise grain	Nylon	Lingerie, lining
Tulle	Fine netting	Nylon, silk	Bridal wear, dance/skating costumes
Velvet	Soft, luxurious fabric with a short, cut pile	Silk, cotton, rayon	Evening wear, upholstery
Velveteen	Pile fabric manufactured in the same way as corduroy but the pile is not cut into ribs	Cotton	Jackets, children's clothing, crafts
Voile	Soft, sheer, plain weave fabric with a crisp hand	Cotton or cotton blends	Curtains, sun dresses

Besides fiber content, another way to identify fabric is by the structure. For instance, velvet is a thick, plush fabric with a "furry" surface but can be made from cotton, silk, or rayon. Terrycloth is a thick absorbent fabric with loops on the surface but may start with cotton or linen fibers. The chart on page 37 offers details about various types of fabric.

When you go to the fabric store to purchase fabric, you will usually find it folded in half lengthwise and wrapped around cardboard (called a "bolt"). Sold by the yard, fabric is measured down the length. The side edges of the fabric are finished; they are called selvages. When the fabric is cut from the bolt, it is cut across the width from selvage to selvage. Fabrics generally come in several standard widths from 36" to 110", measuring across the fabric from selvage to selvage. You may occasionally find other widths, but the ones listed on the chart below are the most common.

When converting from one fabric width to another, there are other considerations for making sure you're purchasing the correct amount:

- If going to a more narrow fabric, make sure that the pattern doesn't have any pieces that are wider than the fabric to which you are converting.
- Remember to allow more fabric for using a napped fabric or for matching plaids or stripes.

Most fabric stores make it easy for you to determine the fiber content (cotton, wool, silk etc.) of a fabric

because it is printed on the end of the bolt. The information includes the name of the manufacturer, the name of the fabric line or collection, the fiber content, the amount of yardage when the bolt is full, the recommended care of the fabric, and the width of the fabric (see chart below). If a fabric is sold as a "flat fold" or off the bolt, it may or may not be tagged with this information. Bargain fabrics are often sold as "indeterminate fiber," leaving you to take a guess at the content and care.

With a little experience, you can often tell the fiber content of the fabric by touch or smell, but there is a simple test you can do at home that is fairly reliable in determining the origin of the fibers that make up the fabric. The burn test is easy but requires a little preparation and common sense to do it safely. You'll need a swatch of the fabric you are trying to identify, long tweezers, a lighter or match, and a metal or glass vessel such as a bowl or pan. The test can also be done in a sink, since being close to water is a good idea.

In a well-ventilated area, you simply hold the swatch down in the vessel with the tweezers, light a corner of the swatch, and immediately blow it out. Look at the charred corner and compare it to the chart below to determine the fiber content of the fabric. Note: This test is fairly conclusive for fabrics of one origin (all silk, all cotton, etc.) but blends that combine two or more fibers do not give reliable results in identifying the multiple fibers.

FABRIC MEASUREMENT CONVERSION

WIDTH	35"–36" JAPANESE PRINTS	39" BATIKS	44"–45" FASHION FABRIC QUILTING COTTON	54" DRAPERY UPHOLSTERY	58"–60" FASHION FABRICS KNITS	108" QUILT BACKING HOME DEC
	1¾	1½	1⅜	1⅛	1	⅝
	2	1¾	1⅝	1⅜	1¼	¾
	2¼	2	1¾	1½	1⅜	¾
	2½	2¼	2⅛	1¾	1⅝	⅞
	2⅞	2½	2¼	1⅞	1¾	1
	3⅛	2⅞	2½	2	1⅞	1
	3⅜	3	2¾	2¼	2	1⅛
	3¾	3¼	2⅞	2⅜	2¼	1¼
	4¼	3½	3⅛	2⅝	2⅜	1½
	4½	3¾	3⅜	2¾	2⅝	1½
	4¾	4	3⅝	2⅞	2¾	1⅝
	5	4¼	3⅞	3⅛	2⅞	1¾

FIBER BURN TEST RESULTS

FIBER	RESULT
Wool	Extinguishes itself, smells of burning hair; leaves an irregular hollow bead residue
Cotton	Yellow flame; smells of burning paper; leaves a dark ash
Silk	Burns slowly; smells of burning hair; leaves an irregular soft bead residue
Linen	Slow to ignite; smells of burning paper; leaves a gray ash
Rayon	Burns rapidly; smells of burning leaves; leaves a soft gray ash
Polyester	Melts; has a chemical smell; leaves a hard black bead
Spandex	Melts; smells of burning rubber; leaves a black ash
Nylon	Melts; smells of celery; leaves a hard black bead
Acetate	Melts; smells of vinegar; leaves a brittle black bead
Acrylic	Melts; Smells of burning fish; leaves a hard black bead

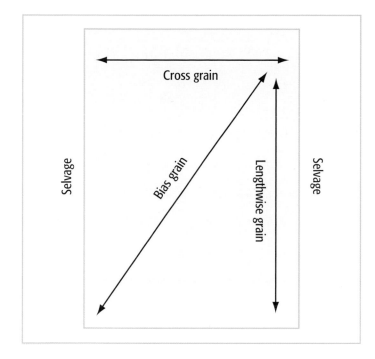

GRAIN LINES

Woven fabrics have directional "lines" created by the weaving of the threads. These grain lines are important for many projects, especially clothing where the fabric will "hang" from the body after it is sewn. The fabric will always find true grain, so if you place the pattern on the fabric off-grain, the garment will hang crooked on your body. Patterns are usually marked with a lengthwise line that should be aligned with the lengthwise grain of the fabric.

Occasionally, a fabric will be distorted when folded and wrapped on a bolt, so when you take yardage home, it is crooked or off-grain. It needs to be straightened before cutting out the pattern. Use the following steps to straighten the grain of distorted fabric.

1. Pull a crosswise thread to find the true crossgrain.
2. Cut along the pulled thread line.
3. Fold the fabric lengthwise, aligning the selvages; if it doesn't align smoothly, it is off-grain.
4. Pull from corner to diagonal corner, pulling away from the distortion to put it back on grain.

A fabric may be so distorted that straightening is not an option. If you choose to use it anyway, be aware that it will be most noticeable if it is a print or plaid (the pattern will be crooked), if making a garment that hangs from the body (it will not drape straight), or if using it to piece a quilt (patchwork patterns will be distorted). It may work fine for small projects such as purses and book covers that do not depend on the grain of the fabric for structure or style.

FABRIC CARE

When selecting fabric, pay attention to the type of care required to get the most use from it. Usually provided on the end of the fabric bolt, international symbols show how to wash, dry, and press fabrics. These symbols are easy to interpret once you become familiar with their meanings. Use the chart at right to understand the care symbols related to your fabric choices.

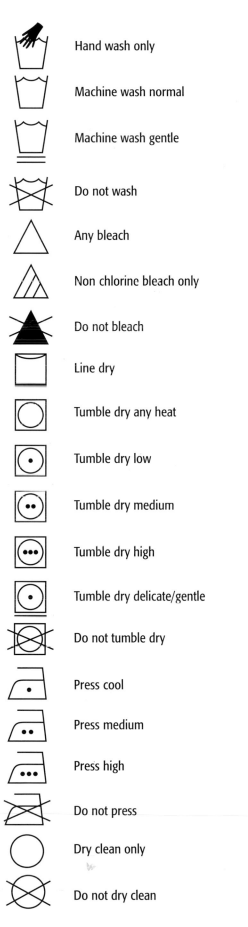

INTERNATIONAL FABRIC CARE SYMBOLS

Hand wash only

Machine wash normal

Machine wash gentle

Do not wash

Any bleach

Non chlorine bleach only

Do not bleach

Line dry

Tumble dry any heat

Tumble dry low

Tumble dry medium

Tumble dry high

Tumble dry delicate/gentle

Do not tumble dry

Press cool

Press medium

Press high

Do not press

Dry clean only

Do not dry clean

Patterns are available for almost any type of project you may want to make.

PATTERNS AND PLANS

Almost every new sewer starts with a pattern although as you build your skills, you may be able to make many things without patterns, especially if they are based on simple shapes such as squares or rectangles. Pillows, tablecloths, and pillowcases are just a few examples of this. Garments can be made without patterns by draping fabric into shape using a dress form. Of course, that is a skill in itself, so for the most part you will use a pattern.

The easiest way to shop for patterns is to browse the pattern books at your local fabric store. All chain stores and many independent fabric stores offer tables with seating, so you can sit and peruse catalogs at your leisure. Pattern companies such as Vogue, McCall's, Butterick, Simplicity, New Look, Burda, and Kwik Sew publish catalogs each season with their full line of patterns. These well-known pattern companies feature all types of garment patterns as well as craft, home decorating, and children's patterns. Besides in-store shopping, these companies have websites for your shopping convenience. In addition to the large pattern companies, there are hundreds of small independent pattern companies offering patterns for everything from garments to crafts to quilts. These patterns are usually found in independent fabric stores and quilt shops, as well as online.

THE PATTERN ENVELOPE

When shopping for patterns, you must know how to decipher the information found on the front and back of the pattern envelope. It can help you decide if you want the pattern, and then, if you purchase it, help you determine the required type and amount of fabric as well as the specific notions needed.

The front of the pattern envelope shows the finished project as an illustration and/or as a photograph of the sewn item. If there are multiple options (short sleeve, long sleeve, crew neck, V-neck, etc.), it usually shows these and labels them with letters (Views A, B, C, etc.). Looking at a photo of the garment made in real fabric usually gives you a better idea of the fit and the flow of the garment, but the illustrations may show some particulars such as seams or closure details that aren't obvious in photos.

When you turn the pattern envelope over to the back, you'll find a wealth of useful information. The first thing to check is the written description, if there is one. This short paragraph may tell you about things you can't see in the illustration or photo such as linings or bias-cut pieces. Next, look at the line drawings of the back of the projects: you'll be able to see more details such as zippers or yokes. There's also a list of suggested fabrics. These will give you the best result but may not be the only options, so don't be afraid to look at other fabrics of similar weight and thickness.

DON'T DO THE NUMBERS

When buying garment patterns, don't expect the sizing to be the same as ready-made clothing. You will probably need at least one size larger, if not two. Wearing a leotard, take your measurements, or, for greater accuracy, have someone else take them. Along with your bust, waist, and hip measurements, you'll need your high bust and back waist length (from the base of your neck to your waistline).

Compare your measurements to the ones listed on the pattern envelope and find the size to which it most closely corresponds. Don't be discouraged if you don't like the size—remember, it's only a number!

When determining the fit of a garment, you need to consider the amount of ease factored into it. Ease is extra fabric built into the garment—added to the body measurement with which the designer starts. There are two types of ease as described below:

WEARING EASE: Extra fabric added to body measurements so clothing will be comfortable, and you can move around in it. If the garment is the exact measurement of your body, it will fit tightly with no room to move and certainly no room for comfort. There are no hard and fast rules about how much wearing ease to add, but it is generally ½"–4" depending on the area of the body to which it is added.

DESIGN EASE: Extra fabric added to body measurements so clothing will fit in a certain way. Typically, the categories are closely fitted, fitted, semi-fitted, loosely fitted, and very loosely fitted. The amount of design ease varies even more than wearing ease. It totally depends on the designer and his or her vision for the garment he or she is designing. What is fitted to one designer may be loosely fitted to another.

The measurements on the back of the pattern envelope are the size of the flat pattern pieces. This includes both wearing ease and design ease. To add to the variables of ease, the type of fabric used can also influence the fit of the garment. A fabric with very little "give" may be uncomfortable when used for a closely fitted garment but one with more stretch or movement may be the perfect choice for fit, comfort, and style. Therefore, while there are no specific answers to the question of ease in garments, it will help if you have an understanding of what the pattern measurements represent.

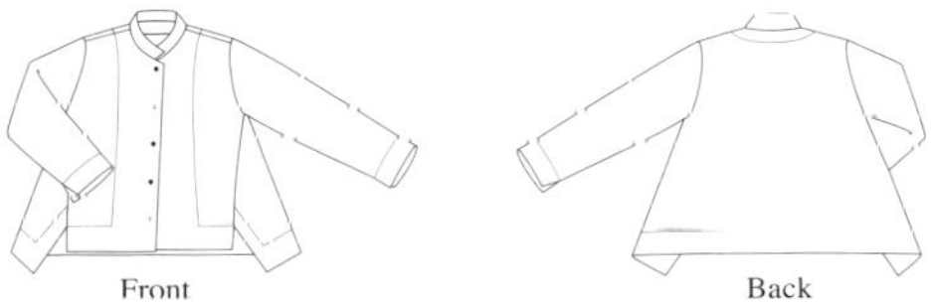

41

Liberty Shirt: Shirt or jacket has diagonal side seams angled to the front, soft stand-up collar, and set in sleeves with vent openings. Asymmetric front and back deep hems with mitered corners. Front topstitching detail and five-button closure.

Fabric Suggestions: Cotton shirting, linen, lightweight wool, crepe de Chine, jersey.

Notions: Five 5/8" Buttons, 1 yd. Fusible Interfacing, Thread.

Fabric Requirements:
*45": 2 5/8 yards sizes XS-M
       2 3/4 yards sizes L-XXL
60": 1 7/8 yards sizes XS-M
       2 1/4 yards sizes L-XXL
*XXL requires 48" fabric width

SIZE MEASUREMENTS

	(XS)	(SM)		(MED)		(LG)		(XL)	(XXL)
SIZE	6	8	10	12	14	16	18	20	22
Bust	31	32½	34	36	38	40	42	44	46
Waist	24½	25½	26½	27½	29	31	33	35	37
Hip	34	35	36	37	39½	41½	43½	45½	47½

LENGTH Finished Back

Shirt	25¾"	26"		26¼"		26½"		27"	27½"

The pattern envelope offers critical information for purchasing fabric and notions. Courtesy of The Sewing Workshop.

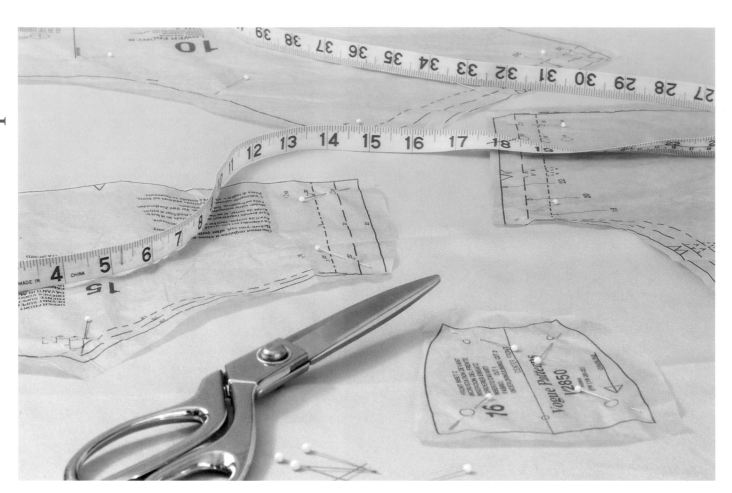

Position and pin pattern pieces with printed grainlines parallel to the selvages of the fabric. Courtesy of Jane Foster Studios.

ADDITIONAL INFORMATION

The pattern envelope can also give you an idea of the complexity of the pattern. Many patterns have labels such as Fast, Easy, or Quick, usually signifying that they are good for the beginner. The number of pattern pieces is often a good indication of the skill level needed to sew the project. Fewer pieces indicate easier while more pattern pieces means a higher level of complexity.

The next important piece of information is how much fabric it takes to make the project. Noted in yards, this amount includes any fraction of a yard needed and is listed according to the width of the fabric. In most cases, you need the amount listed first, but if you look down the list you may see an amount needed for fabric with nap. This refers to fabric that has texture such as velvet, corduroy, or fleece. Because the nap can be brushed in different directions, up or down, it has the possibility of reflecting light differently, making it look as if it is different colors. To avoid this, all pattern pieces should be placed on the fabric in the same direction, which requires a bit more fabric.

Other situations that call for napped layouts are uneven plaids, directional prints, and uneven stripes. You'll need the extra fabric to match these or to make them run in the correct direction. If you want to be more specific in calculating fabric for patterned fabric, use this formula:

Measure the repeat (from start to end of one set of plaids, patterns, or stripes) and add this number to each yard required. For instance, if the repeat measures 5" and the garment requires 3 yards, you will require 3 yards and 15" (3 repeats); round up to 3½ yards, and you'll have enough to match the patterns as you make the project.

Also listed on the back cover are required amounts of lining fabric, interfacing, and trims. Finally, the back cover lists any notions you need to complete the project—not sewing supplies, but specific items such as buttons, zippers, and thread.

THE PATTERN PIECES

The tissue paper pattern pieces and the instruction pages called guide sheets are inside the pattern envelope. The first thing to do is to open the guide sheet and get the "lay of the land." If you've never used a pattern, read the opening information about using the pattern, deciphering the pattern markings, and understanding the sewing directions. Next, unfold the pattern pieces and determine which ones you need to use. Using scissors designated for paper, cut the pieces apart, trimming along the printed cutting lines. Press the pieces with a dry iron to remove creases and flatten the pattern.

Find the layout diagram that corresponds with the view and size you are making. Circle or highlight it for easy

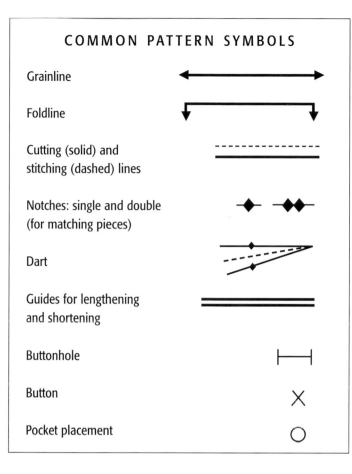

COMMON PATTERN SYMBOLS

Grainline

Foldline

Cutting (solid) and
stitching (dashed) lines

Notches: single and double
(for matching pieces)

Dart

Guides for lengthening
and shortening

Buttonhole

Button

Pocket placement

After cutting out the pattern pieces, it is important to transfer any markings (using chalk, water-soluble or air-soluble marker, tailor tacks, etc.) from the paper pattern pieces to the fabric. These markings indicate seam lines, gathering lines, pocket placement, pleat lines, buttonhole placement, etc. Careful marking can mean the difference between smooth construction and a struggle to put it all together.

PATTERN SOFTWARE

Today's technology has added a custom element to patterns. You can create your own and print them on your home computer. There are several programs available, most offering free demo versions, so you can try them before making a purchase. Some programs require you to input your measurements, so you can make garments that fit your body. Programs also offer the ability to create your own design, changing elements to give a unique look to your garment. Whether garment-related, quilt design or craft-based (purses, accessories, etc.), these programs offer the ultimate in creating custom projects.

reference as you sew. Also circle any lining and/or interfacing layouts that apply to your project. Next, prepare your fabric for cutting — launder it as you expect to launder the finished project (hand wash or machine wash and line dry or machine dry or, dry clean), then fold it according to the layout diagram you have circled, usually in half lengthwise, right sides together, matching the selvages. Position the pattern pieces on the fabric, consulting the diagram for placement and orientation (right or wrong side up). Pin the pieces to the fabric or use weights to hold them in place.

Patterns should follow the grain lines of the fabric. This is especially important when sewing garments, because it will determine how the finished garment will hang from your body. To make sure you have correctly positioned the pattern piece on the fabric, locate the printed line which indicates lengthwise grain. Measure from this line to the side of the fabric (either the folded edge or the selvage) in several places to make sure the edge of the fabric is parallel to the printed line. If it is not, make the adjustments needed to correct this.

Once all of the pieces are correctly positioned and pinned or weighted, cut along the cutting lines of the pattern piece using bent-handled shears. For the most accuracy, keep the outer edge of the lower blade of the scissors in contact with the table and take long, smooth cuts. Do not remove the pattern piece from the fabric; if you used weights instead of pins, temporarily pin the paper pattern to the fabric in one or two places.

PAPER PATTERN TIP

Once the guide sheets and tissue paper patterns have been removed from the envelope and used, it is almost impossible to refold everything so it fits easily back into the envelope. Try this trick, and you'll have no trouble keeping your patterns neat and organized. Refold the pattern pieces to be the approximate size of the folded guide sheet, but don't worry about how flat or neat the pattern pieces are. Place the tissue paper between the sides of the folded guide sheet and compress the layers between your fingers. Now you can slide the guide sheets and pattern pieces into the original pattern envelope without a problem!

UNDERNEATH IT ALL

Interfacings and stabilizers appear to be similar materials but are used for different purposes and in different sewing situations. Become familiar with the types available and when they should be used, so your projects will have a professionally-sewn look.

INTERFACING

Interfacing is used to add body, structure, and shape to a project such as when adding stability to a waistband, adding body and buttonhole support to a shirt placket, and preventing the stretching of a neckline. It can be a sew-in or fusible type and will stay in the project after it is sewn. Most garment patterns give cutting and construction instructions for interfacing. Interfacings are usually available in white, off-white, gray, and black.

The three major types of interfacing are:

TRICOT: Available as a fusible, this type of interfacing is lightweight and has stretch across the width and is used for light to medium weight knits as well as wovens. Its often used as an underlining because it can be fused to the entire body of a garment without changing the hand of the fabric. Tricot interfacings have more drape and are more flexible than other types.

NON-WOVEN: Available as sew-in or fusible versions, this type of interfacing is made of synthetic materials (polyester, nylon, and/or rayon) that are bonded together. It does not ravel and there is no grain, so it can be cut in any direction. It may have stretch in one or more directions (this varies with brand and type), which should be taken into consideration. There is minimal shrinkage with non-woven interfacings.

WOVEN: Available as sew-in or fusible versions, this type of interfacing should be cut with the grain the same as fabric or on the bias for soft shaping. Often used for shaping in tailored garments, woven interfacing generally offers the most strength and stability. Made from cotton, polyester, or blends, it includes every weight from lightweight sheer to heavy canvas; canvas interfacings may include goat hair or wool fibers and are used in tailored garments, usually coats and jackets. Fabrics such as organza and batiste are sometimes used as interfacings, usually in projects made of sheer or lightweight fabrics.

When selecting interfacing, decide on the weight and degree of crispness needed for your project. Is it a fluid garment with a soft drape that only needs interfacing at the neckline, a smartly tailored shirt requiring interfacing for a crisp collar and cuffs, or a highly structured jacket that uses interfacing to shape the lapels and collar? Make your selection accordingly to get the results you want. In general, fusibles add more firmness than sew-in interfacings.

When deciding whether to fuse or sew, consider first your fabric. Certain materials such as velvets, plastics, and beaded, or delicate fabrics cannot take the heat needed for fusing. Open weave or lace fabrics also don't work

Interfacing is available in several neutral colors: white, black, grey, and beige.

well with fusibles, as the adhesives will come through to the right side of the fabric. Be aware that once a fabric is fused, it is difficult to un-fuse if a mistake needs to be corrected. When fusibles were first introduced to the home sewer, they were stiff and unreliable and often did not give the desired results, but in the 25 to 30 years since, great improvements have been made, and now they are often the choice of many stitchers. Fusibles are generally faster and easier to use than sew-in types, which may require basting or hand stitching. Most sew-ins are pinned or basted in place and then stitched in permanently with the garment seams. Heavier canvas interfacings are stitched by hand because the seam allowances are trimmed to remove bulk. Ultimately, the choice is just a matter of preference, taking into account what is available for the type of project being made.

Pre-treat woven sew-in interfacings in the same way as your project fabric: machine washing, hand washing, or dry-cleaning. It is best to pre-shrink fusible interfacing but be careful to avoid disturbing the fusible adhesive. For woven and knit fusibles, submerge in warm water and make sure they are entirely wet. Squeeze (don't wring) the excess water and let air-dry. Hang woven interfacing over a shower rod but dry tricot flat. Non-woven interfacings can be pre-shrunk using a steam iron. Hold the iron 1"–2" above the non-fusible side of the interfacing and steam for about 10 seconds, taking care not to touch the surface of the interfacing.

When using fusibles, always do a test swatch to see how the interfacing adheres to the fabric and to check the bond created by the fusing. Every brand and type of fusible interfacing has slightly different properties, so it is important to follow the directions of the manufacturer. In general, you need to pay attention to the temperature and the time required (too hot and/or too long may melt the adhesive and too cold and/or too short may not allow it to bond). It is also important not to slide the iron but to apply pressure in an up-and-down motion. Once the fusing is complete, let the fabric cool completely before handling it. When it is cool, check the feel of the fabric—is it too stiff or too soft? Also fold it and roll it to check the bond and the shaping properties to determine if it will work in your project.

STABILIZERS

Stabilizers are materials that add temporary support to fabric for decorative stitching. After the stitching is complete, the stabilizer is removed. If stabilizer is needed and not used, the stitches will pucker or tunnel the fabric. Stabilizers are also used extensively in machine embroidery to prepare fabrics for embroidery designs and are called backings or toppings. Available in different weights, stabilizers are usually identified by the method used to remove them from the project after the stitching is complete.

TEAR-AWAY: Use for woven fabrics. Available in light, medium, and heavy weights, this stabilizer is easy to remove by tearing it close to the stitching; hold the stitches to protect them as you tear. The portion left in the stitching will soften with washing. For easier removal, it is sometimes better to use two layers of lightweight instead of one medium or heavy. When selecting a tear-away, be aware that different brands may tear more easily in one direction or another and some may tear more cleanly than others.

45

Stabilizers are categorized by their method of removal: cut-away, wash-away, and tear-away.

CUT-AWAY: Use for knit fabrics. This stabilizer comes in all weights and is removed by cutting it away close to the stitching. The portion left in the stitching will soften slightly with washing. Depending on the project, you may want to leave the entirety of this stabilizer in for added body.

WASH-AWAY: Use when you don't want any stabilizer left in the design. This type is available as a clear, "plastic-like" film or as a white material similar to paper. Both types will completely dissolve when rinsed with water. The clear type is not as stable but can be used as a topping that is placed on top to keep the stitches from sinking into the pile of the fabric; this is especially helpful when stitching on terrycloth or velvet. The white type of wash-away stabilizer has less stretch and is used on the back of the project. Both may be washed away but it may take several rinsings to completely remove all of the stabilizer, depending on the weight used.

HEAT-AWAY: Remove this type of stabilizer by using a dry iron to dissolve it after stitching is complete. Heat causes the stabilizer to turn brown, and then it crumbles and can be brushed away using a soft toothbrush. Choose this type when the fabric and/or stitching is too delicate to use a tear-away or too sheer for a cut-away. This is a good choice for a fabric that tolerates heat but not moisture.

Choosing a stabilizer starts with the fabric but also needs to take into consideration what you are stitching. You should match the weight of the stabilizer to the weight of your fabric. In general, the denser the stitching, whether decorative stitches from the sewing machine or an embroidery design, the sturdier the stabilizer needs to be.

The stabilizer is usually placed on the wrong side of the fabric. In the case of machine embroidery and some free-motion sewing machine stitching, the layered fabric and stabilizer are hooped as one to prepare for stitching. Temporary spray adhesives or basting sprays, made especially for use on fabric, can be used to bond the stabilizer to the fabric to make it easy to treat them as one.

Also available are adhesive-backed stabilizers in tear-away, cut-away and wash-away versions. These are used mostly for machine embroidery in situations where the item being embroidered cannot be hooped. This includes collars, cuffs, caps, and tote bags, as well as thick fabrics such as terrycloth. The stabilizer is hooped and the protective paper in the hoop is removed to reveal the adhesive. The hard-to-hoop item is smoothed into place on the adhesive, ready for stitching.

STABILIZER TIPS

- Don't be tempted to use materials other than quality stabilizers for your projects. Using paper, dryer sheets, or coffee filters may seem like good ideas, but you may run into problems because these materials may have stretch in them and will not be stable enough to give you the best results. They may also create lint or fuzz and/or have foreign matter in them that may be deposited into the working parts of your machine, possibly causing damage now or at a later date.

- If you are planning to use a wash-away stabilizer or topping, make sure your fabric will handle wetness without staining.

- If using a film type of water-soluble stabilizer, you can layer it for heaver support. Use a dry iron (steam will dissolve the stabilizer) to meld the layers into one.

- When selecting stabilizer, sew a test with fabric to make sure it gives good results before beginning your project. This is especially true with embroidery designs but is also a good idea for decorative stitching and machine techniques that call for stabilizer.

- There are so many types of stabilizers it can sometimes be confusing. To be ready for most sewing and embroidery situations, be sure you have one of each of the three basic types (cut-away, tear-away, wash-away) in your stash.

- Stabilizers look so similar, it's sometimes hard to tell them apart. When you open a new package of stabilizer, cut an 8" square and label it with its name using a permanent ink marker. Keep the squares as references so you can always know what you have. Note: Some stabilizer companies have sample packs that include labeled swatches of their entire line.

- The general rule of stabilizers is to use cut-away with knit fabrics and tear-away with woven fabrics.

- To remove water-soluble stabilizer, cut or tear most of it away. Place a towel over the remaining stabilizer and press lightly using a steam iron. This dissolves the stabilizer without having to get the project wet.

- Use the color of stabilizer most appropriate for your fabric: white for light color fabrics, beige for white or beige fabrics, and black for black or dark fabrics.

pressing

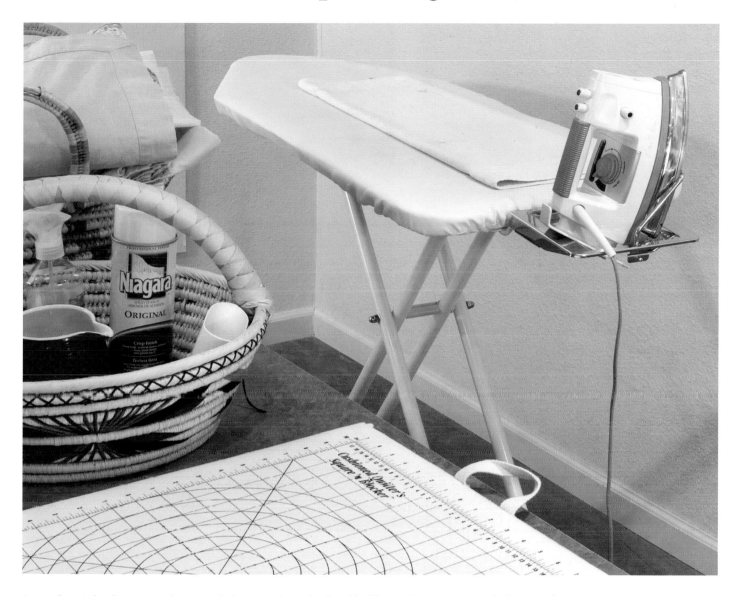

A pressing station in your sewing room helps result in professional-looking projects. Courtesy of Diana McClun.

PRESSING

Often overlooked, pressing is one of the most important steps in sewing. If you want your projects to be professional and avoid that "homemade" look, pay attention to pressing techniques and take advantage of the tools that make them effective. Ironing and pressing are different techniques for different situations, and it's important to understand the difference to avoid making irreparable mistakes. Ironing involves moving the iron across the surface of the fabric to flatten it and remove wrinkles. Pressing is more of an up-and-down motion, applying pressure to set stitches or shape the fabric in a certain way.

In most cases, pressing is required throughout the sewing process, usually after each sewing step. Press each seam before sewing across it; steam and shape individual parts such as collars before attaching them to another part of the project.

PRESSING EQUIPMENT FOR EVERY SEWER

IRON: The only piece of equipment that is absolutely essential for pressing is the iron. When selecting an iron for the sewing room, look for a good, solid iron that has both dry and steam settings; it also needs a wide range of temperature settings to accommodate a wide variety of fabric types. Select one that has a smooth soleplate that is easy to clean. "Surge of steam" and spray button features are good to have on your sewing iron, especially if you do custom tailoring. When comparing irons, look at the point at the front; a long, narrow point makes it easy to get into small areas such as between buttons or tight corners, letting you easily press all parts of your project. Many irons today are equipped with an automatic shut-off feature that can be an annoyance in the sewing room. As you move back and forth between the sewing machine and the iron, you'll spend a great deal of time waiting for the iron to re-heat before you can continue pressing. In this case, the latest new feature may not be the best choice. If you do a large amount of sewing or work with large projects such as bridal wear or draperies, you may want to have an iron equipped with a separate water tank/steam generator.

IRONING SURFACE: Most sewers use an ironing board; be sure it's sturdy and level. An adjustable height feature lets you set the ironing board to suit your height whether standing or sitting. The surface should be padded and usually the foam pad that comes with it needs to be enhanced with layers of wool or cotton batting. Avoid ironing board covers that are made of a reflective material as they may hold too much heat and can cause fabrics to scorch. If working with oversized projects such as draperies, a pressing table large enough to lay out the fabric and support its weight will make the job easier. A large pad that fits over your cutting table may be a workable alternative to a permanent pressing table. Also available are vacuum suction pressing boards. These are similar to large ironing boards and are used with steam systems or irons with separate water tanks. Usually operated by a foot control, the suction draws the steam through the fabric, and the vacuum dries it for a clean, crisp finish.

PRESS CLOTH: This simple item can go a long way in protecting the surface of your fabric during pressing. A large square of white 100% cotton or linen fabric can be used as a press cloth. Printed or dyed fabrics are not good choices because the dye or pattern may transfer to your project. Placing the press cloth over the area to be pressed forms a barrier between the iron and fabric surface, preventing scorch marks and burns. Another press cloth option is called an appliqué or Teflon® press cloth. This durable, plastic-like material is heat-resistant and is especially useful when working with fusibles and fabric glues. The smooth, glossy surface of this pressing sheet doesn't stick to the adhesives and protects your iron and ironing board from sticky build-up.

USEFUL ACCESSORIES FOR MOST SEWERS

PRESSING HAM: Also called a tailor's ham, this useful pressing surface gets its name from its ham shape. It is for pressing shaped areas, usually in garment making. Useful for pressing darts, collars, sleeve caps, and curved seams, the ham is made of wool (for fabrics requiring low to medium temperatures) on one side and cotton (for fabrics requiring medium to high temperatures) on the other. Traditionally stuffed with sawdust, some instructions for making your own suggest using scraps of wool as a stuffing. Whatever the filling, pack it tightly, as the surface of the ham should be very hard. For the most stability, use the ham with a stand, usually available separately.

USEFUL ACCESSORIES: From the top, seam roll, point presser/clapper, pressing mitt, seam stick, pressing ham with stand.

SEAM ROLL: The seam roll is similar to a ham but a different shape. It is a long, round pressing surface for pressing narrow areas such as sleeves and pant legs. A wooden tool with similar uses, called a seam stick, is flat on one side and rounded on the other.

CLAPPER: Use this oval-shaped piece of wood to open and flatten seams, bulky facings, pleats, and collar edges (typically in wool but can be used on any fabric). Use the iron to generously steam the fabric, then place the clapper over the steamed area and apply pressure; the result is a flat, crisp press.

POINT PRESSER: A narrow wooden piece used to press narrow seams in hard-to-reach areas such as belts, cuffs, collars, etc., it's often mounted on a wooden base that serves as a clapper.

SLEEVE BOARD: Resembling a mini ironing board, this accessory is helpful in pressing sleeves and other small areas. It can be used on top of your ironing board and may be portable with a collapsible base or made of wood with a wooden base. Either type has a padded cover on the pressing surface.

PRESSING BOARD: This long, flat board was traditionally made of wood; today's versions are padded and covered with a silicone-treated fabric. Slip the board into pant legs to aid in pressing the seams open.

PRESSING MITT: A padded mitt that fits over your hand, slip it into areas of your project that are too small to fit over a tailor's ham and press over the mitt.

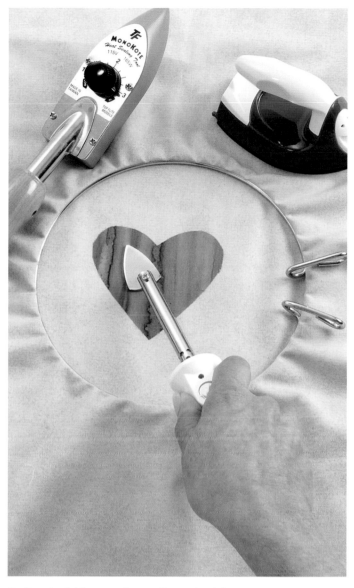

Craft and mini irons make small pressing jobs easy.

SPECIALTY PRESSING EQUIPMENT

CRAFT AND MINI IRONS: A small iron or wand iron is perfect for taking to classes or pressing at your sewing machine. The size allows easier manipulation in tight spaces and more control doing small detailed pressing. It's also good for small pressing jobs, for example, when sewing children's clothing, patchwork blocks, and items such as ties, ribbons, binding, etc.

TABLETOP STEAM PRESS: This item is great for fusing large areas and is also good for heat transfer designs. Use it to apply fusible interfacing to fabric before cutting out the fabric pieces. It does require table space although some models have stands that can be purchased separately.

NEEDLE BOARD: This pressing surface is covered with tiny stainless steel pins. Fabric that has a nap or pile such as velvet or corduroy is placed face down on the pins for pressing. This keeps the pressure of the iron from crushing the nap of the fabric.

GENERAL PRESSING TECHNIQUES

Before pressing any project, consider the type of fabric and select the correct iron temperature; test it on a left-over piece of the project fabric, checking to see if steam is acceptable. Use a press cloth or press from the wrong side to avoid damage to the right side of the fabric. The key to pressing or shaping with steam is that once you have applied heat and moisture, the fabric needs to dry completely without being disturbed. Let it sit until the surface of the fabric is dry to the touch. This will set the fabric and is especially important when pressing sharp creases or shaping areas such as collars and lapels.

SIMPLE SEAMS

Every straight seam should first be pressed in the direction it was sewn with the seam allowances together. This sets the stitches and melds them into the fabric. After setting the stitches, open the seam allowances and press the seam flat.

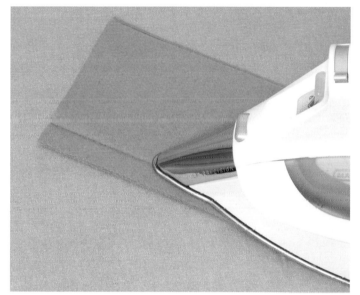

Setting the stitches.

Pressing the seam open.

GATHERED SEAMS

When pressing gathers in puffed sleeves, gathered waists, etc., use the tip of the iron to move between the gathers in the fabric. Avoid pressing any sharp creases into the fabric.

Move the tip of the iron into the gathered edge to avoid pressing sharp creases into the fabric.

CURVED SEAMS

An example of curved seams is princess seaming used to fit a garment over the bust. The major difference in pressing a curved seam rather than a flat one is that you need a curved surface such as a pressing ham or seam roll to maintain the shape of the seam. The first pressing step is the same as for the flat seam—set the stitches by pressing with the seam allowances together. Next, lay the seam over the pressing ham and open the seam, clipping the allowances where necessary to help it lay flat.

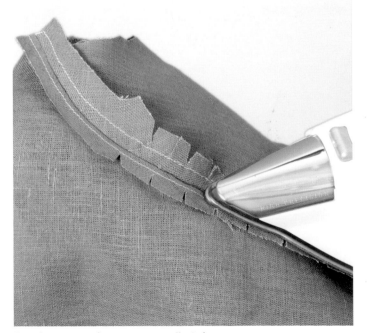

Pressing a curved seam over a tailor's ham.

ENCLOSED SEAMS

When finishing seams that will be inside such as in cuffs, collars, or facings, they must be pressed before and after turning the fabric to the right side. Trim the corners at a diagonal. Using a point presser and the tip of the iron, press the seam allowances open (Step 1). Next, place the piece on an ironing board with the seam allowances turned toward the underside; press (Step 2). Turn the piece to the right side and press from the underside (Step 3).

Step 1

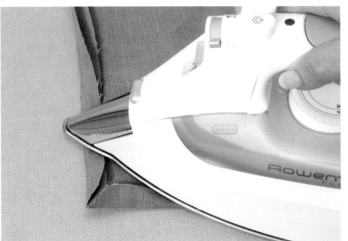

Step 2

Step 3

DARTS

Darts are used to shape the fabric to fit the body. For this reason, they should be pressed on a curved surface such as a pressing ham to maintain the shape. Before placing the fabric over the ham, press the dart flat as it was sewn. Press horizontal darts down and vertical darts toward the center. Darts in heavy fabric can be slit along the fold to about ½" from the point and pressed open to reduce bulk.

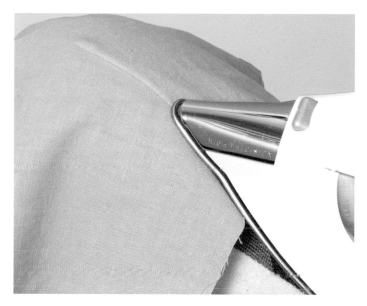

Press darts over a pressing ham to set the shape.

PLEATS

After pleats have been stitched, fold the fabric the entire length of the pleat, pinning or basting the lower edge if needed to hold them in place. Press to set the pleats, using steam as needed, and avoid pressing over the pins or basting thread.

Press pleats with brown paper "protectors."

SLEEVES

Using a seam roll or sleeve board, press the seam open. Press from the right side, then the wrong side.

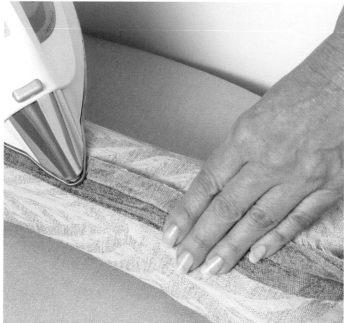

Insert a sleeve roll into the sleeve for pressing the seam open.

51

PRESSING TIPS

- When pressing from the wrong side, avoid "pressing shadows" on the right side of the fabric by slipping pieces of brown craft paper (can be cut from grocery bags) under the seam allowance, dart, or pleat before pressing. The paper keeps the seam allowances from making impressions that show through on the right side of the garment.
- Always press with the grain of the fabric using an up-and-down motion to avoid stretching or pulling the fabric. This is especially important when pressing bias-cut pieces.
- Each seam or dart should be pressed after stitching, making it as flat as possible before joining to another piece of fabric.
- Avoid pressing over fabric markings, pins, and basting threads as they may leave marks in the fabric.

An organized sewing space makes it easy to be productive.

ROOM TO SEW

A corner, a closet, a spare room, or the entire West wing—no matter how much space you have for sewing, two things are true. One, it will never be enough, and two, you'll make it work. As long as you have a place to set up your machine and somewhere you can spread out for cutting, you'll have room to sew. More space is nice and allows you more storage for fabrics, notions, and equipment, but it's not absolutely necessary. Ample space also lets you always have your sewing machine ready and waiting, rather than in the closet, waiting to be set up. This makes it easier to sew in short bursts and lessens the frustration of having to "get ready" to sew.

Usually, the amount of space we have is determined by where we live and who lives with us. Many sewers never have a dedicated room until the kids are grown and on their own. However, whatever your space, you want to make it as comfortable and as functional as possible. Use these guidelines for efficient and ergonomically friendly selection of sewing room elements.

CUTTING TABLE: To find the correct cutting height for you, stand with your arms to your sides and measure up from the floor to your elbow. Subtract 4" to find a comfortable cutting height that doesn't require

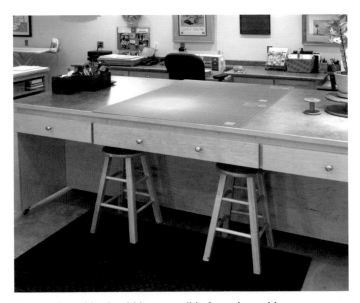

Your cutting table should be accessible from three sides.

continually bending (too low) or excessive lifting of your arms (too high). An easy way to add height to a regular table is to use bed risers under the legs. You can find these at specialty bed and bath stores or on the Internet. For the easiest use of a cutting table, place it so it is accessible

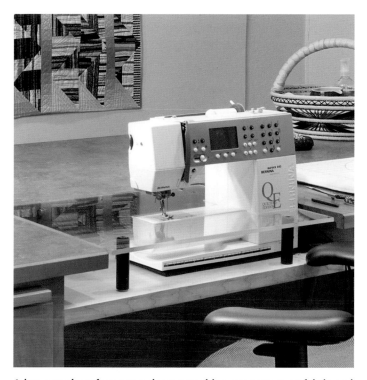

A large work surface around your machine supports your fabric and helps when managing large projects.

PLACEMENT OF FURNITURE/EQUIPMENT

The same as in your kitchen, your sewing room is most efficient if you have a work triangle connecting the different stations needed for sewing. The basic stations are cutting, sewing, and pressing, Depending on the type of sewing you do, you may also need to add any or all of these stations or areas: serging, embroidery, computer, fitting, quilt designing. If it sounds like you really will need the West wing, don't worry—many of these areas overlap or do double-duty, and some you may only set up as needed, especially if you don't have a dedicated sewing space. You may also find sewing room furniture that easily accommodates several pieces such as your machine, serger, and computer in an efficient arrangement using only one or two fixtures.

If you are planning a space dedicated to your craft, start with a diagram of the area and plan it on paper first. Use graph paper so you can plan in proportion to make sure everything fits as needed. You can try several possibilities without the strain of moving furniture and equipment. Arrange the basic stations in a U-shape, L-shape, galley (along parallel walls), or on a single wall. Even if you sew in a temporary space, where you set your equipment up and take it down frequently, considering the work triangle makes it easier and more efficient while you are sewing.

on at least three sides. If your cutting table has drop-down work surfaces, allow enough room to easily lift and lower the sides as needed.

SEWING MACHINE: Sit with your feet flat on the floor. Bend your arms at a 90° angle. This is where the bed of your machine should be (usually about 29"–30" from the floor), whether it sits on a table or fits down into a cabinet. If you have trouble finding a table or cabinet the correct height, invest in an adjustable-height office chair and adjust it to the table. A minimum of two feet of workspace on each side of the machine gives you enough room for sewing in comfort without feeling cramped.

SERGER: Has similar requirements as the sewing machine but these useful companion machines usually sit on a table, not in a cabinet. This is where the adjustable chair really comes in handy. A minimum of two feet of workspace on each side is also needed for the serger.

PRESSING STATION: Your ironing board should be about 3" higher than your cutting table for ironing from a standing position. You can also adjust your ironing board to about 24" from the floor and iron from a sitting position. This is most useful if you can set your ironing surface next to your machine at a right angle. If your chair has wheels, you can easily swing around to press after stitching.

EMBROIDERY MACHINE: You don't need to sit at the embroidery machine, so the height of the table is not as important as with the sewing machine. It works well to put the embroidery machine on a tall table or counter, ideally with the screen at eye level. This makes it easy to change settings, attach the hoops to the machine, and change threads from a standing position without the need to bend over.

A triangular work pattern is the most efficient when arranging work stations.

Keep all stations within easy reach of each other to minimize effort.

The layout and cutting area may be completely removed from the other stations.

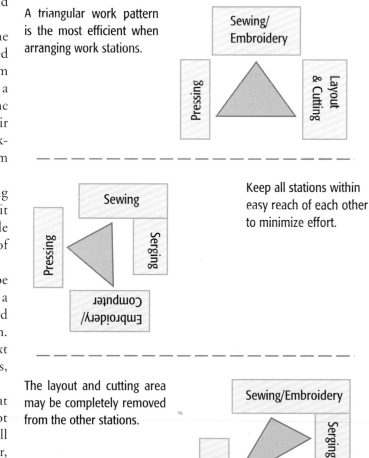

BEYOND FURNITURE

Other considerations for making your space as workable as possible are electrical power, lighting, flooring, and organization "extras." Take these points into account as you plan your dream sewing space.

LIGHTING: Natural lighting is best, so a room with windows and/or skylights is great. Even if you have natural light (and especially if you don't), you'll need ambient and task lighting, so you can see every detail of your work. Full-spectrum lamps that simulate daylight are available in desk and floor models to give you optimum lighting situations in your sewing space. If the light on your sewing machine is not adequate, place a table lamp behind and slightly to the left of the needle. To avoid eye strain, direct more light on your work, making sure that it doesn't shine in your eyes and doesn't cast shadows on your work. Light-colored walls help reflect the light and make it easier to see your work.

Task lighting is especially important for accuracy in the sewing room.

ELECTRICAL POWER: Important in your sewing room, place enough outlets in appropriate places to accommodate your machines, iron, and lamps. Think about the placement of the cords, positioning them out of the way, making it easier to move around your space without fear of tripping over them. Use a surge protector for computerized sewing machines to protect them from power surges; it also allows you to turn off multiple machines with the flip of one switch. If possible, have a separate circuit for your iron as it draws more power than lamps or machines and can overload an already heavily used circuit.

FLOORING: Hard flooring such as tile, wood, and laminates are best so pins, needles, and thread don't collect in carpet fibers. If you do have carpet, consider using a plastic mat (available at office supply stores) under your chair, so you can easily roll around your work area as needed.

MIRROR: If you have room, a full-length mirror is valuable when trying on garments to check fitting and fabric drape. This is especially true if you sew for others. A clear area of 4'–5' in front of the mirror gives enough room to make it useful.

Natural light is great for any sewing space. Courtesy of Jane Foster.

Organize and store similar items together for efficiency.

MEDIA: With all of the sewing and quilting TV programs, instructional tapes, and DVDs available, it is useful to include the equipment needed for viewing them in your sewing room plans. If you don't have the floor space, look up. Consider a wall-mounted swivel shelf to hold a television and DVD or tape player. Place it where it is visible from as much of the room as possible and be sure it is sturdy and securely attached.

DRESS FORM: If you sew garments, using a dress form can make the process easier with more satisfying results. Even though you can certainly make clothing without a dress form, being able to work in 3-D and see the garment from all angles adds accuracy and precision to your sewing. If the dress form is an exact copy of your figure, you can fine-tune your fit until it's perfect for your body.

There are several types of forms available, from high-end body casts that are exact duplicates of your shape to mass-produced adjustable forms that come close but can be flimsy. There are also foam forms that you can pad to match your measurements and inexpensive types made of papier-mâché or duct tape that are easy to make yourself but require a partner to tape your body and help with the process. Dress forms can be purchased at chain fabric stores or over the Internet. Thrift stores and garage sales may also offer real finds, but it's a long shot to find a second-hand size and shape that matches your body.

DESIGN WALL: Often employed by traditional and art quilters to plan and design layouts, this tool is useful for other types of sewing, especially if you plan your own designs, selecting and combining fabrics and experimenting with unique color schemes. Your design wall may be large or small, permanent or temporary, padded or not to suit your sewing situation. The surface should be covered with flannel or batting so fabrics stick to it without pins or tape. Covering insulation board or foam core presentation boards makes a permanent design wall to attach to the studs of the wall in your sewing room. If possible, it's best to be able to stand 5'–8' away from the wall when evaluating fabrics, colors, and blocks. A large piece of felt (at least one square yard) can serve as a temporary design wall and be folded and taken with you to classes or on trips. Keep the color light (white, off-white, light grey) to avoid color distortion of your fabrics.

A design wall is useful for all types of stitching, especially quilting.

Using a dress form can streamline the garment-making process.

Plastic boxes and bins are useful to hold specific sewing supplies.

NOTION STORAGE: Corralling all of the paraphernalia that goes with sewing is an ongoing challenge in our sewing spaces. Pegboard, slat wall, and corkboard are materials that can help with this, as can plastic bins, baskets, boxes, drawer organizer trays, and rolling drawers. Along with fabric and quilt shops, office supply, hardware, and discount stores offer a multitude of choices for storing, organizing, and maintaining many of the notions and supplies you keep in your sewing room. Try a few of these ideas if you are looking for ways to control the clutter.

PLASTIC BOXES AND BINS: These can act as "buckets" to hold a variety of items, but you'll also find some that seem to be custom made for certain notions. Presser feet fit into the small drawers of plastic chests found at hardware stores. Some thread companies offer sectioned boxes to hold and separate spools of thread. Keep your eyes open to make your own discoveries that fit specific items in your sewing room.

BASKETS: Used as bins in a bookcase or on open shelving, baskets give a warm, natural look to your sewing space, while keeping things organized and easy to find.

OFFICE SUPPLIES: Cute, coordinated desk accessories such as in and out trays, folder holders, and CD boxes can all be useful in the sewing room. Think beyond the original use for which the article was designed and you may be able to repurpose items you already own.

PLASTIC CHEST OF DRAWERS: These inexpensive storage units are useful for several reasons. They offer a lot of storage in a small amount of space. It's easy to organize multiple items—just label each drawer with a type of notion (cutting tools, markers, pins and needles, etc.) and then throw all related items into the drawer for quick organization. The drawer sets usually come with casters, making them easy to move around your sewing room for the most versatility.

PEGBOARD, GRID WORK, AND SLAT WALL: These offer ways to give a home to almost any type of notion. Pegs, hooks, bins, and shelves keep everything in view, making it easy to find what you need at a glance.

OPPOSITE PAGE: Unique storage containers for sewing supplies and fabrics can add to the room décor. Courtesy of Diana McClun.

CORKBOARD OR MAGNETIC MESSAGE BOARD: Great for holding design ideas, pattern instructions, and construction notes, this useful accessory can be decorative and practical at the same time. Corkboard can be painted and/or framed before mounting on the wall. Make a magnetic board by covering a piece of metal with fabric (pull it around the back and secure with packing tape); add magnets to the back of interesting buttons for note holders. Mount the board to the wall with double-sided mounting adhesive.

FINDING THE RIGHT SEWING ROOM CHAIR

- Should have adjustable height, back, and seat position.
- Back should be padded and have support for the lower back.
- Wheels or casters are useful, but you should be able to lock them for stability.
- Seat should be padded and contoured so your body weight is distributed evenly.
- Seat should have a "waterfall" (sloped) front edge to keep from cutting off leg circulation.

hand sewing

IT IS ONLY SINCE THE INDUSTRIAL Revolution in the late eighteenth century that ready-made clothing has become easily available. As commercially made garments became more and more affordable and readily accessible to most people in the second half of the twentieth century, home sewing, in general, fell out of favor. Sewing was no longer a necessity, so why do it? Most people who sew today use it as a creative outlet and not as a required means to improving their fundamental quality of life. However, even if we don't have to sew for survival, every person should, at the very least, have a few basic sewing skills to get them through the day-to-day responsibilities of caring for and maintaining the clothing and soft furnishings they buy with their hard-earned money. Sewing on buttons, repairing tears, and shortening or lengthening hems are just a few tasks that can save you money and give you the satisfaction of being self-sufficient in keeping the contents of your household in good repair. These basic skills are accomplished with a simple needle and thread and a few elementary techniques.

Even if you create your own garments or fashions for your home using the sewing machine, certain hand stitches are a part of the process. Very few sewing projects are made entirely on the machine. Securing hems, tacking down facings, and adding custom hand-worked details such as saddle stitching or buttonholes can take your machine-sewn garments from well made to custom couture.

SUPPLIES: Tape measure, needle grabbers, hand sewing needles, assortment of threads, needle threaders, straight pins, pincushion, seam gauge, thread snips, trimming scissors, thread cutter, thimbles, beeswax.

HAND SEWING TOOLS

Hand sewing takes only a few tools, all of which are portable and several are the same as those used in machine sewing. Create a small mending basket that holds a collection of these useful tools, ready for an evening in front of the TV while catching up on your mending and hand sewing.

NEEDLES

Hand sewing needles come in several types, related to the tasks for which they are used. Each type is available in multiple sizes, to suit the fabric being sewn. Often found in assortment packages, needles are also sold in individual packets of one type and/or size. They are sized counter-intuitively, meaning the larger the number, the smaller the needle. This is the opposite of sewing machine needle sizing.

THREAD

Most threads are used for both machine and hand sewing, although there are some that work especially well for hand sewing. Mercerized cotton thread is strong and resists tangling, so it's perfect for hand sewing. Use silk thread for hand stitching on silk and woolen fabrics. In general, select thread with a fiber content (cotton, rayon, polyester) close to the fiber content of your fabric. For more information on thread fibers, see page 75.

NEEDLE THREADER

Even if you can see well enough to thread a needle easily, having a needle threader is a good idea. Using specialty threads or sewing in a low-light situation may require you to have some help getting that narrow little strand through that tiny little hole. If you've been sewing long enough to develop "mature eyesight," you'll appreciate a little help with this necessary step in the hand sewing process. There are a number of needle threaders on the market, and the selection is simply a matter of personal choice, so try a few until you find one that works for you. You may already have one if you own a serger; the looper threader generally works with hand sewing needles, also.

THIMBLES

Sewing by hand can be hard on the fingers, which is one reason a thimble comes in handy. Usually worn on the second finger of your sewing hand, most thimbles are made of metal but can also be leather or plastic. Again, the one you use is a matter of choice, and you'll need to try a few until you find your personal favorite. It may be

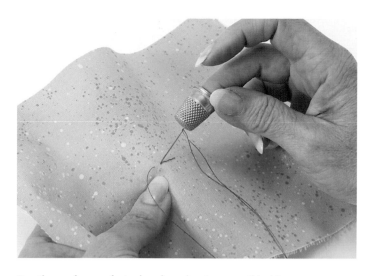

Practice makes perfect when learning to use a thimble.

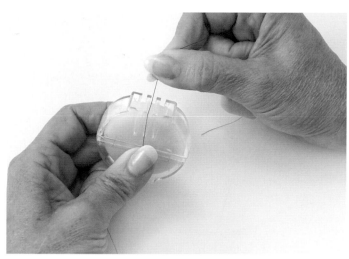

Beeswax makes thread smooth, strong, and sturdy for hand sewing.

awkward at first if you are not used to wearing a thimble, but not only does a thimble protect your finger, it allows you to sew through thick or dense fabric with ease, so it is well worth the effort to learn to use one.

TAPE MEASURES AND SEAM GAUGES

The same types of tape measures and seam gauges used for machine sewing also come in handy for hand sewing. A measurement product developed specifically for hand sewing is a tape called Tiger Tape™. This adhesive-backed tape has evenly-spaced markings. Adhere it to your project and use it as a guide to keep stitches and spaces consistent and even.

BEESWAX

Used to coat thread for hand sewing, beeswax strengthens the thread, making it smooth and sturdy as well as helping to keep it from tangling. The thread is also less likely to catch or snag the material while sewing. This is a must when working on a large project such as hand tailoring a jacket.

HAND SEWING NEEDLES

Sharp	Of medium length, sharps are the most common type of needle used for a variety of sewing tasks. Available in sizes 1 to 12. Sizes 10 and 11 are used for appliqué.
Between	Short needles that offer more control, making them good choices for fine detail work including hand tailoring and quilting. Available in sizes 1 to 12, sizes 7 to 9 are most often used for quilting.
Embroidery	Sometimes called crewel needles, these needles are the same as sharps but have a longer eye to accommodate thicker embroidery flosses. Available in sizes 1 to 10.
Milliner	Also called straws, these needles are longer than sharps and are used for basting, pleating, and millinery (hat making). Available in sizes 1 to 10.
Chenille	Large, sharp pointed needles used for heavy embroidery on closely woven fabric. They are available in sizes 13 to 24.
Tapestry	The same length as the chenille needles, tapestry needles have longer eyes and blunted points. Available in sizes 13 to 26.
Darner	A long needle used for basting and mending available in sizes 1 to 12.
Yarn Darner	Heavy darning needles used with wool fibers, these needles are available in sizes 14 to 18.
Beading	Long needles used to attach beads and sequins to fabric. They are available in sizes 10 to 12.
Self-Threading	Sometimes call calyx-eyed, these needles have a slot in the top to eliminate the need to feed the thread through the eye of the needle.
Ballpoint	This specialty needle is for sewing knits and has a rounded point to avoid snagging the fabric. They are available in sizes 5 to 10.
Doll	These long thin needles (2.5"–7") are for soft sculpting such as when creating facial features.
Leather	Also known as glovers, these needles have a triangular point that pierces leather, suede, plastic, and vinyl without cutting it. They are available in sizes 3/0 to 10.
Sailmaker	Used for sewing thick canvas and heavy leather, these needles have a longer triangular point than leather needles; available in sizes 14 to 18.
Tatting	Long needles used to tat lace; they are the same thickness along the entire shaft and are not pointed at the end; available in sizes 0 to 9.
Upholstery	Long heavy needles used for heavy fabric, upholstery, tufting and tying quilts. These needles come in both straight (sizes: 3"–12") and curved (1.5"–6")
Bodkin	This is a long, thick needle with a ballpoint end and a large, elongated eye. Flat or round, it is generally used for threading elastic, ribbon, or drawstrings through casings and lace openings.

GETTING STARTED

THREADING THE NEEDLE

Cut an 18"–20" length of thread from a spool. If the thread is much longer than this, it will tangle easily and result in frustration and annoyance when stitching.

Clip the end of the thread at an angle and put it through the eye of the needle, pulling about 5"–6" through to the other side.

TYING A KNOT

Tie a knot in the end of the long side to keep the thread from pulling through the fabric once you start sewing. The easiest way to tie a knot is to hold the thread in one hand and twist the end around the index finger of your opposite hand 2–3 times. Pinch the twisted loops between your thumb and finger, pulling until it is tight.

After threading the needle, tie a knot in the end of the thread to keep it from pulling through the fabric.

BEGINNING AND END

Take a few small stitches on the wrong side of the fabric at the beginning and end of the seam to secure the stitching. For basting, do the same but leave the stitches loose, as they will be removed.

THREADING TIPS

- For better visibility, hold the needle and thread over a piece of white paper.
- For more control, stiffen the end of the thread by coating it with beeswax.
- Use tweezers to put the thread through the eye of the needle, grasping the thread close to the snipped end; the closer you are to the nend, the more control you have.

BASTING STITCHES

There are several hand-basting techniques suitable for different sewing situations. In most cases, basting is designed to hold two pieces of fabric together temporarily and is usually removed once permanent stitching is in place. Lightweight basting thread is recommended and you should avoid pressing over it especially if you have basted across the surface of the fabric; heat and pressure can cause thread lines (permanent indentations in the fabric).

COMMON BASTING: Good for all fabrics, this type of basting is used to ensure accuracy when machine stitching pieces together or when fitting a garment before permanently sewing the seams. Use a running stitch with the needle going from front to back, and then going from back to front further along the same line with the same spacing. Long stitches and short spaces (called uneven basting) works for most basting situations. If you are working on something needing more control, such as curved seams or setting in a sleeve, make the stitch shorter, the same as the spaces between them (called even basting).

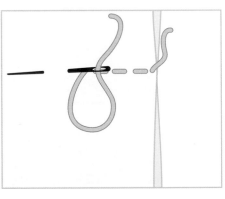

SLIP BASTING: Used for matching plaids, stripes, or patterns, this type of basting works on all fabrics. Fold the seam allowance of one piece to the wrong side and position the fold along the seamline of the second piece, matching the pattern; pin through all layers. Come up from the back next to the seam line through the single layer of fabric. Take a tiny stitch through the fold of the first piece of fabric. Continue, spacing stitches about ¼" apart.

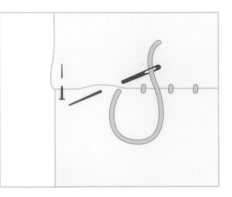

DIAGONAL BASTING: This basting technique is a fast way to attach layers of fabric together and is a good way to hold interfacing, interlining, and lining temporarily to the wrong side of fabric. Even though the thread shows in a large diagonal pattern, the stitches are small and horizontal. Sewing from right to left, take a small horizontal stitch. The second stitch should be about 2" below and parallel to the first. Continue making vertical rows of stitches in this manner to cover the entire surface of the fabric.

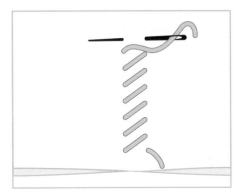

SEAMING STITCHES

Hand sewn seams are not as sturdy as machine sewn but are useful in some situations. Take care to work the stitches evenly and avoid pulling the thread too tightly as it will curl and pucker the fabric.

RUNNING STITCH: This is a row of simple "in-and-out" stitches similar to common basting but in a shorter length. The stitches are about ¼" long and the spaces between them are the same. For faster stitching, weave the needle in and out of the fabric several times before pulling the thread through the fabric.

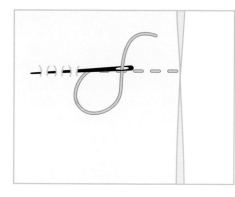

BACKSTITCH: One of the strongest hand stitches, the backstitch is good for stitching or repairing seams. It shows as small stitches on top of the fabric and overlapping stitching on the underside. Bring the needle up from the wrong side and go back down into the fabric about ⅛" behind that point, coming up about ⅛" in front of it. Continue this, starting at the last stitch you took.

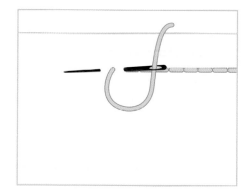

LADDER STITCH: This stitch is almost invisible and works well for closing an opening such as a ripped seam or a seam on a project after it has been stuffed (pillow, toy, etc.). Take a tiny stitch on one side of the opening, and then take a tiny stitch on the other side. Continue this, moving back and forth to form a "ladder." The opening closes and the stitches are hidden when the thread is pulled snug.

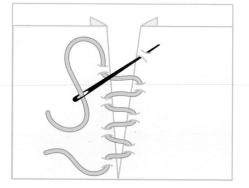

PRACTICAL STITCHES

This group of stitches is the most functional in everyday life. Mending torn fabric or frayed buttonholes, finishing the edge of a garment and sewing on buttons take care of most household sewing needs. Learn these stitches along with a hemming technique or two, and you'll have the skills you need to care for clothing and soft goods for your family.

DARNING STITCH: Mending tears and repairing holes is simple to do and can give new life to a favorite garment. Trim stray threads on the torn edges. Fuse a piece of lightweight interfacing behind the torn area. Place the torn area in a small spring embroidery hoop. Starting above the patched area, sew a row of small horizontal running stitches, working right to left. Turn the work and stitch a second row, again working right to left, and staggering the stitches with the first row. Continue to turn the work and sew rows of staggered running stitches until the damaged area is covered.

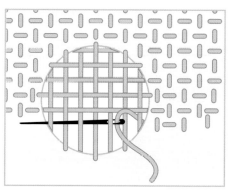

BLANKET STITCH: A quick way to add a decorative edge to jackets, blankets, and table toppers, the blanket stitch is often worked using embroidery floss or topstitching thread. It is usually sewn on a finished edge or on fabric such as fleece that does not fray. Decide how wide you want the finished edging to be; measure that distance from the fabric edge and insert the needle at that point, starting at the left and working toward the right. Keeping the needle perpendicular to the fabric edge, make sure the thread is behind the needle. Pull the thread through the fabric. The stitch will form as you snug the thread. The

cross thread of the stitch should fall on the edge of the fabric.

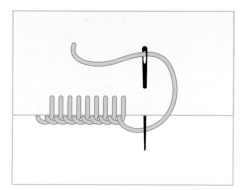

BUTTONHOLE STITCH: Similar to the blanket stitch, the buttonhole stitch is, as the name implies, for making buttonholes and also for repairing frayed buttonholes. It is worked over the edges of a slit with small stitches sewn very close together. Working from right to left, insert the needle into the fabric at the desired outer edge of the buttonhole and then insert it through the slit. The thread should be behind the needle and to the left. Pull the thread through the fabric, snugging it to the edge of the slit. Once the edges have been sewn, make a bar tack at each end to finish the buttonhole.

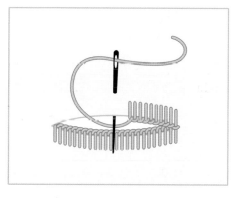

SEWING ON BUTTONS: Probably the most common repair is replacing buttons that fall off ready-made garments. Flat buttons with two or four holes are simple enough to attach but the step most people overlook is the making of a thread shank behind the button. The purpose of a thread shank is to give the garment room to lie flat once it is buttoned. Without it, the buttoned area looks bunched and puckered. To determine how long the shank should be, measure the thickness of the garment and add 1/16"–1/8". To sew on a button, you simply run the threaded needle in and out of the holes, creating a simple bar tack that holds the button onto the fabric. To create a thread shank, place a toothpick over the holes before stitching in and out of the holes. This creates slack in the thread, attaching the button loosely. Without clipping the needle thread, remove the toothpick and pull the button away from the fabric as far as possible. Wind the needle thread around the stitches, and then tie-off the thread by taking a few small stitches before clipping the thread.

TAILORING STITCHES

The process of tailoring a garment involves a number of hand stitches to add structure, define shape, and complete the finishing touches. Even though many of these stitches are not visible in the finished article of clothing, they are the mark of a well-made custom garment.

TAILOR TACKS: Used to transfer pattern markings to fabric, tailor tacks are often used when tailoring a garment or in other sewing situations where chalk or fabric markers may not be suitable. The tacks are made after the pattern has been cut

out but before the paper has been removed from the fabric. Thread the needle with a double length of thread in a color that contrasts to the fabric and leave it unknotted. Working from the top, take a small stitch through the pattern and both layers of fabric, leaving a 2" thread tail. Take a second stitch in the same place but do not pull it flat, leaving a loop of thread on the surface. When finished, carefully pull the two pieces of fabric apart. Clip the threads between the layers of fabric, leaving a tailor's tack on each piece.

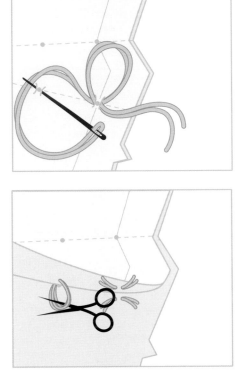

PAD STITCHING: Similar to diagonal basting with shorter stitches, pad stitching is used to permanently secure interfacing to fashion fabric. This type of stitching is also used when attaching layers of interfacing to help shape and form pieces such as collars and lapels.

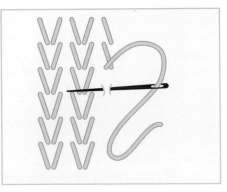

BAR TACK: These are heavy stitches used to reinforce areas of stress such as pocket corners. Take three long stitches the desired length of the bar tack. Take a series of closely spaced stitches around and perpendicular to the three stitches, working from one end to the other.

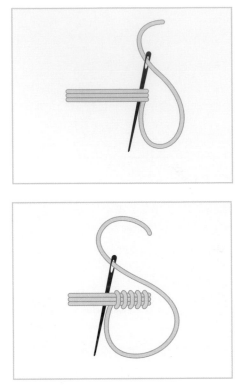

FRENCH TACK: A French tack is similar to a bar tack but is worked "in the air," not on fabric. It is used to loosely connect two separate pieces such as a coat and lining, leaving room for movement. Take a small stitch on the inside of the garment near the top of the hem allowance. Leaving about 1"–2" of thread between the two parts of the garment, take a similar stitch in the corresponding position on the lining. Take 2–3 additional stitches in the same place and the same manner. Take a series of closely spaced blanket stitches, perpendicular to the three stitches, working from one end to the other and covering the threads.

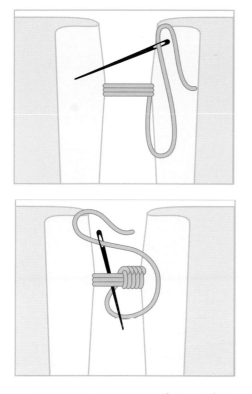

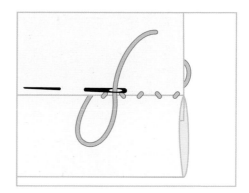

SADDLE STITCH: This stitch is similar to a running stitch with longer stitches and heavier thread. Used as a topstitched accent, it is typically sewn with buttonhole twist, topstitching thread, or embroidery floss in a color that contrasts to the fabric color. Starting from the back, bring the thread through the fabric to the front and take a series of running stitches about ¼"–⅜" long with spaces of the same length between the stitches.

garment. Finish the raw edge of the garment with stitching or hem tape and fold the hem in place; press and pin. Fold the hem edge back about ¼"; take a tiny horizontal stitch in the hem allowance and then pick up 1–2 threads in the garment at a slight diagonal. Continue in this manner, keeping the stitches fairly loose to avoid puckering. Once the hem is stitched, the edge of the hem will cover the stitching. This stitch is also good for discreetly securing facings on the inside of a garment.

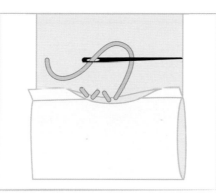

SLIP STITCH: An inconspicuous stitch, the slip stitch is used for hemming most light to medium weight fabrics and is also good for invisibly attaching pockets and trims. Slip the needle into the fold of the upper edge of the hem, then pick up 1–2 threads of the garment. Sew a line of these stitches, spacing them evenly, about ¼" apart.

LOCK STITCH: The lock stitch is a secure hemming stitch and works well for hemming draperies and most garments. Because each stitch is locked, the advantage is that if the thread breaks, the entire hem will not come out. Pick up 1–2 threads in the garment and then 1–2 threads in the hem allowance. Loop the thread around the needle and pull the thread through the fabric. Continue making stitches in this manner, spacing them about ½" apart.

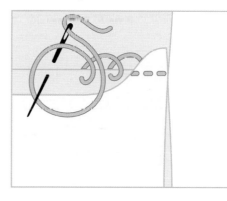

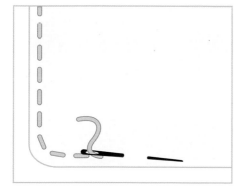

HEMMING STITCHES

The final step in most sewing projects is hemming. The method you choose depends on the type of project, the fabric selected, and the finished look you want. In the most commonly used methods detailed here, you should find a way to hand-stitch almost any hem.

BLINDSTITCH: The blind-stitch works on almost all fabrics and is invisible on both sides of the

A SIMPLE GIFT

A thoughtful gift for someone going off to college or setting up house-keeping, the well-stocked mending basket should have several spools of all-purpose, neutral-colored thread in light, medium, and dark values, a seam ripper, thread snips, small scissors, beeswax, a selection of needles with a threader, thimble, pincushion, tape measure, a few safety pins, and an assortment of shirt buttons. Collect these items and place them in a small basket or decorative box that has a lid, so they'll always be ready for any kind of sewing emergency!

machine sewing

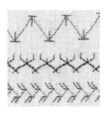 WHETHER YOU ARE SEWING ON A HAND-me-down sewing machine or a new top-of-the-line sewing computer, you need to have an understanding of how to use it and how to take care of it. With all of the changes and advancements made in sewing machines over the last few decades, it's amazing that they all do basically the same thing—sew fabric together. The parts and pieces of most sewing machines are similar, even though they may have special functions or advanced features added to them.

It's not uncommon for sewers today to have several sewing machines, plus an embroidery system, a serger, perhaps a blind hemming machine or needle punch machine, and/or a quilting frame that makes it easy to quilt large quilts using a sewing machine. If you are fortunate enough to be able to invest in multiple machines, take the time to get to know each and every one, so you can smoothly and easily enjoy your passion. Read the manuals, take classes, surf the net, and explore the machine until you have made friends with it and know how to use it to your advantage.

This chapter offers general information on the most common types of machines used for home sewing. It can make the basics clear and answer some of your questions, but don't forget, your machine manual and, most of all, your sewing machine dealer, have specific information related to your machines.

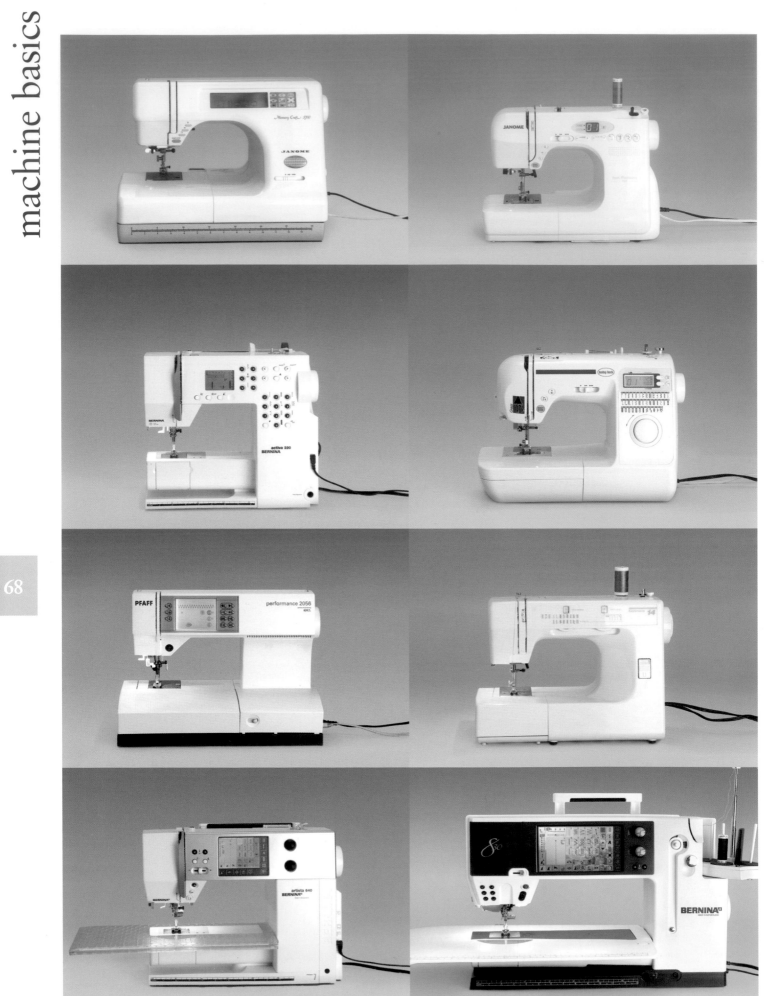

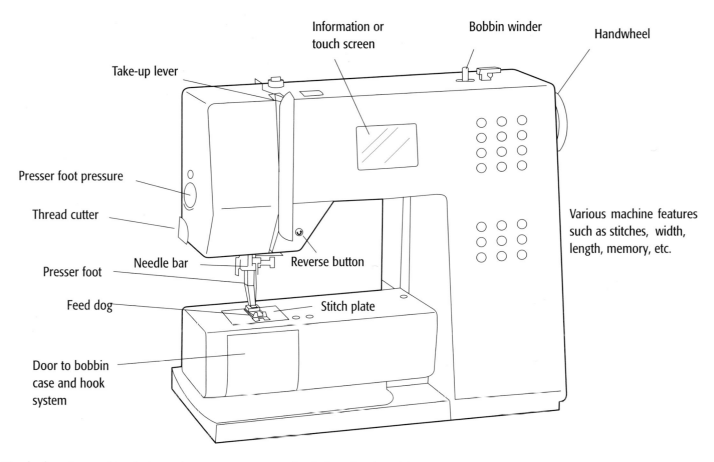

Standard sewing machine features shown may vary according to brand and model.

ANATOMY OF A SEWING MACHINE

If you are new to using a sewing machine, the best thing you can do is acquaint yourself with the basic working parts.

HANDWHEEL: Found on the right side of the machine, the handwheel lets you manually move the needle up and down. The important thing to remember about the handwheel is that, on most machines, you move it toward you. Moving it backward, or away from you, may affect the timing (the coming together of the needle and bobbin threads) and could necessitate a visit to the service technician.

FOOT CONTROL: This detachable pedal powers the machine when you press it with your foot. It has a cord that attaches to the machine, and the pedal is placed on the floor. Some newer machines have pushbutton or slide power options, and do not require foot controls.

NEEDLE BAR: This part of the machine is where the needle is inserted. It moves up and down when the foot control is pressed to move the needle in and out of the fabric.

FEED DOG: Sometimes called feed teeth, this moveable piece on the bed of the machine directly under the needle moves from front to back to transport the fabric under the needle. The presser foot holds the fabric down on the saw-tooth feed dog to move it smoothly. On most machines, you can lower or cover the feed dog, so you can move the fabric as

you want (called free-motion stitching). Some machines have directional feed dogs that also feed fabric side to side.

STITCH SELECTOR: The method of moving from stitch to stitch. Usually on the front of the machine, this can be a dial, a lever, a button, a slide, or a touch screen, depending on the machine.

REVERSE: Often positioned near the needle area, this is a button or lever that causes the machine to stitch backward while it is being pressed. It's used to back-tack at the beginning and end of seams to secure stitching. Some machines have a continuous reverse feature, enabling the machine to sew in reverse until the feature is disengaged.

TAKE-UP LEVER: Part of the threading path, this device regulates the thread as it comes off the spool, pulling just the right amount for each stitch.

BOBBIN WINDER: Automatically winds thread onto a bobbin, often with an automatic stop feature when the bobbin is full and a thread cutter to snip the thread after winding it. Bobbins come in several types and sizes, and you must use the type required by your machine.

STITCH LENGTH AND WIDTH CONTROLS: May be knobs, buttons, or touch screen, these separate controls regulate how long or how short the stitch will be. Most computerized machines have automatic or default

OPPOSITE PAGE: Sewing machines today are available in a variety of brands, each with a choice of models and feature packages.
LEFT COLUMN: Janome MemoryCraft 5700, Bernina activa 220, Pfaff performance 2056, Bernina artista 640
RIGHT COLUMN: Janome Gem 760, Babylock Grace, Kenmore 14, Bernina 830.

settings that can be changed if desired. These settings must be made manually on mechanical sewing machines.

STITCH PLATE: Sometimes called a throat plate or needle plate, this metal piece fits around the feed dog and usually has markings to aid in precise stitching. These plates are usually removable, so that lint can be cleaned from around the feed dog. The stitch plate has an opening for the needle to go into the bobbin area to join the two threads. This opening can be a small hole for straight stitch only or a wider hole to accommodate zigzag and decorative stitches.

SHUTTLE/HOOK SYSTEM: The mechanism that holds the bobbin (lower thread), the shuttle has a hook that grips a loop of needle thread as the needle brings it down; the movement of the shuttle wraps it around the bobbin thread, tightening it to form a stitch. Some hook systems are rotary systems that move in a complete circle; others are oscillating systems that move back and forth in a semi-circle.

BOBBIN CASE: This case regulates the tension of the lower thread and may be fixed in the machine or may be a separate piece of equipment. The bobbin fits into the bobbin case, and the thread is placed into a tension spring. The bobbin tension is set at the factory, and it is usually suggested that only a trained technician make changes to it. When using a heavy decorative thread for bobbin work, the tension is loosened to allow the stitches to form, and it is recommended that a separate bobbin case be used so the tension setting of the original case is still set for regular sewing.

FAVORITE FEATURES

Many features and functions on sewing machines are nice to have but there are several that not only make your sewing easier but will also save time, letting you produce more in less time. That leaves you more time to sew!

AUTOMATIC THREADING: Most machines today use slotted threading, which means you only have the needle to actually thread—the rest of the path has slots to drop the thread into. Many machines also have automatic needle threaders, so you don't even have to worry about

the needle. You'll also find a few of the latest machines that make it so easy you just lay the thread on a designated path, push a button, and that's it! The faster you get the machine threaded, the faster you get to start sewing.

CONSISTENT TENSION: In the history of the sewing machine, tension issues have ranked highest in frustration for sewers. Many machines take a great deal of testing and adjusting to get them to sew correctly. It doesn't have to be that way. A machine that has consistent tension, letting you move from one fabric to the next is not only a time-saver but lets you enjoy sewing rather than dread it.

PRESSER FOOT LIFTER: Every machine has a way to raise and lower the presser foot, so the fabric can be positioned and held for stitching and removed when the stitching is complete. Most machines have a lever on the back or the side near the needle; the lever is manually lifted (usually by your right hand) to raise the foot and then lowered to place it in the down position (which also engages the needle tension). Some machines have more efficient ways to raise and lower the presser foot that can actually speed your sewing and increase your production. It may be a knee-activated lever that is operated by pressing your right knee against a bar that extends from the lower right front of the machine. Other machines have computerized functions operated by pushing a button or by selecting the "up" or "down" icon on the touch screen. This feature is one that is difficult to appreciate until you have actually used it and can see firsthand how beneficial it is.

NEEDLE DOWN: In the past, most machines quit sewing when you lifted your foot from the foot control and the needle stopped wherever it happened to be, down in the fabric or up in the air. Then, to pull the fabric away from the needle or to start sewing again, you turned the handwheel to raise the needle to the highest position. Some machines still do this, but many machines today have features that let you control where the needle stops each time you stop sewing, usually by pushing a button to engage this feature. There are also machines that let you tap the foot control or push a button to raise or lower the needle as needed.

VARIABLE MOTOR SPEED: It may sound crazy but slowing down can sometimes save you time. Being able to adjust the speed of the machine can be useful for situations such as teaching kids to sew, an adult beginning sewer, techniques where stitch placement needs to be precise such as heirloom sewing, free-motion stitching, piecing quilts and blanket stitch appliqué.

KNOW YOUR MACHINE TIP

Place the manual that came with your machine next to your bed for a little late-night reading. It's amazing what you can learn by reading a page or two each night before retiring. If your manual is not spiral-bound, consider taking it to your local copy shop and having it disassembled and spiral-bound. It will lie flat and be much easier to use as a reference at your machine.

Consider all of the options when shopping for a new sewing machine.

MECHANICAL VS. COMPUTERIZED

Most machines today are computerized, at least in part, but there are some mechanical models still out there. The biggest difference between the two is how the machines receive their instructions. A mechanical machine has levers, knobs, and dials that have to be manually adjusted to move the machine parts into place as you select a stitch, set the length and width, change the needle position, etc. You must know how to do this, you must remember the settings for each stitch, and you must take the time to get the machine ready to sew.

A computerized machine receives its instructions electronically, usually when you push a button that activates a circuit board, sending impulses to the machine. This type of machine also knows the usual or typical settings for each stitch and can often remember changes you have made to them, so you don't have to adjust the settings each time you stitch a certain technique. Another type of computerized machine is actually a sewing computer that has an operating system and functions much like a computer. Many top-of-the-line machines are sewing computers and are preprogrammed with intricate stitches,

automatic functions, and programmable features. They often operate using a screen that shows the options and settings available. These screens may be touch-activated or the settings may be adjusted by buttons, dials, or knobs, and the screen shows the settings you have made.

Even though the mechanical machines are simple in their makeup, the computerized machines are much easier to use. The machine does much of the work for you; you spend less time getting ready to sew and more time sewing. Computerized machines also offer a wider range of decorative stitches and creative functions (such as half pattern and mirror image) that mechanical machines cannot. Sewing computers are more complex and may take a lesson or two to get used to how they operate, but they offer the most in creative options and automatic features. One type of machine is not necessarily better than another; it simply depends on your preference, your comfort level, and the type of sewing you want to do.

THE LOWLY STRAIGHT STITCH

The foundation of almost all sewing, the straight stitch, is the soul of the sewing machine. For years, it was the only stitch on all sewing machines, before cam-driven technology existed and a computerized machine was not even a gleam in a mathematician's eye. Understanding the straight stitch, how it is formed, and how it can be used will help you no matter what fabric and thread you sew.

The straight stitch is created using two threads, one threaded through the eye of the needle and one wound on the bobbin; the needle thread shows on top of the fabric, and the bobbin thread is on the underside. The stitch is formed when the sewing machine loosely knots the two threads together, and then tightens them to pull the knot, so it is hidden between the layers of fabric. The correct tension on the threads determines if they meet precisely between the layers of fabric. If not, loops of thread will result, depending on whether the tension is too loose or too tight. If the tension is too loose, loops will show on the underside of the fabric; if the tension is too tight, loops will form on the upper fabric. On most sewing machines, a zero setting is no tension, 3–5 is normal, and 8–9 is very tight.

The weight of the thread plays an important part in getting a balanced stitch. If the same thread is used in both the needle and the bobbin, the tension should need little or no adjustment and the stitch will form correctly. However, if one thread is much heavier than the other, some adjustment will be needed. For instance, if a 30 weight embroidery thread is in the needle and a 60 weight bobbin thread on the bobbin, the needle tension needs to be loosened (turned to a lower number) until the bobbin thread is no longer pulling to the front. Note: Most tension problems are solved by adjusting the upper tension. The bobbin tension has been set at the factory and rarely needs adjusting. If it does, it is usually best to have it corrected by an authorized technician.

To visually check the balance of the tension on your machine, thread the needle and wind the bobbin with the same type of thread (weight, ply, and fiber) in contrasting colors. Sew a line of stitching; you should be able to see only one color of thread on the top of the fabric and the other color on the underside.

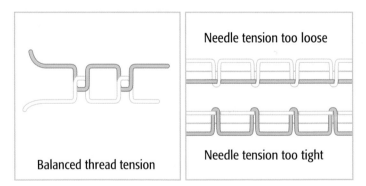

Balanced thread tension

Needle tension too loose

Needle tension too tight

SEWING MACHINE NEEDLES

If the straight stitch is the soul of the machine, the needle is the heart. Sewing machine needles can affect the performance of a machine more than any other part, causing skipped stitches, poor stitch formation, and even damage to the machine itself when the wrong needle or a bent needle is used. When troubleshooting stitch problems,

always try a new needle as the first possible solution. Many times, this solves the problems and your machine will stitch as good as new. Change the needle frequently, putting in a new one at least at the beginning of each new project.

There are more details to a sewing machine needle than you would think given its tiny size. The diagram below shows the different parts, each precisely engineered to do a particular job in the process of carrying the upper thread to meet the lower thread and form a stitch. When selecting a needle for your machine, there are three things to consider.

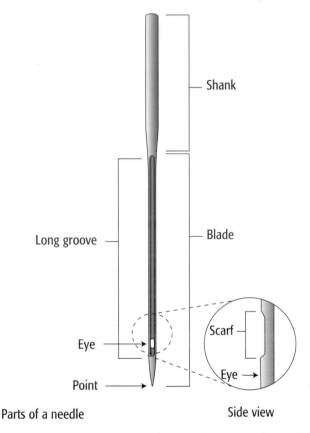

Parts of a needle

Side view

Shank

Blade

Long groove

Scarf

Eye

Eye

Point

NEEDLE SYSTEM: This is the type of needle your machine was manufactured to use. Your owner's manual will tell you which type your machine takes; this is non-negotiable because each machine is engineered to accept only one type of needle. Using a different system may cause damage to the machine. Most machines (but not all) use the system 130/705. There is often a letter or letters after the system number to designate the type of needle (e.g., H = household, MET = metallic, Q-H = household quilting, etc.).

NEEDLE POINT: Select the type of point by matching it to the type of fabric being used and/or the technique being stitched. For example, a universal point works for most fabrics, a ballpoint is for knits, and a leather point is for sewing leather.

NEEDLE SIZE: Select the needle size for the type of fabric and thread being used. Use the smallest point possible for the fabric and select the size of thread that fits in the groove on the front of the needle, filling the hole that the needle makes in the fabric. Needle packages show the sizing in two numbers, European and American. (Refer to the charts on the next page.)

NEEDLE NOTES

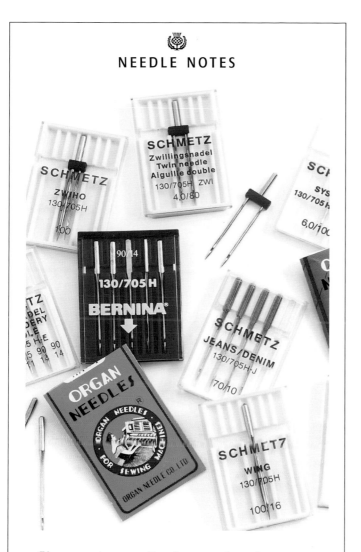

- Change the needle frequently, about every 4–6 hours of sewing. A good rule of thumb is to start each project with a new needle. Don't shortchange yourself and your stitching results by adopting a sense of false economy. The needle is one of the most inexpensive parts of the machine and giving it the respect it deserves can avoid damaged fabric and/or time-consuming machine repairs.
- Safely discard a broken or bent needle by taping it to a piece of paper or scrap fabric, then wrapping it up before you throw it in the trash. You can also put used needles in leftover pill bottles or film canisters for disposal.
- If your needle makes a "popping" sound as it goes into the fabric, the point is dull. Replace and discard it to avoid damaging your fabric and possibly breaking your thread.
- If you break a needle, stop sewing immediately and replace the needle. Be sure you retrieve all of the broken pieces, which may include removing the bobbin and inspecting the hook area. Even a tiny point can cause damage if it obstructs any part of the machine from operating.

NEEDLE SIZE EQUIVALENTS

EUROPEAN	AMERICAN
70	10
75	11
80	12
90	14
100	16
110	18

FABRIC AND NEEDLE SIZE COMPATIBILITY

FABRIC TYPE	FABRIC EXAMPLES	NEEDLE SIZES
Very light	Organdy, organza, tulle, chiffon, batiste	60–70
Light	Broadcloth, jersey knit, handkerchief linen	70–80
Medium	Flannel, challis, wool jersey, cotton knits, medium weight denim	80–90
Heavy	Heavyweight denim, coatings, burlap, brocade, fleece	100–110
Very heavy	Upholstery, canvas, ticking	110–120

STANDARD NEEDLES

There are a few needles that meet most everyday sewing needs and work well on a wide variety of fabric types. Keep a supply of these on hand, and your machine will always be ready for sewing.

TYPE	USES	AVAILABLE SIZES
Universal: Slightly rounded tip that stitches between the fibers rather than cutting through them; the elongated scarf makes the bobbin and needle threads consistently meet to form a stitch.	Great all-purpose needle; works with most fabrics including wovens and most knits.	60–120
Ballpoint: Sometimes called a jersey, this needle has a more rounded tip than universal, making it easier to slip between the loops of knitted fabric.	Good for most knit fabric and some stretch fabrics such as spandex.	70–100
Stretch: Has a ballpoint tip with a specially designed scarf and eye; minimizes skipped stitches.	Use for elastic and stretch fabrics such as spandex.	75 and 90
Jeans: This strong needle has a reinforced shaft and a modified sharp tip for penetrating heavy fabric and multiple layers.	Good for coating, quilts, and denim (minimizes deflection in the twill weave, resulting in even, consistent stitches). Also good for tightly woven fabrics such as satin.	70–110

SPECIALTY NEEDLES

A wide variety of needles are available for special sewing situations such as quilting, using metallic thread, and sewing on leather. Purchase these needles as the need arises to make all of your sewing as effortless as possible.

TYPE	USES	AVAILABLE SIZES
Topstitch: Made for heavy or multiple threads, this needle is extra sharp with a large groove (to accommodate the heavier threads) and a 2mm eye.	Perfect for topstitching, embroidery, and bobbin-work on most fabrics.	80–100
Quilting: The tapered tip of this needle pierces firmly woven fabrics without damage.	Great for piecing patchwork patterns; especially good at penetrating multiple layers where seams meet.	75 and 90
Metallic: With this needle that has an elongated eye and large groove, the friction is reduced when using metallic thread, minimizing shredding and fraying.	Good for all sewing and embroidery where metallic thread is used.	80 and 90
Microtex: Has a narrow point that pierces densely woven fabrics.	Best for microfibers and imitation leathers such as Ultrasuede or Pleather.	60–90
Leather: The wedge-shaped point of this needle easily penetrates leather skins.	Use for natural or tanned leather but not for imitation leather and suede.	70–110
Embroidery: With an enlarged eye and groove, this needle is perfect for the fast pace of machine embroidery stitching.	Good for the more delicate embroidery fibers such as rayon to minimize fraying and shedding.	75 and 90
Gold Embroidery: This titanium-coated needle has an enlarged eye and slightly rounded point for use with delicate threads.	Use for machine embroidery. Also good for penetrating very coarse fabric.	75 and 90
Wing Needle: Sometimes called a hemstitch needle, this needle has flat extensions or "wings" on each side that work with decorative stitches to create embroidered holes.	Use with natural fiber fabrics and multi-motion decorative stitches to create texture and decorative embroidery effects.	100 and 120
Double Eye Needle: This needle with a universal point has two eyes for using two threads at once.	For sewing on most medium weight fabrics including wovens and most knits.	80
Self-Threading Needle: This universal needle has a slot in the eye to make threading easy.	For sewing on most medium weight fabrics including wovens and most knits.	80 and 90
Spring Needle: A needle with a spring around it, this needle is used without a presser foot.	For free-motion stitching such as quilting and thread painting, the spring keeps the fabric from "flagging" (traveling up the needle). Allows more visibility of the stitching area.	80

MULTIPLE NEEDLES

Using double or triple needles can create unusual special effects with very little effort. Once the machine is threaded and the needle is inserted (all needles are mounted on a single shank, so they are inserted the same as a standard needle), all you do is sew as usual and the machine stitches double or triple rows. These needles have two numbers listed in the front of the package (e.g.: 3.0/90). The first number is a measurement in millimeters and indicates the distance between the needles (between the right and left on the double needle and between the inner and outer on the triple needles). The second number is the size of the needles.

TYPE	USES	AVAILABLE SIZES
Universal Double Needle Two needles with slightly rounded tips that stitch between the fibers rather than cutting through them; both needles are attached to one shank.	Used for decorative stitch work, pintucks, stitched hem, and parallel sewing on most fabrics, woven and knit.	70–100 (1.6, 2.0. 2.5, 3.0, and 4.0mm) 100 (6.0 and 8.0mm)
Stretch Double Needle These two needles, attached to one shank, have ballpoint tips and specially designed scarves and eyes to minimize skipped stitches.	Use for parallel sewing on knits, elastic and stretch fabrics such as spandex. Especially good for topstitching a stretch hem on knits.	75 (2.5 and 4.0mm)
Jeans Double Needle These strong needles have reinforced shafts and modified tips for penetrating heavy fabric and multiple layers; two needles are attached to one shank.	Good for parallel stitching on coating, quilts, and denim (minimizes deflection in the twill weave, resulting in even, consistent stitches).	100 (4.0mm)
Metallic Double Needle The elongated eyes and large grooves of these needles reduce friction when using metallic thread, minimizing shredding and fraying.	Good for tightly woven fabrics. Good for parallel stitching on most fabrics.	80 (2.5mm) 90 (3.0mm)
Embroidery Double With enlarged eyes and grooves, these needles are perfect for the fast pace of machine embroidery stitching; two needles are attached to one shank.	Good for parallel stitching using delicate embroidery fibers such as rayon to minimize fraying and shedding.	75 (2.0 and 3.0mm)
Double Wing Needle Combination of a wing needle and a universal needle on one shank.	Use with natural fiber fabrics and multi-motion decorative stitches to create texture and decorative embroidery effects.	100 (2.5mm)
Universal Triple Needle Three needles with slightly rounded tips that stitch between the fibers rather than cutting through them; all needles are attached to one shank. The width measurement (2.5mm or 3.0mm) is the distance between the inner and the outer needles.	Used for decorative stitch work, pintucks, stitched hem, and parallel sewing on most fabrics, woven and knit.	80 (2.5 and 3.0mm)

Good-quality thread adds to the value and excellence of your project.

THREAD

The selection of thread available for sewing seems to grow on almost a daily basis. New colors, unique finishes, and interesting textures can add to the style of your project, but there are other considerations that make a difference in your thread selections.

Look for long staple thread; it is smoother and creates less lint in your machine. Long staple simply means that long fibers or filaments are twisted together to make the thread. Beware of using bargain thread (several spools for $1). Made of short staples, the thread is uneven in texture and the result is less than perfect stitching. In the long run, it can impede the performance of your machine. When lint and fuzz get into the tension mechanism of your machine, it can affect the tension setting, causing poor stitching.

Select a fiber that is compatible with the fabric, requiring similar care. Fibers commonly found in sewing stores today:

COTTON: Strong thread that's good for construction, especially on natural fiber fabrics; has a soft look. Mercerized cotton has been treated to be smoother and straighter with less fuzz than other cotton threads.

POLYESTER: Strong and colorfast, this is an all-purpose thread that is good for construction. Polyester embroidery thread has a high sheen and is abrasion resistant.

COTTON-WRAPPED POLYESTER: An all-purpose thread that combines the strength of polyester with the properties of cotton; good for natural and blended fabrics.

SILK: Strong and lustrous, this thread is used for construction and stitched details such as buttonholes and topstitching. Use on silk and wool fabrics. Silk has also gained popularity as a quilting thread, resulting in beautiful quilting designs on cotton fabric.

RAYON: High sheen thread not strong enough for construction; used mainly for decorative work such as embroidery and decorative stitching; not always colorfast so test a stitched sample by soaking it in hot water.

METALLIC: Sometimes metal wrapped around a polyester core and sometimes made of pure metal, this thread can be used to add sparkle to your work but requires some adjustments such as loosened needle tension, larger needle, and slower sewing speed.

In general, the higher the weight number, the finer the thread will be. The relationship between the sewing machine needle and the thread selected is critical to good

---

SPECIALTY THREADS

Along with construction and decorative threads, there are a few unusual threads made for specific sewing tasks.

- NYLON THREAD: Also called "monofilament" or "invisible" thread, quilters use this when they want to emphasize the design, rather than the stitches themselves, or when stitches need to be invisible such as when doing appliqué. Look for size 0.004; larger sizes will have trouble going through most sewing machines. Even though it is the strongest of all thread, nylon has its drawbacks. It melts with heat and doesn't stand up to moisture and mildew well.

- BASTING, VANISHING, WASH-AWAY THREAD: Good for temporary stitching that you want to remove later, this thread disappears by washing or spraying the fabric with water.

- FUSIBLE THREAD: This thread melts with heat, bonding two layers of fabric together. It can be especially useful for hemming. Place a length of fusible thread in the fold of the hem and press with the iron, following the manufacturer's directions. The hem is securely held in place for stitching. Another practical use for fusible thread is to wind it onto a bobbin for stitching bias binding onto a raw edge. Then, fold the binding around the raw edge and press in place. The fusible thread will melt, bonding the binding to the fabric. Stitching can be added for extra security.

stitch formation. The thread should fit in the groove that runs down the front of the needle—it should not have extra room or be too large to fit. The size of the needle and thread should both be similar to the fabric weight: small needles and fine thread for sewing fine fabrics such as batiste, large needles and heavier thread for heavier fabrics such as wool. The thread weight information below offers some guidelines, but experiment and see what you like for the project you are sewing.

There are many types and brands of thread from which to choose when planning your next project. With the multitude of choices, you should have no problem finding the perfect thread for construction and embellishment. Exploring new thread options can add life to your projects and enhance what you sew, so keep your eyes open and be willing to investigate new ones that you see.

BOBBINS

The lower thread that joins with the needle thread to form stitches is wound onto a small metal or plastic spool. Each machine requires a particular size and type of bobbin. Many of them use a common size, but some machines need specially designed bobbins available from the dealer and will not operate with a "generic" one. Use the bobbin winder of the machine to evenly wind the thread onto an empty bobbin. For a balanced stitch with little tension adjustments, use the same thread in the bobbin as you do in the needle.

PRESSER FEET

The purpose of the presser foot is to hold the fabric in place against the feed dog. The feed dog moves the fabric to the back while the needle moves up and down, forming stitches. Every sewing machine comes with several presser feet. Even the most basic machine has three or four, usually an all-purpose foot, a zipper foot, a buttonhole foot, and often a blind hem or edgestitch foot. If you are like most people, you use the all-purpose foot unless there's

an obvious reason to use something else. For instance, the zipper foot lets you get closer to the coils of the zipper than the all-purpose foot. Some machines come with 10–12 presser feet, which is only the beginning of what may be available.

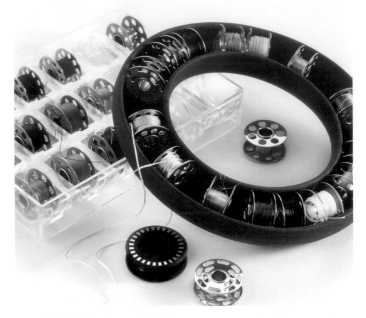

Organize bobbins in small, plastic compartmentalized boxes or in a rubber Bobbin Saver.

Check with your sewing machine dealer for presser foot options made for your brand and model of machine.

☙ THREAD WEIGHTS

- **12- to 20-wt.:** Use for couching and as a decorative thread for bobbinwork.
- **30-wt.:** Good for some embroidery and can be used as a decorative thread for bobbinwork.
- **40-wt.:** Most common; good for general construction, quilting, and embroidery.
- **50-wt.:** Good piecing thread and will also work as a bobbin thread for regular sewing.
- **60-wt.:** Use for lingerie and heirloom sewing; also good for appliqué and as a bobbin thread for decorative stitching and regular sewing.
- **80-wt.:** Use for extra fine lingerie and heirloom sewing.

NOTE: Some presser feet are "generic," meaning they fit several brands of machines, but some brands will only take feet designed specifically for their machines. If using a generic foot, you usually need to know if your machine has a low, high, or slant shank, and then buy accordingly. The number and type of presser feet vary from brand to brand, so check with your local sewing machine store to see what is available for your machine.

If you have never explored the use of a variety of presser feet, you should keep one thing in mind: Never underestimate the power of presser feet! Using the "correct" one (one designed specifically for the sewing task you're attempting) can improve your sewing immediately, give you more professional-looking results, speed your sewing, and/or open creative avenues you never realized were there.

Many sewing tasks can be completed with any of several presser feet, some more effectively than others, and you can sew for years without investing in a collection of presser feet. However, once you understand how they work and what they can do for your sewing, you'll be able to decide what works for the type of sewing you do.

On today's machines, presser feet are usually easy to change and often don't require any tools such as a screwdriver. Some are "snap-on" feet with interchangeable soles that simply snap onto a permanent shank on the machine. Others are one-piece (shank and sole together) and easily clip onto the machine at the top of the shank. Check your machine manual for the specifics about your machine.

To understand the functionality of presser feet, there are three parts to consider:

BOTTOM OF THE SOLE: If the foot has been designed to accommodate specific materials such as heavy thread, decorative cords, strands of beads, etc., the bottom of the sole will have one or more grooves, tunnels, or indentations (rather than being flat like an all-purpose foot). This tells you it was designed to ride over something. Embroidery, appliqué, piping, and cording feet have specially designed soles.

TOP OF THE SOLE: Look for holes, grooves and other openings to allow materials such as yarns, ribbons, and heavy decorative threads to be held in place for the needle to stitch over. The sole may also be more open than usual to allow more visibility of the stitching area. Couching, cording, and embroidery feet often have one or more of these features.

Look for holes or openings on the top of the sole for feeding yarns, ribbons, and cords.

ATTACHED GUIDES: Some feet have guides attached to the side, center, or top of the sole to provide a method of measuring or tracking where the needle goes. Edgestitch, piecing, and blind hem feet are examples of this.

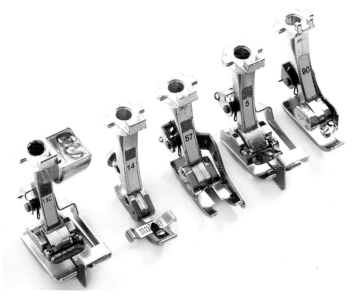

Some presser feet have added guides to measure or track the path of the needle.

If you are sewing a technique and the result doesn't look quite right to you, check your presser foot. Buttonholes can usually be made with an all-purpose foot, but because the bottom of the foot is flat, it drags on the heavy thread of the buttonhole beads, inhibiting the feed and resulting in adequate, but not beautiful, buttonholes. Using a buttonhole foot corrects the feed and gives full, satiny buttonholes—all with a simple change of the presser foot!

The bottom of the sole may have grooves or channels that ride smoothly over heavy thread, cord, etc.

Create a reference book for machine stitches and techniques to help in planning your sewing projects.

STITCH-O-LOGY

Even the most basic machines today go beyond the straight and zigzag stitch. They all have stitches designed for specific techniques such as overcasting edges or sewing knits and most have decorative stitches (sometimes hundreds!) that you can creatively use for decoration and embellishment. Look for these types of stitches on most machines:

FUNCTIONAL STITCHES: These start with the straight and zigzag stitches but may also include stretch stitches for sewing knits, overlock stitches for overcasting edges, blind stitches for invisible hems, running or serpentine stitches for sewing elastic, gathering or bridge stitches for gathering, and more. Some of the names are consistent from brand to brand but others may have different names for the same or similar stitches, depending on the make of the machine. Functional stitches are often used for construction but can also be used in decorative ways, especially when stitched using a double or triple needle. Included in this group are pre-programmed functions used to accomplish such tasks as sewing on buttons or darning torn fabric.

ORNAMENTAL STITCHES: These stitches contain a wide variety of decorative patterns including flowers, vines, hearts, bells, bows, geometric designs, etc. Some are open, stitched as outlines, and others are heavier designs sewn with satin stitches. For the heavier designs, use an embroidery or appliqué foot that has an indentation or cutout on the sole to allow the thread to pass under the foot without inhibiting the feed of the fabric. Some machines have groups of stitches designated for specific types of sewing such as quilting or home dec, but, of course, they are your stitches so you can use them for any type of sewing!

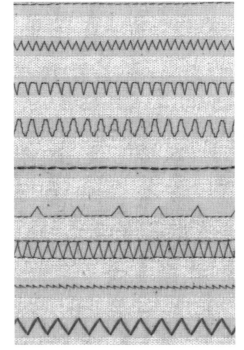

Functional stitches

Ornamental stitches

Create a stitch/technique book that catalogs the stitches of your machine. Sew lines of stitches on stabilized swatches, so you'll have a record of what the stitch actually looks like on fabric. Most machine manuals show drawings of the stitches, many bearing little resemblance to the sewn stitch. You'll consult your stitch book over and over again when selecting stitches for your next project.

STITCH ATTRIBUTES

Every stitch has several changeable traits, depending on your machine, to suit your taste and your project. The stitch width and length are the two most common attributes that make a stitch look the way it does. Needle position and presser foot pressure are two other settings that can make your stitches more versatile and useful.

Some sewing machines automatically make the stitch width and length settings that work best for each stitch. In most cases, you can make changes, so play around and adjust the stitches to do what you want. In the case of decorative stitches, you may find adjustments that give you other decorative possibilities. The needle position is important for placing the stitch exactly where you want. This gives you the precise stitching you need for techniques such as edgestitching, bias binding, and blind stitching. Some sewing machines offer multiple needle positions for selected stitches and others have more versatility with adjustable needle positions for every stitch.

Another variable is presser foot pressure. It refers to how light or how hard the foot sits on the fabric. The correct pressure is important for proper feeding of the fabric. You may need a lighter than normal pressure for the proper feeding of thick or textured fabrics such as fur. Slippery or sheer fabrics may need a heavier than normal pressure to hold the fabric in place and feed it under the needle.

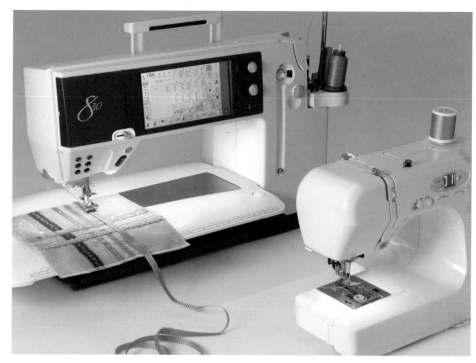

No matter what type of machine you want, you have lots of options.

THE SEARCH FOR THE PERFECT MACHINE

If you are in the market for a new machine, shop carefully to make sure you get the machine that is best for you. The perfect machine for you may not be the same as for the next person. Start with research—talk to friends, surf the Internet, and read today's sewing and craft magazines. Select 2–3 brands of machines that appeal to you. You may want to shop one brand at a time over several shopping trips, or make it one long excursion and see them all in one day. Many sewing machine stores carry multiple brands, so it may not be difficult to compare the ones that interest you.

A word about the cost of sewing machines—most people start shopping for a machine by deciding how much they want to spend. As we all have boundaries and limits to the amount we can spend, this is definitely something to consider. Machines are available in all price ranges, from less than $100 to over $10,000 so finding something to fit your budget is always possible. If you haven't shopped for a machine in a while, be prepared for sticker shock but realize that you get

a lot more for your money when you buy a machine today than you did even 20 years ago. So decide on a price range but keep an open mind and an objective eye when making your final decision. After all, the machine you choose will give you years of use and hours of creative satisfaction!

Think about the type of sewing you do and the features that are useful to you. Do you need a machine that has an easy way to make beautiful buttonholes for your custom-made garments? Is it important that your machine is small and portable to take to classes or to your vacation cottage? Start a list of everything you want the machine to do. Once you start shopping, you'll find things that you didn't even know machines could do (especially if you've been using the machine you inherited from your grandmother), but the place to start is with what you know you need. Look at the machine you have now and list three features you love about it and note three things you definitely don't want on your next machine.

Consider also your personality and methods of doing things. Do you like to fiddle with settings and tinker

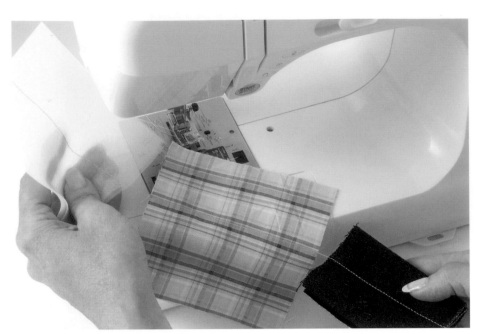

A good machine should sew well on a variety of fabric types and thicknesses.

with machines? If so, you may want to look for a mechanical model that lets you make all of the settings. Are you someone who wants a fast, direct way to set your machine so you can get on with the business of sewing? A push-button, computerized machine that automatically makes typical settings for you may be the answer. Or, are you a technophile who loves to have the latest in computer technology and gadgets? A top-of-the-line sewing computer will offer you layers and layers of technology to keep you entertained for years to come.

Next, prepare your materials for your shopping trip. Most sewing machine store personnel are ready to demonstrate the machines and show you the highlights of what they can do, but there are several things you need to check if they don't show up in the demo. Put together a small swatch kit to take with you to make

⚜

SHOPPING TIP

Make a kit for each brand you are investigating and put the contents in plastic zipper bags. Keep them separated as you shop, so you can look at them later and make comparisons as you narrow your search.

sure you run each machine through its paces. The kit should include:
• 3–4 swatches of fabric (about 6" square) that vary in type and weight. Tricot, quilting cotton, and thick wool are good choices. Test the machine that interests you by stitching on these fabrics, one after another, to see how easily the machine transitions from one weight of fabric to another. Check to make sure the tension is consistent. You should not have to greatly change or adjust the tension to sew on different fabrics.

• Take several swatches of a sturdy fabric such as denim to see how the machine sews through multiple layers. Does it run smoothly with no hesitation, or does it grind and falter as it tries to move through the thickness?

• Look around your sewing room and select 3–5 types of fabric that you use consistently, especially if they are unusual or difficult to sew. Try these on your potential new machine to see how it performs.

• If you use unusual threads, such as metallic or topstitching, take these and ask to see how the machine handles them. You may also pick up a few general tips for using them such as type of needle to use, adjusted tension setting, etc. as you talk to the staff of the sewing machine store.

• Include a small notebook and pen to make notes or jot down questions.

Take note of any features that are new to you so you can ask about them at the next stop. You may think you'll remember later, but it will all start to blur after a few hours of shopping!

Once you start your hunt, make sure you try out each machine. Test it out as you would new furniture. Sit down in front of the machine, look at the controls, and see how convenient they are. How easy are they to access, and how comfortable are they to adjust? If the machine has a screen, note the location. Is it easy to see while keeping your eye on your sewing or is it in an inconvenient location that is awkward to visually transition to and from? Sew on the machine to get the feel of it and hear the sound. Does it run smoothly and quietly, giving the feel of quality and durability? Is it loud and rough? If the demonstration does not answer the issues addressed with your swatch kit, take out your fabrics and see what the machine can do.

One feature often overlooked by most sewing machine shoppers is the establishment from which you are purchasing. Buying a machine off the shelf at a local discount or chain store may the quickest and in some cases the least expensive (not always!), but it guarantees you will be missing an extremely important component of a new machine. You want someone who will teach you to use the machine, answer your questions about sewing, and be there to service the machine on a routine basis and if problems arise. Even if you have sewn for years, knowing how to sew is not the same as knowing how to use your machine to its fullest. Many sewers are self-taught or learned years ago in junior high and have managed fine for years but have no idea of the advancements made in techniques, notions, and equipment over the years. Not only can your sewing be easier with results that are more professional, it can be more fun! Consistent service (once a year) from an authorized dealer is extremely important to maintaining a healthy machine with which you can have fun expressing your creativity. It's also good to know you have someone to rely on in case of problems because even the highest quality machines can hit a bump in the road. They are, after all, only machines!

Purchasing from an authorized dealer also has other advantages. They often take older machines in on trade for a new machine. If you are planning to replace your existing machine with a new one, go prepared with the following information about your current machine: brand, model, approximate date you purchased it, and any extra accessories you are including with it. Be aware that working with a dealer who carries the same brand you are trading will often get you a higher trade value as he or she usually has a customer base looking for that brand and model. Ask the dealer about any additional items he or she offers that add value to your purchase. This may include optional accessories, extended warranties, free or discounted service, free classes, etc. Make sure you have the full story of what you are purchasing before making your final decision. Many dealers also offer free classes to potential buyers as a way to let you try the machine you are considering, get the feel of using it, and gain more information with which to make your decision.

Some last advice for purchasing a new machine: collect brochures and business cards for each machine, add them to your swatch results, and take them home for consideration. Think again about the type of sewing you do and what you want from a machine. Once you decide on a brand and model, consider moving one step up if your budget allows. This will give you what you are looking for but will also allow you to grow and expand your sewing experiences as you learn your new machine and explore new creative horizons. You want your new machine to give you years of satisfaction before you outgrow it and move on to the next great model!

ROUTINE CARE

To get the best performance from your machine, it is important to routinely clean and care for it. Do this frequently, especially if your machine is running noisier than normal or having unusual tension problems. Your machine manual should give specific details for taking care of it, but these are the basic steps to follow, starting with an unthreaded machine, disconnected from the power outlet.

GETTING READY
- Remove stitch plate.
- Remove bobbin.
- Remove needle.
- Remove bobbin case if applicable.
- Remove hook system if applicable.

CLEANING
- Using a lint brush, make-up brush, or soft toothbrush, clean all lint and debris from the feed dog and bobbin areas. Be careful about using canned air to blow out the lint, as it is difficult to keep from blowing some of it into the machine, which could cause future problems.
- Brush each side of the upper thread tension discs (do this with the presser foot in the up position so the tension discs are open).
- Use topstitching thread to "floss" on each side of the discs to clear any stray threads that may be down in the tension area.

OILING
- Place one or two drops of oil in the hook area and any other place your manual directs (most machines today need a minimum of oil). Use only the type of oil recommended for your machine; do not over oil.
- Run a swatch of fabric under the needle several times to get rid of any excess oil.

FINISHING
- Replace hook system and bobbin case if needed.
- Replace stitch plate.
- Insert a new needle.

One of the best things you can do to prolong the life of your machine is make a yearly visit to an authorized technician for deeper cleaning and lubrication. Schedule it for your birthday month, so it's easy to remember or during your vacation when you won't be using the machine.

Routine care of your machine will help it sew well for years.

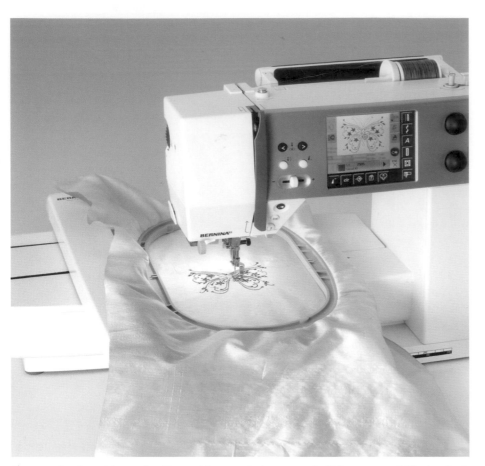

Computerized machine embroidery adds an entirely new embellishment possibility to all of your sewing projects.

EMBROIDERY MACHINES

The latest and strongest trend in home sewing is machine embroidery. Digitized designs stitched by sewing computers give professional results that in the past were available only from commercial embroiderers. Introduced in 1990, the first home embroidery machine stitched beautiful 4" x 4" designs. Today's embroidery machines have gone far beyond this, enabling you to customize designs and stitch up to 16" x 10" in one hooping. Now you can personalize everything with richly-colored designs and lettering stitched in your sewing room.

When shopping for an embroidery machine, there are three main points to consider:

1. Determine how much space you have to devote to embroidery. Do you have room for another machine in your sewing area?

2. How computer literate are you or do you want to be? If all you want to do is stitch preprogrammed designs, you don't need as elaborate a machine as you do if you want to customize and digitize your own designs.

3. Think about the type of projects you want to embroider—do you want to only stitch simple monograms on terry towels or are you planning lavish designs across the backs of jackets?

Embroidery machines are sold as stand-alone machines that only do embroidery, or they are part of a system made up of a sewing machine and a separate unit added to the machine to stitch embroidery designs. If you have the room for a separate machine, the stand-alone machine offers you the opportunity to embroider designs at the same time you are using the sewing machine. The single machines are usually more limited in features and in maximum design size but offer you the opportunity to get into machine embroidery for less money. Combination machines sometimes offer more in the way of features and design size and are priced accordingly.

Designs are available in a variety of file formats, each one unique.

Most machines read one format but files can usually be converted to other formats using the computer and a conversion program. Many embroidery software programs include a conversion feature.

Design styles range from beautiful florals to outline redwork to funny cartoons. Any style of artwork can be digitized and turned into a stitched design. When purchasing designs, especially over the Internet, make sure you are buying from a reputable design house. The quality of digitizing that goes into the design makes a huge difference in how it stitches and in your satisfaction. Look for designs that are attractive and detailed without having too many small details. They should sew out with a minimum of color changes and jump stitches that need to be trimmed. Multiple fill stitches with different patterns sewn at different angles add depth and dimension to a design.

Correct hooping is one of the most important elements of good embroidery. The fabric should be taut in the hoop but should not be stretched or distorted. If you pull the fabric too tightly, it will pucker around the design once the fabric is released from the hoop.

BASIC HOOPING STEPS:

• Open the outer hoop (usually by loosening a screw on the rim) and place it on a flat surface such as a table or counter.

• Place a single layer of fabric (with stabilizer if needed) over it. If hooping a ready-made garment,

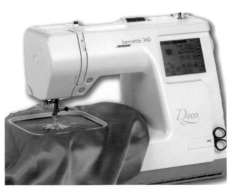

Machines that embroider only are available as companions to sewing machines.

Digitized embroidery designs are available in any style you can imagine. Courtesy Oklahoma Embroidery Supply and Design.

be sure that other portions of the garment are out of the way.

- Position the inner hoop over the fabric and push it down into the outer hoop. Smooth the fabric and pull it taut without stretching or distorting it. Tighten the screw of the hoop.
- Use the plastic template provided with most machine embroidery hoops to make sure the fabric is hooped on-grain and the placement is as desired.

MONOGRAMS/LETTERING/FONTS

Most embroidery machines have one or more fonts that can be used to create monograms or personalize embroidery designs. Some machines have advanced manipulation functions such as kerning, leading and baseline adjustments that let you position each letter exactly as you want. Look for monogramming functions that give you options for stylizing one or more letters into decorative monograms.

Besides stitching monograms and names, embroidery machines can be used for creative writing. Birth and marriage announcements, pithy sayings, words of wisdom, fabric books and poetry can be stitched on fabric or paper for artwork, toys, and gifts.

QUILTING IN THE HOOP

Beautiful outline designs used to quilt layers of fabric and batting give a rich quilted look in a fraction of the time needed for free-motion quilting. Embroidery machines are generally set with a fairly tight bobbin tension and a looser needle tension, which makes for good-looking designs with the needle thread pulling slightly to the back to keep bobbin thread showing on the front of the project. This works for most projects but isn't the best option if you want the back of a quilt to look as good as the front. You can make tension adjustments on the machine, or you can stitch the embroidery designs through the quilt front and batting, adding the backing after all of the embroidery designs are stitched, and then use stitch-in-the-ditch and/or free-motion stitching techniques to complete the quilt and stitch all layers together.

To stitch the quilt, use water-soluble stabilizer that can be dissolved when the stitching is complete. The best method of preparing the quilt is to place one or more layers of stabilizer behind the batting and hoop all layers, being careful not to distort the fabric. For small areas and simple designs, you can hoop the stabilizer only and use temporary spray adhesive to hold the quilt in the hoop.

For design placement, the most accurate method of positioning requires a design template. Stitch it in the desired size and make photocopies of it. Position the templates on the quilt as desired and mark the placement for stitching.

After hooping and stitching the designs, remove the fabric from the hoop and cut away the excess stabilizer. Dissolve any remaining stabilizer with water. Finish the backing and binding of the quilt as desired.

IN THE HOOP PROJECTS

Small projects can be stitched mostly or entirely in-the-hoop, allowing the embroidery machine to construct as well as embellish. Card cases, pocket purses, paper dolls, and cosmetic bags are examples of projects that can be made. Some of these are digitized to stitch completely in-the-hoop and once the stabilizer (usually water-soluble) is removed, the project is finished. Others are created in pieces and once the parts are embroidered, they are removed from the hoop and construction is completed using the sewing machine.

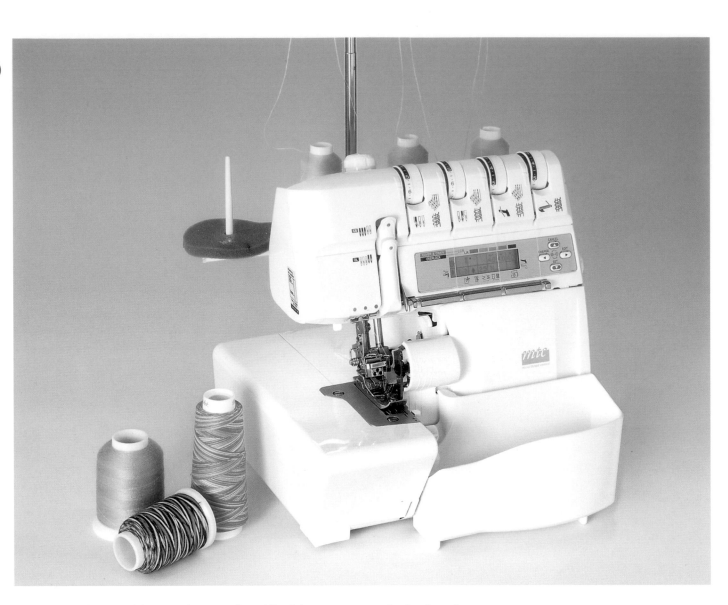

Sergers have the potential to speed your sewing while giving you more professional results.

84

SERGERS

Available to home sewers since the 1980s, sergers are machines fashioned after commercial equipment used in factories to speed garment production and produce more professionally finished clothing. Considered a companion to the sewing machine, the serger will perform certain functions such as seaming, seam finishing, and hemming but is not able to do other tasks such as basting, topstitching, buttonholes or intricate decorative stitching.

Even though the serger is not as versatile as a sewing machine, it is considered by many sewers to be a necessity in the sewing room. It runs faster (around 1500 stitches a minute) than sewing machines and actually does three operations (trimming, seaming, and overcasting) in one pass under the needle. The speedy result is a professional-looking seam similar to that found in ready-to-wear.

Learning to use a serger can be intimidating simply because it is very different than a sewing machine and looks more complicated because most of the working parts are exposed when the front cover is opened. The secret to becoming comfortable with the serger is to remember that it is a specialty machine and therefore has fewer functions to learn. Take a class (usually offered as part of the purchase) and read your manual—before long, you'll wonder how you got along without it!

CONE HOLDER: Serger thread is sold on cones and the plastic cone holders keep them seated more securely on the spindle. Cones hold more thread than regular spools, which is useful because a serger stitch requires more thread than a sewing machine stitch. Thread on regular spools can be used on sergers (without the cone holder) but will need replacing more frequently.

THREAD GUIDES: Each thread has a unique path with guides to keep the thread in place. The thread guides on most sergers are color-coded, so it is easy to follow the path to the needle or looper.

TENSION DIALS OR LEVERS: Each thread has its own tension dial. Tensions are adjusted individually to form each type of stitch. Usually low numbers indicate less tension and high numbers signify more tension. Some sergers have a tension release (no tension on the thread), activated by raising the presser foot, to make the threading or unthreading process easier.

NEEDLES: Most sergers use standard sewing machine needles but usually in a more narrow size range. Size 80 and 90 universal needles are most commonly used in sergers.

LOOPERS: Found in the lower part of the serger, these metal "arms" have holes in the ends to feed thread through. For most stitch formations, the upper looper forms a loop of thread on the right side of the fabric and the lower looper forms a loop on the underside of the fabric.

CUTTING KNIVES: The nice clean stitches that sergers make are due, in part, to the fact that the edge of the fabric is trimmed just before the fabric goes under the needle. Most sergers have an upper knife and a lower knife that work together in a manner similar to scissors. The knives generally last quite a long time but can be replaced (see your manual) once they start cutting poorly. The knives on most sergers can be disengaged when desired and some stitch formations require the fabric to be uncut.

CUTTING WIDTH: The stitch width of serger stitches cannot be set in the same way it can on a sewing machine, however the amount of fabric that is trimmed from the fabric edges can be adjusted, affecting the width of the final stitch formation. Usually a dial turns to move the lower knife from side to side, positioning it closer or farther away from the needle. The tension of each thread is adjusted, if needed, so they overcast the seam allowance without curling the edge of the fabric or looping over it.

HANDWHEEL: Sergers have handwheels on the right side of the machine, similar to sewing machines. Turning the handwheel raises and lowers the needle and moves the machine through the stitch formation process. An important point to remember— never turn the handwheel backward away from you. This could affect the timing of the machine and require a trip to the technician.

DIFFERENTIAL FEED: Some sergers have more than one set of feed dogs that work simultaneously and also independently of each other,

depending on the setting you select. The purpose is to make it possible to handle all types of fabric, resulting in smooth, flat serger stitches. If using a lightweight fabric that tends to pucker at normal settings, you can adjust the feed so that one set of feed dogs inhibits the feed (usually a low number), pulling the fabric taut as it goes under the needle. For knit fabrics that tend to stretch as they are stitched, change the setting (usually to a high number) so that one set of feed dogs pushes the layers under the foot, keeping them flat as they are stitched.

STITCH LENGTH: Adjust the length of the stitch much the same way as a sewing machine stitch. A lower number indicates a shorter stitch length and gives a "filled-in" look to the stitch—a setting often used with rolled edges and flatlock stitches. A higher number makes the stitch longer and is used on heavier fabric and for specific techniques such as gathering.

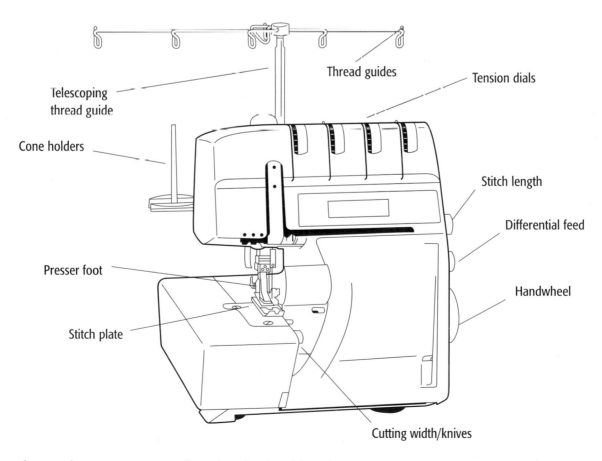

Telescoping thread guide

Cone holders

Thread guides

Tension dials

Presser foot

Stitch plate

Stitch length

Differential feed

Handwheel

Cutting width/knives

Standard serger features shown; may vary according to brand and model.

STITCH POSSIBILITIES

Serger stitches are created using 2, 3, 4, or more threads, multiple needles and mechanisms called "loopers" in the lower part of the serger. The looper threads meet on the edge of the fabric, thus the name, overlock, which is another name for serger. Here are the most commonly used serger stitches and the general uses for each.

OVERLOCK: Used for construction and edging, this stitch is formed with one or two needles, the lower looper and the upper looper. The outer needle thread stitches on the seam line and the two looper threads meet at the edge of the fabric to overcast the edge. The 3-thread version of this stitch is flexible and a good stitch for knits; the 4-thread version sews a line of stitching down the center of the 3-thread stitch formation and is the stronger of the two. It works well on woven fabrics and for construction.

Balanced 4-thread overlock stitch

FLATLOCK: A decorative stitch, the flatlock can be used as a seam to join two pieces of fabric or as a decorative line of stitching across the surface of the fabric. As a seam, the flatlock stitch is not very strong, so it should not be placed in areas of stress. A wide flatlock stitch uses two loopers and the left needle; a narrow flatlock stitch uses two loopers and the right needle.

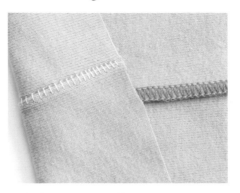

Flatlock seam (reversible)

ROLLED HEM: This inconspicuous stitch actually rolls the fabric under and covers the rolled edge with thread. Most often used as an edging on items such as napkins and scarves, it can also be used as a seam on sheer or lightweight fabric. This stitch has a 3-thread formation using the right needle and both loopers. Some sergers will also form a 2-thread rolled hem (right needle and one looper) for a more delicate look.

Rolled edge

CHAIN STITCH: Available on some sergers, this stitch is formed using one needle and the chain stitch looper. Good for basting and decorative work, the chain stitch is also useful in place of a sewing machine straight stitch.

Chain stitch

COVER STITCH: The cover stitch is similar to a stitch found on many ready-to-wear items. Using two or three needles, it resembles double or triple needle stitching on the top with looped thread on the underside. Excellent for knit fabric and active wear, the cover stitch can be used for seaming, hemming, and binding.

Cover stitch

SERGER LEARNING TIP

Most sergers have color-coded thread paths to make it easy to learn and remember the threading process. Thread each path using the assigned colors, creating a multi-colored stitch. This helps you to see the part each thread plays in forming the stitch, and it also lets you see how tension adjustments affect the individual threads.

BASIC SERGER TECHNIQUES

STARTING TO SERGE

When starting to sew, lift the front edge of the foot and place the fabric under it. Most serger presser feet are long and spring loaded and the fabric will be pulled under the needles for stitching.

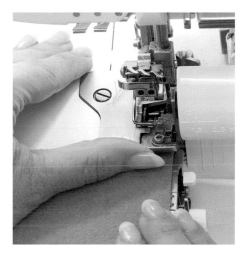

Place the fabric under the front edge of the presser foot to start serging.

SEAMING

When stitching a seam, feed the fabric under the needle and serge the length of the seam, continuing to serge after the fabric is behind the foot. Serge off the fabric, leaving a 4"–6" chain of thread; clip the thread, leaving about 2"–3" behind the foot and on the fabric.

The knife trims the seam allowance so the stitch can form over the fabric edge.

LOCKING A SERGER STITCH

Even though the serger stitch looks as if it will not come apart, the threads are actually loosely intertwined and not secure. Fasten or "lock" the serger stitches using one of the following methods:

- Put a drop of seam sealant on the last stitch; let it dry and trim the thread tails.
- Slip a hand tapestry needle into the row of serger stitches, with the eye exposed. Thread the tail through the eye and then pull the thread through the line of stitches.
- Tie an overhand knot in the thread tail next to the fabric; trim excess.

Apply seam sealant to the thread and let dry.

Bury the end of the thread tails in the serger stitch.

Tie the thread tails into a knot.

SERGING AN OUTSIDE CORNER

For serging corners on projects such as scarves, napkins, placemats, and tablecloths, try this easy technique:

Serge one side of the project, sewing off the edge at the corner; serge the next side, going over the previously serged edge. Put a drop of seam sealant on the corner; let it dry and trim the thread tails.

This easy corner technique is great for napkins, placemats, and other square projects.

SERGING AN INSIDE CORNER

Useful for sleeve vents, neck openings, and slits, this serger manipulation is easy to learn.

Clip about ¼" into the corner. Serge until the front of the presser foot reaches the corner; stop with the needle in the fabric. Raise the presser foot, then open the fabric into a straight line. Lower the foot and continue serging, taking care to avoid pleats and puckers at the corner area.

Serge until the front of the foot is at the clipped inside corner.

Straighten the fabric into a straight line and continue serging.

SERGING A CIRCLE

Great for circular applications such as edging round placemats, table toppers, and tablecloths, this technique works well for any flat, curved edge.

Trim about 1½" times the width of the seam allowance from the edge of the circle. Position the needle at the cut area to begin serging the circle. Lower the foot and serge along the edge of the circle, overlapping the beginning stitches to finish. Note: If the edge of the circle ripples or waves as you serge, adjust the differential feed setting to a higher number; if it puckers, adjust it to a lower number.

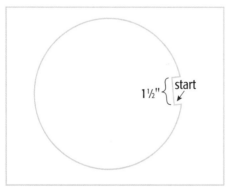

Overlap the beginning and ending stitches when serging a circular shape.

SPECIALTY EQUIPMENT

As we push the boundaries of creativity, we find more equipment to help us design and craft fabric fashions. Specialty machines are available to add to your sewing skills and expand your creative horizons. You just have to find the room!

BLINDSTITCH MACHINE

This small machine sews a single stitch for making invisible hems on all types of garments. This hem is similar to garment industry techniques and is often employed by professional dressmakers and in alteration shops.

INDUSTRIAL SEWING MACHINE

Commercial or semi-industrial sewing machines are heavy-duty machines that sew faster than household machines. They are usually mechanical models that have limited stitch packages, designed for specialized techniques and increased production. Cottage industries often use these machines for producing sewn items for sale.

QUILTING FRAME

A freestanding frame equipped with a sliding tray that holds a regular sewing machine, giving some of the benefits of a longarm quilting machine. Extended arm sewing machines let you stitch the quilt in the shortest time, but these frames will work with a variety of sewing machine models.

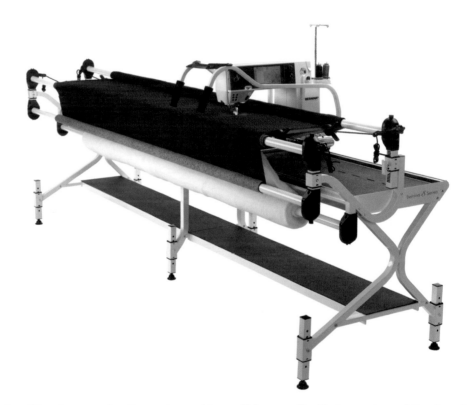

A quilting frame makes it easy to machine quilt large quilts. Photo courtesy of Bernina of America.

NEEDLE PUNCH MACHINE OR ATTACHMENT

This craft requires either a specialized machine or a special accessory that attaches to a sewing machine, depending on the brand. This technique uses no thread and the machine or attachment has a series of barbed needles that "punch" fibers down into the surface of fabric, creating texture and design.

A needle punch attachment makes fast work of felting.

LONGARM QUILTING MACHINE

This type of sewing machine has been manufactured to provide additional room between the side of the machine and the needle. It works with a frame that a quilt is rolled onto, allowing the stitcher to stand and move the machine across the quilt. Once the width has been stitched, the quilt is rolled to expose an unquilted area. Plan ahead when you purchase one of these, as the frame is 10'–12' wide.

MULTI-NEEDLE EMBROIDERY MACHINE

Six, ten, or twelve needles make stitching with these embroidery machines quicker than home embroidery machines and easier to use with fewer thread changes. These computerized machines have a smaller footprint than commercial embroidery machines and are gaining popularity with home embroiderers.

A multi-needle embroidery machine eliminates the need to stop and change threads.

construction essentials

 MOST SEWING PATTERNS OFFER DIRECTIONS for specific parts of the projects such as sleeves, collar, lining, etc. and then give assembly directions for putting them all together. As with the majority of creative and artistic endeavors, there are multiple ways to create fabric projects—some easy, some more involved, and others that have not even been developed yet! However, if you don't have the time and energy to come up with new construction methods, it's a good idea to follow tried and true ways to sew. This chapter starts with the common seam and moves through some of the more widely used techniques and their variations. A creative tip: It's easier to imagine new methods if you are familiar with the usual ways to cut, stitch, and assemble your fabric creations!

If some of these construction techniques are new to you, test them first before stitching on your garment fabric. At the end of this chapter, you'll find small scale practice patterns that will make it quick and easy to become familiar with the steps discussed on the following pages. Photocopy the patterns, enlarging them 200% for easy handling and work your way through the process for each technique. You'll use less fabric and the sewing will go more quickly than if you were working full scale. You can also keep the finished pieces as references for later sewing sessions.

These small-scale garments were made using the patterns on pages 120–125. Perfect for practicing new garment techniques, the patterns are also just the right size for 18" dolls.

SEAMS AND SEAM FINISHES

One thing that almost all sewn items have in common is the seam—two pieces of fabric sewn together a short distance from the edges. Usually the fabric pieces are placed right sides together, matching the raw edges. Once the seam is sewn, the seam allowances (fabric edges extending past the line of stitching) are pressed open or both pressed to one side, depending on the project. The most common type of seam is sewn with the straight stitch, but there are specialized seams for particular fabrics and sewing situations.

CONSISTENT SEAM ALLOWANCES

Accuracy is important when stitching seams, especially when sewing a garment that you want to fit or piecing patchwork shapes that form a pattern. With experience and practice, you'll be able to sew a seam with consistent seam allowances, but if you are new to sewing or if you are sewing a project that needs exact precision, there are guides that will help. Try any or all of these methods to find the ones that work for you.

STITCH PLATE: The stitch plates of most sewing machines are marked with grooves or printed lines that give you visual references for seam measurements. There are usually lines for several common measurements such as ¼", ½", and ⅝". Simply guide the edge of your fabric along the appropriate mark, and,

with the needle in center position, you'll have consistent seam allowances of the correct width.

PRESSER FOOT AS A GUIDE: You can also use the side of your foot as a guide. If the width is appropriate for the project you are sewing, place the outer edge of the foot along the edge of the fabric while stitching. You can vary the width of this method by adjusting your needle position, making it closer or farther away from the fabric edge. Using the presser foot as a guide is also a good way to stitch closely-spaced parallel rows of topstitching.

BED GUIDES: If you are using very wide seam allowances or stitching farther into the fabric, you can place a guide on the bed of the machine to the right of the stitch plate. Some machines have these included, and they attach to the machine with a screw; there are also magnetic ones available that work on all machines with metal beds. An easy way to create a guide of this sort is to measure the desired distance from the needle and put a piece of tape on the bed of the machine. Use painter's tape or another low-adhesive type, so you don't leave residue on your machine.

SEAM GUIDE: Most machines have a seam guide available that fits on the back of some presser feet. Set this for the distance desired and then let it follow the fabric edge or previous line of stitching for consistent seaming or parallel rows.

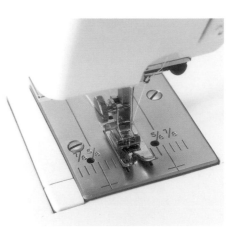

Most stitch plates have markings that help keep the seam allowances consistent.

Aligning the edge of the presser foot with the edge of the fabric is one way to sew even seams.

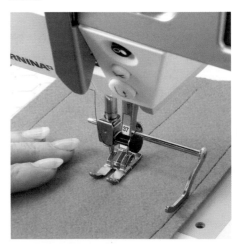

Seam guides that attach to the presser foot let you sew wide seams or parallel rows of stitching.

✾ SEAM ALLOWANCES

The size of seam allowances may vary from project to project but, generally, these measurements are used:

- ⅝"—most commercial garment patterns
- ½"—most home decorating projects
- ¼"—patchwork quilt patterns
- ¼"—knit garments

SEAMS FOR WOVEN FABRICS

Even though the plain straight seam is by far the one used most often for woven fabrics, there are other options you may need for certain sewing situations. Become familiar with these and you will be able to sew most fabrics successfully.

STRAIGHT SEAM: Place fabric pieces right sides together and pin about every 2"–3". Sew along the seamline, backstitching about ½" at the beginning and end of the seam. Remove pins as you come to them; never sew over pins. Press the seam open for most garment applications or to one side for patchwork. Note: When sewing patchwork, you do not need to backstitch as most seams are secured when crossed by another seam.

Straight seam

CORNER SEAM: Turning corners when stitching a seam is easy but may not be obvious if you haven't done it before. Sew a seam down one side of the fabric as described above for straight seams. When you get to the place where the seamline intersects with the seamline from the next side, stop with your needle down in the fabric. Hint: If you activate the Needle Stop Down feature (if available), the machine will stop with the needle down automatically. Lift the presser foot and turn or pivot the fabric 90°, then continue seaming. This type of seam is usually an enclosed seam because you will turn the fabric to the right side, causing the seams to be on the inside. Before turning, trim the point off the corner, so the fabric is flat after it is turned.

Corner seam

CURVED SEAM: This seam shapes fabric into smooth curves for example in the princess seaming used to fit a jacket or dress over a bust-line. Necklines and armholes are also places that require curves. Curved seams require a few more steps than straight seams because the fabric doesn't naturally want to follow a curve. The extra effort involves the following steps:

1. STAYSTITCHING: This is a line of straight stitching sewn on a single layer of fabric; it is sewn on the seam allowance next to the seamline, about ½" from the fabric edge. Its purpose is to keep the curved edge from stretching out of shape and to help in creating a smooth curve. Staystitching is sewn before the fabric pieces are sewn together and remains on the fabric; it should not show once the garment is complete. It sometimes seems that this is an unnecessary step, but don't skip it if your pattern directions tell you to do it. The final smoothness of the curved edge will be your reward!

2. CLIPPING: Inside curves such as necklines and armholes require clipping to release the fabric and allow for shaping into a curve. Use the tips of very sharp scissors and clip up to, but not through, the line of staystitching. Some clipping, such as on the inward curved piece of a princess seamline, is done before seaming.

3. NOTCHING: Outward curves as on a round collar require notches to be cut from the seam allowances to reduce the bulk and allow a smooth turn of the fabric. These notches are cut after the seam is sewn and the cuts should go up to, but not through, the staystitching.

A princess seam joins an inward curve with an outward curve. To sew it, first staystitch both curved edges. Clip the inward curved seam allowance up to the staystitching. Pin the two curved edges right sides together, spreading the inward clipped edge to match the outward curved edge.

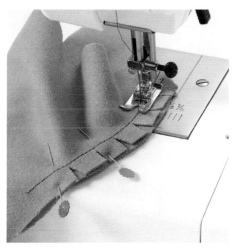

Princess seam

Position the pinned fabrics under the needle with the clipped piece on top and stitch the seam, removing the pins as you come to them. Notch the outward curved piece and press the seam open over a tailor's ham.

BIAS-CUT SEAM: When sewing bias-cut seams, care must be taken not to stretch the fabric or allow it to be distorted. If both edges being joined are bias, carefully hand-baste the seam before sewing with the machine. Letting the garment hang for 24 hours before seaming gives it a chance to relax and helps to avoid puckered seams. Placing the two layers of fabric on tissue paper and sewing through all of the layers will help control the seam and avoid stretching the fabric. If only one edge is bias, carefully pin, and then baste the bias edge to the straight edge without stretching. Stitch the two pieces together with the bias edge on top; if the bias edge is on the bottom, it will be pulled by the feed dog, stretching and distorting it.

SEAMS FOR KNIT FABRICS

One of the benefits of knit fabric is that it stretches to move with your body, making it comfortable even when it fits closely. Because of this, it requires a seam that will stretch with it while securely holding the fabric together. There are several choices to make this happen.

ZIGZAG STITCH: A simple tiny zigzag stitch (width = 0.5mm, length = 1mm) has more "give" to it than a straight stitch and is better for knit fabrics than a straight stitch. To test the seam once it is sewn, stretch the knit fabric to its fullest. If the stitches break, the seam does not have enough stretch and an alternative should be used. This type of seam can be pressed open or to the side.

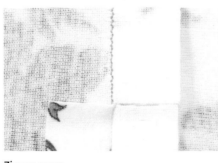

Zigzag seam

STRETCH STITCH: Most sewing machines have a stretch stitch that is flexible and will move as the knit is stretched. This is a narrow stitch and will allow you to press the seam open as you would with a straight stitch. Check your machine manual for the specifics of this type of stitch on your machine.

Stretch seam

MACHINE OVERLOCK STITCH: Most sewing machines also have at least one overlock stitch. This type of stitch is made for knit fabrics and gives about a ¼" seam allowance. You sew the stitch along the seamline and then trim the excess fabric next to the stitching. Again, check your machine manual for the specifics of this type of stitch on your machine.

Overlock seam

KNIT TIPS

- When cutting or stitching fabric, do not let it drape over the edge of your sewing table as it will stretch the fabric and/or distort the stitching.
- Universal needles work on many knit fabrics, but if you experience skipped stitches, switch to a ballpoint or stretch needle.
- Do not let the sewing machine stretch the fabric as it moves it under the needle. Use a walking foot and/or lighten the pressure of the presser foot.
- Some sergers have differential feeding systems that let you adjust the way the knit is moved under the foot to avoid stretching and rippling the fabric.

GUIDE TO SMOOTH SEAMS

When turning a project to the right side, seam allowances must be reduced in order to get a smooth, bulk-free look from the right side of the fabric. This guide shows how to handle each type of seam allowance.

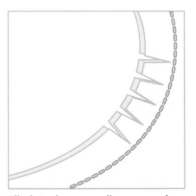

Clip into the seam allowances of inner curves.

Cut notches into the seam allowances of outer curves.

Trim corners at a diagonal, tapering the seam allowances.

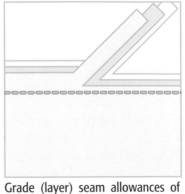

Grade (layer) seam allowances of enclosed seams.

SERGED SEAMS

Sergers are great for woven fabrics but also work well for knits as the stitches are looped together and have a lot of stretch to them. There are several choices for serger seams, depending on the type of fabric you are using.

OVERLOCK SEAMS: The basic serger seam, this can be stitched as a 3-thread or a 4-thread stitch. The 4-thread stitch is the strongest and will work on knits and most wovens, except for extremely loosely-woven fabrics that ravel easily. The 3-thread stitch has the most stretch and is good for very stretchy knits. A 3-thread stitch can also be a narrow seam for lightweight fabrics such as batiste.

FLATLOCKED SEAMS: Flatlocking is a visible, decorative technique that can be a seam, using 2 or 3 threads. It is not a very strong seam and should not be used in areas that will receive a lot of stress or strain. Set the serger for a flatlock stitch (see your manual). Place the fabric wrong sides together and stitch. Then gently pull to flatten the stitch. This type of stitch can be reinforced with a machine straight stitch to make it stronger or a "faux" flatlock stitch can be used, which is a serger seam stitched with the fabric wrong sides together, leaving the seam allowance on the outside of the garment. The seam allowance is pressed to one side and topstitched to the fabric.

ROLLED SEAMS: This type of seam is very delicate and will work on lightweight fabric. It is not a strong seam but can be used for sheer fabric on garments and projects that will not receive stress or strain. As it is a decorative stitch, the seam allowances can be on the inside or outside of the garment, as you prefer. Thread the serger for a rolled hem and adjust the tensions as needed (see your manual). Place the two layers of fabric together and roll the edges as one. The seam can be reinforced with a straight stitch sewn immediately next to the rolled stitched.

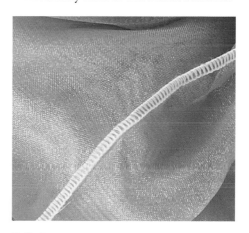

Rolled seam

Overlock seam

Flatlock seam (reversible)

Sergers work on almost any type of fabric but are especially useful with knits because serger stitches have more "give" to them than most sewing machine stitches.

SPECIALTY SEAMS

There are certain sewing situations that call for unusual seam techniques because of the type of fabric selected or the type of project being made. Here are some of the most common applications.

FRENCH SEAMS: This enclosed seam is used most often on sheer fabric where the seam allowances are visible and works best on straight edges. It starts with the fabric placed wrong sides together, opposite from the usual. Stitch about ⅜" from the edge, and then trim the seam allowance to ⅛". Press and turn the fabric to the wrong side, placing the stitched seam exactly on the fold. Stitch along the original seamline, which should be ¼" from the folded edge. This technique can also be used in unlined jackets or other places where the seam allowances will be seen.

FLAT-FELLED SEAMS: A sturdy enclosed seam, this stitch is often used on men's shirts, jeans, and children's clothing. Place fabric wrong sides together and stitch on the seamline. Press the seam open and then to one side. Trim the lower seam allowance to ⅛" and press ¼" under on the other seam allowance. Stitch this folded edge to the fabric, covering the trimmed seam allowance and making sure the line of stitching is parallel to the original stitched seamline. Some sewing machines have feller feet that will fold and hold the seam allowance in place for stitching.

Flat-felled seam

WELT SEAMS: This seam is similar to a flat-felled seam but does not have the enclosed bulk. You start with a plain seam stitched on the seamline; press to one side. Trim the lower seam allowance to ¼". From the right side, topstitch a scant ⅜" from the seamline, through the upper seam allowance only. For a double welt seam, add topstitching close to the seamline, parallel to the first line. Flat-felled seams are completely finished on the inside but the seam allowances show with welt seams although they are secured with the topstitching.

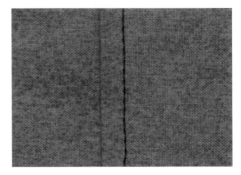
Single welt seam

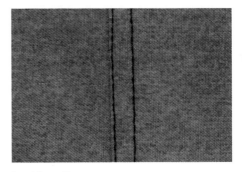
Double welt seam

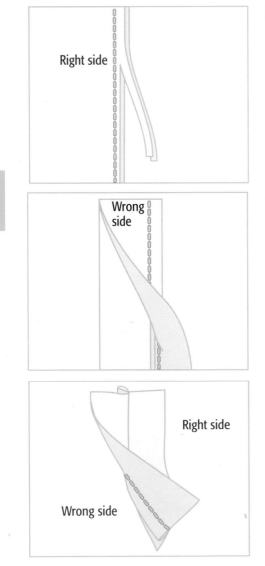
French seams are narrow and totally enclosed.

Flat-felled seams are totally enclosed.

SEAMING AND FINISHING TIPS

- To check the fit or deal with difficult fabrics, baste by hand or using a long machine stitch before sewing a permanent seam.
- When notching and clipping the seam allowances of curved seams, cut each seam allowance separately and stagger the clips and notches with the opposite seam allowance. This reduces bulk while preserving the integrity of the seam.

SEAM FINISHES

One of the benchmarks of quality-made clothing is the neatness of the inside of the garments. Loose threads, raveled edges, and poor-quality stitching are signs that a garment is not well-made and will probably not last long. Finishing seam allowances extends the life of the garment and makes the inside as beautiful as the outside.

PINKED EDGES: This is one of the simplest ways to finish your seams and works on many woven fabrics, especially ones that don't easily ravel such as wool. You merely trim the edges with pinking shears; for more protection, stitch ¼" from the edge before pinking. It does not stop loosely woven fabrics from raveling.

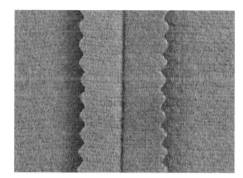

Pinked edges

CLEAN FINISHED EDGES: Also easy, this method works best on light and medium weight fabrics that are not bulky. Turn the edge of the fabric under about $3/16$" and edgestitch the fold. Trim the extra fabric close to the stitching and press.

Clean finished edges

OVERSEWN EDGES: Good for fabrics that tend to ravel, this method uses a medium zigzag stitch (width and length = 2mm–3mm) on the edge of the fabric. The right swing of the stitch should go into the air next to the fabric, causing the stitch to wrap the edge.

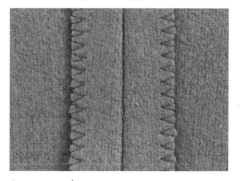

Oversewn edges

SERGED EDGES: Sergers are great for finishing seams quickly and neatly on almost any type of fabric. Set the serger for a 3-thread overlock stitch and serge along the edge, trimming the fabric slightly. A 2-thread balanced stitch can be used on lighter weight fabrics.

Serged edges

HONG KONG FINISH: This couture seam finish is good for medium to heavyweight fabrics and works especially well on bulky fabrics. It completely encloses the fabric edge, so it is excellent for fabrics that tend to ravel easily. Using 1" bias tape or bias cut lightweight fabric strips, sew to the fabric about ¼" from the edge. Fold the bias around the edge and stitch in the ditch to secure; trim the extra bias fabric from the back of the seam allowance.

Hong Kong finish

BIAS BOUND EDGES: Similar to the Hong Kong finish, this method uses double-fold bias tape, wrapped around the edge and stitched in place and is often used as a seam finish in unlined coats and jackets. The purchased tape is folded off-center, so one side is wider than the other one. Fold the tape around the fabric edge with the wider allowance underneath. Stitching on the edge of the upper allowance will automatically catch the lower edge.

Bias bound edges

CLOTHING CONSTRUCTION STANDARDS

When constructing clothing (or purchasing ready-made), you should know the standards that show quality construction. For a finished, professional look, keep these in mind and strive to make your garments as close to these standards as possible.

DETAIL	STANDARDS
Buttons	• Appropriate size for garment • Accurate placement with even spacing • Fastened securely • Neatly stitched with beginning and ending stitches hidden behind the button
Buttonholes	• Accurate placement with even spacing • Placed at stress points • Appropriate type and color of interfacing used • Appropriate size; fits selected buttons • Center cut neatly open; all loose threads trimmed
Collars	• Edges are smooth—no bulky seam allowances • Understitching holds under collar in place • Shape is symmetrical • Appropriate interfacing is used • Rolls smoothly or lays flat as needed • Smooth curves and sharp points where appropriate
Cuffs	• Edges are smooth—no bulky seam allowances • Under cuff does not show • Shape is symmetrical • Appropriate interfacing is used
Darts	• Smoothly tapered with no bubble or pucker at point • Pressed correctly—horizontal, down and vertical, to the center • Attractive and appropriate placement
Facings	• Smooth; lays flat • Edges finished to prevent raveling • Understitched to keep facing from rolling to front • Seams clipped, notched and/or graded as needed
Fasteners (hooks, eyes, snaps, etc.)	• Stitching neat/inconspicuous; doesn't show on outside • Placed ⅛" in from edge • Reinforced with interfacing • Garment lays flat when fastened
Gathers	• Appropriate fullness (2–3 times the finished area) • Smooth, evenly distributed across area
Hems	• Even in width; parallel to the floor • Stitches are inconspicuous unless the hem is decorative • Smooth and bulk-free (allowances graded and trimmed as needed) • Evenly eased, without pleats or puckers • Appropriate technique used for the style and fabric
Interfacing	• Type, color, and weight compatible to fabric • Not visible on inside and outside of fabric • Adds no bulk to garment • If applicable, fusing is smooth and even
Lining	• Adds no bulk; fits smoothly inside garment • Fabric type is appropriate for garment • Hem 1" shorter than garment; sleeve hem is ½" shorter • Facings smooth and flat • Attached linings have ease pleat(s) • Free-hanging linings have French tacks at seams
Pleats	• Discreet and inconspicuous • Uniform in width; pressed as needed • On the straight of grain • On the straight of grain; evenly spaced

DETAIL	STANDARDS
Pockets	**Patch Pockets** • Flat and smooth with no added bulk • Straight stitching • Upper corners reinforced • Smooth curves and square corners where appropriate • If lined, lining does not show from the front • Appropriate placement for garment **In-Seam Pockets** • Flat and smooth, adding no bulk to garment • Inconspicuous, tucking completely into the garment **Welt Pockets** • Flat and smooth with no added bulk • Appropriate size welt • Even in width with straight sides and square corners
Seams	• Straight stitching; appropriate stitch length and tension setting • Fullness eased in as needed • Clipped, notched, graded as needed • Pressed correctly • Intersecting seams positioned correctly • Understitched where appropriate • Plaids or patterns matched as needed • Edges finished in an appropriate manner
Sleeves	**Set-in Sleeves** • Fullness evenly eased or gathered as applicable for garment • Smooth and even seam around the cap • Underarm portion of seam reinforced and trimmed • Pressed toward sleeve • Edges finished in an appropriate manner **Raglan or Kimono Sleeve** • Seams pressed open • Seams clipped and reinforced as needed • Edges finished in an appropriate manner
Waistbands	• Smooth and flat with no excess bulk • Cut on grain with square corners • Appropriate interfacing is used • Sets exactly at the top of the zipper • Skirt or pants treated in the appropriate manner (easing or darts) to fit waistband • For traditional waistband, the overlap is even with the placket and has a 1" extension on the underlap of the waistband • Fasteners (buttons, hooks, etc) securely stitched and properly located
Zippers	• Zipper placket is smooth and flat with no puckering • Stitching is straight and even • Zipper covered or exposed as appropriate • Ends in appropriate place: for skirts and pants, at the band; for necklines, ½" lower to allow for hook and eye • Edges at the top of the zipper are even

DARTS

Darts shape fabric to fit around the body. Common places to find darts are at the bust, waist, and shoulders. Commercial garment patterns have the dart placement printed on them and the markings should be transferred to the fabric using tailor tacks, chalk, or a fabric marker. When stitching a dart, a smooth taper and a sharp point are important to avoid puckering at the end of the dart.

ONE-POINT DART: Used to shape the bust or waist area of a garment, this dart starts at the side or waistline seam and tapers to a point over the fullest part of the bust or hip.

1. Fold the fabric right sides together on the center line and pin.

2. Stitch along the outer line, tapering the line of stitching to a point at the folded edge. Stitch off the edge and tie the threads to secure the line of stitching.

3. Press the dart down or to one side using a pressing ham to shape the fabric.

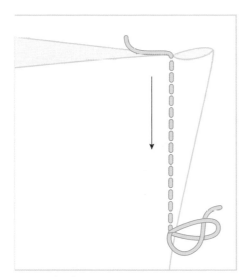

One-point dart

CONTOUR DART: This vertical dart is used to shape the waistline of a garment without a waistline seam; it is widest in the center and tapers to a point at each end.

1. Fold the fabric right sides together on the centerline and pin.

2. Starting at the center point, stitch along the outer line, tapering the line of stitching to a point at the folded edge. Stitch off the edge and tie the threads to secure the line of stitching.

3. Return to the center and overlapping a few of the beginning stitches, stitch the remaining side of the dart in the same manner as the first side.

4. Press the dart to one side using a pressing ham to shape the fabric.

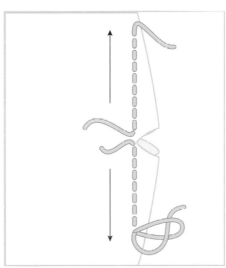

Two-point dart

DART TIPS

- To avoid bubbles and puckers, do not backstitch at the point of a dart. Instead, take a few stitches on the fold at the point and leave a 5" tail; tie the tail into a knot.

- Most commercial patterns use darts designed for B-cups. If you are larger or smaller, be sure to check the placement and adjust it as needed.
- When pressing darts, use kraft paper (brown grocery bags) to avoid pressing marks on the right side of the garment. Slip a piece between the dart and the garment before pressing.
- When pressing a contour dart, clip the center so the dart will lie flat.

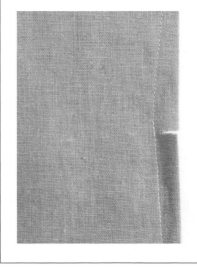

Edgestitch pockets to garment for a crisp tailored look.

POCKETS

Pockets are everywhere: on shirts, jackets, skirts, pants, children's clothing, even on pillows and wall organizers. Try some of these common methods for making pockets of almost any style.

PATCH POCKET

The easiest type of pocket to make, the patch pocket, is used on camp shirts, dresses, jumpers, children's clothing, and men's shirts.

UNLINED PATCH POCKET

1. Cut out the pocket. Note: The pocket pattern piece should be the finished size and shape desired with 1" added to the upper edge for a facing and one seam allowance (½"–⅝") on all other sides.

2. Hem the upper edge by turning ¼" to the wrong side twice. Topstitch it in place and press.

3. Fold the hemmed edge to the wrong side on the upper pocket edge. Starting at one upper edge, stitch the side of the facing continuing to stitch on the seamline (stay stitching) and finishing on the remaining facing.

4. Trim upper corners at a diagonal and turn the facing to the wrong side.

5. Turn the side and lower edges to the wrong side using the staystitching as a guide; press.

6. Position the pocket as desired on the project; pin in place.

7. Using a regular straight stitch (2.5mm stitch length), sew the pocket to the project along the sides and lower edges.

Step 3

LINED PATCH POCKET

1. Cut out the pocket. Note: The pocket pattern piece should be the finished size and shape desired with one seam allowance (½"–⅝") on all sides.

2. Cut a lining piece the same as the pocket. Note: If using light or medium weight fabric, the lining can be the same fabric as the pocket. For heavyweight fabric, use a lightweight or lining fabric.

3. Place lining and fabric right sides together; pin.

4. Using a regular straight stitch (2.5mm stitch length), sew the pocket and lining together along the seam line, leaving a 2"–3" opening along the lower edge for turning.

Step 4

5. Trim the upper corners at a diagonal, clip curves as needed, and turn the pocket to the right side. Press the pocket, folding the seam allowances of the opening in.

6. Position the pocket as desired on the project; pin in place.

7. Using a regular straight stitch (2.5mm stitch length), sew the pocket to the project along the sides and lower edges, closing the opening in the process.

In-seam pockets are inconspicuous.

IN-SEAM POCKET

These flat pockets are sewn as part of the side seam and are tucked inconspicuously into the side seam of skirts and pants.

1. Cut out two pocket pieces for each side using a lightweight lining fabric.

2. Place each pocket section right side down on the garment seam allowances (2 side fronts and 2 side backs); pin.

3. Using a regular straight stitch (2.5mm stitch length), sew the pocket pieces to the side seam allowances as pinned.

4. Place the garment front and back right sides together; pin.

5. Stitch the upper side seam, pivot at the pocket and then sew around the pocket, pivoting again to continue and complete the side seam.

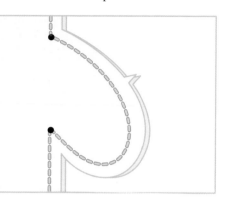

In-seam pockets may be cut as part of the garment or as a separate piece sewn to the seam allowances (Step 3).

PATCH POCKET TIPS

- The pocket can be sewn to the project using an all-purpose presser foot, but an edgestitch foot ensures that your stitching is close to and parallel to the pocket edges.

- For an inconspicuous and hand-sewn look, use a narrow blind-stitch and thread that blends when attaching the pocket to the project.

- If the project and pocket are both cut from the same print, align the pocket pattern piece to match the segment of the print over which the pocket will be placed.

- For perfect rounded edges, use a pocket template for shaping the lower edge.

INSEAM POCKET TIPS

- To make the pockets as inconspicuous as possible, replace the first 2"–3" of the upper portion of the pocket with the same fabric as the garment (seam it to the lining fabric).

- To reinforce the pocket, stitch the pocket seam allowance a second time on top of or next to the first line of stitching.

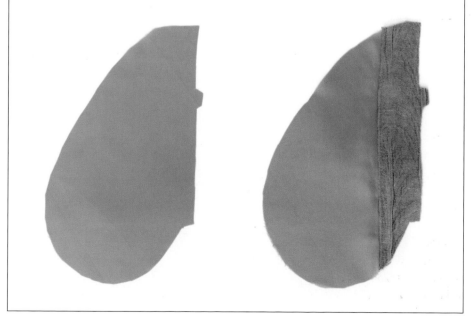

FACINGS

Facings are fabric pieces used to finish edges such as necklines, armholes, and waistlines; stitch facings to the outside of the garment and turn to the inside to hide them. shaped, cut-on, and bias are three common types of facings. Insert zippers at necklines and waistlines before attaching facings.

SHAPED FACING

Provided as a separate pattern piece, this type of facing is used for places such as necklines and armholes.

1. Interface the garment and/or the facing as directed by your pattern instructions.

2. Prepare the facing by stitching any seams (such as shoulder or underarm seams) and finishing the outer edges with serging, turning and stitching, or binding.

3. Place the prepared facing right side down on the outside of the garment, matching the raw edges.

4. Stitch the facing to the garment.

5. Trim, clip, and/or notch the facing seam as needed. Turn the facing to the inside of the garment; press.

6. To keep the facing from rolling out to the front of the garment, understitch the seam allowances to

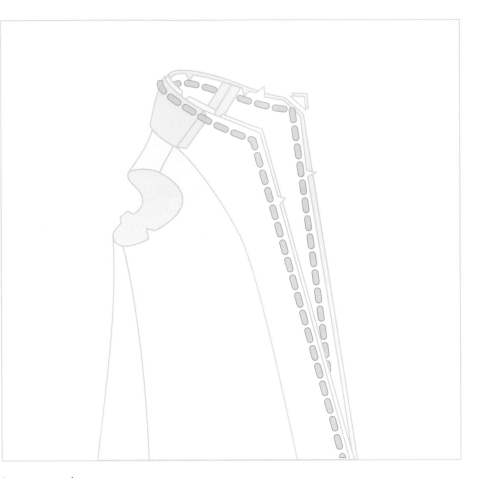

Steps 3, 4, and 5

the facing. Flatten the facing and garment with both seam allowances under the facing. Stitch next to the seam line through all layers.

7. Secure the facing to the garment by hand-tacking it to the seam allowances. An alternative is to stitch-in-the-ditch at the seams (shoulders, side seams, etc.) from the right side of the garment through the seam allowances and facing.

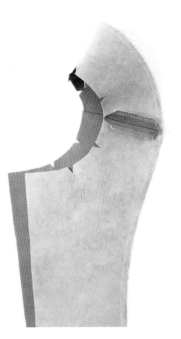

A shaped or contour facing is cut separately from the garment.

Understitching is one of the most important steps in sewing a professional-looking faced edge.

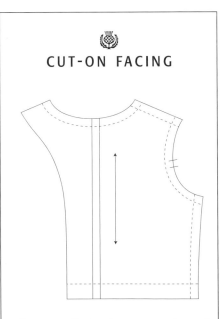

CUT-ON FACING

A cut-on facing is an extension of the garment piece, eliminating the need to sew the facing onto the garment. A little faster and easier to stitch, the cut-on facing is often seen on blouses and shirts.

BIAS FACING

A bias facing works on almost any type of garment but is especially useful for sheer fabric where the facing may show or for bulky fabric where two layers are too cumbersome.

1. Cut a bias strip of lining or lightweight fabric:
   - Width—four times the finished desired width plus ⅜";
   - Length—add 2" to the edge of the garment.

2. Fold the strip in half lengthwise with right sides together. Press, using steam to shape the bias to fit the edge being faced.

3. Place the folded strip along the garment edge; pin in place.

4. Using a ¼" seam allowance, sew the bias facing to the garment.

5. Clip the seam allowances and trim the bias strip ¼" past the garment edges.

6. Turn the bias facing to the inside of the garment, rolling so it doesn't show on the outside of the garment.

7. Slipstitch by hand or topstitch by machine to hold the facing in place, turning the raw edges in at the ends.

A bias facing may be topstitched in place or can be slip-stitched by hand for an invisible finish.

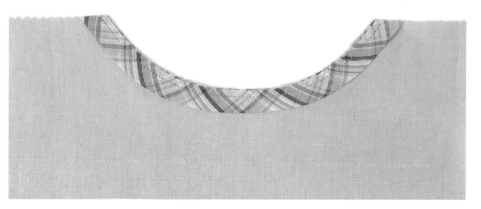

A bias facing adds a minimal amount of fabric to the inside of clothing and works well for unstructured garments.

✿ FACING TIPS

- Use an edgestitch foot to make understitching easy. Place the guide of the foot in the well of the seam and adjust the needle position to stitch beside the seam. Keep the guide in the seam as you stitch and the stitching will be parallel to the seam.
- Before stitching a bias facing to a garment, use steam to shape it to fit the curved edge of a neckline or armhole. Place the folded bias strip on the ironing board and shape it into a curve. Hold the iron over it and steam the strip. Let the curved bias strip dry, then carefully pin it to the garment edge for stitching.
- To hold facings in place, hand-tack or stitch-in-the-ditch along shoulder seams, sewing through all layers of the facing and garment.
- If the pattern is altered, be sure to make any corresponding alterations to the facings. For example, if the neck edge is enlarged, make the same change to the neckline facing.

COLLARS

Collars often determine the look or style of a garment while providing a finish for the neckline. There are three basic types of collars, each with several styles, variations or names. A collar can be flat (peter pan, sailor), standing (mandarin, banded, stand-up), or rolled (shirt, shawl, notched). While each type has some unique characteristics, they all have similarities. When assembling a collar, you will have an upper collar and an under collar (sometimes called a collar facing). Under collars are generally interfaced to add support and body; in some cases, such as a standing collar, the upper collar is interfaced also.

FLAT COLLAR

Often used on children's clothing this type of collar may have two sections meeting in the centers of the front and back necklines. Be sure to cut mirror image versions of the pattern.

1. Interface the under collar with sew-in or fusible interfacing as desired.

2. Place the upper and under collars right sides together. Stitch along the seamlines, leaving the neckline seam open.

3. Trim and grade seam allowances to reduce the bulk and avoid "show-through" once you turn the collar to the right side. Clip and notch as needed for a smooth turn.

4. Before turning to the right side, press the seam allowances: first, open and then toward the under collar.

5. Optional: Understitch the outer edge, stitching close to the seamline on the under collar, through the seam allowances.

6. Turn the collar to the right side, pushing corners and curves out with a point turner as needed.

7. Press the collar, rolling the upper collar lightly to the back so it will not show.

8. Pin or baste the raw edges of the collar to the neckline and finish as directed in your pattern with a facing.

Steps 2 and 3

Steps 6 and 7

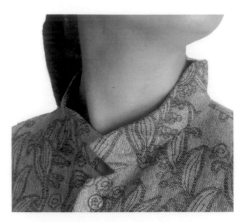

A standing collar can be narrow and crisp or it can be wider and softer as shown here.

STANDING COLLAR

1. Interface the front collar (upper collar) with sew-in or fusible interfacing as desired. If working with a one-piece collar, interface the entire piece of the fabric if it is not too bulky.

2. Place the upper and under collars right sides together. Stitch along the side and upper seamlines, leaving the neckline seam open.

3. Trim and grade seam allowances to reduce the bulk and avoid "show-through" once you turn the collar to the right side. Clip and notch as needed for a smooth turn.

4. Before turning to the right side, press the seam allowances: first, open and then toward the under collar.

5. Turn the collar to the right side, pushing corners and curves out with a point turner as needed.

6. Press the collar, rolling the upper collar lightly to the inside so it will not show.

7. Pin or baste the raw edges of the upper collar only to the neckline.

8. Stitch the collar along the neckline, leaving the lower edge of the under collar free.

9. Fold the seam allowance of the raw edge of the under collar to the wrong side and pin to cover the neckline seam allowances.

10. Secure the folded edge of the under collar by edgestitching with a straight stitch. If you do not want the stitching to show on the outer garment, slipstitch the edge by hand.

A Peter Pan collar is an example of a flat collar.

A rolled collar should turn smoothly at the neck and have flat, bulk-free edges.

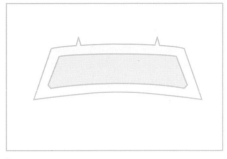

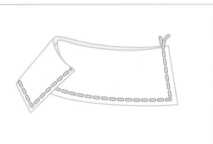

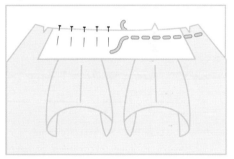

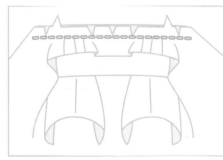

ROLLED COLLAR

This type of shirt collar, sometimes called a convertible collar, works with the facing of the shirt to form a notch collar and lapel similar to a blazer.

1. Interface the under collar with sew-in or fusible interfacing as desired. Using a firm interfacing, trim the corners at a diagonal and trim about ½" from the seam allowances.

2. Place the upper and under collars right sides together. Stitch along the seamlines, leaving the neckline seam open.

3. Trim and grade seam allowances to reduce the bulk and avoid "show-through" once you turn the collar to the right side. Clip and notch as needed for a smooth turn.

4. Before turning to the right side, press the seam allowances: first, open and then toward the under collar.

5. Optional: Understitch the outer edge, stitching close to the seamline on the under collar, through the seam allowances.

6. Turn the collar to the right side, pushing corners and curves out with a point turner as needed.

7. Press the collar using a pressing ham to shape it, rolling the upper collar slightly to the back, so it will not show.

8. Pin or baste the raw edges of the collar to the neckline.

9. Finish as directed in your pattern with a facing.

ROLLED COLLAR TIPS

- Hide the seam of the upper collar by trimming about ¹⁄₃₂"–¹⁄₁₆" from the under collar. Match the edges as usual when seaming and the upper collar will favor the under collar (roll slightly to the underside).

- Use a sleeve board when pressing collars; the curved portion of the board will support curved seams and the straight portion works for the straight edges.

- Do not skip Step 4. Pressing the seam allowances open and then to the side gives a crisp sharp edge for a professional look.

- Insert neckline zippers before joining the collar and facings to the garment; attach hooks and eyes after.

WAISTLINES

When making pants and skirts, one consideration is the method for finishing the waistline. Two of the most common ways are the standard waistband for a tailored look and the elastic casing for a softer style.

STANDARD WAISTBAND

1. Sew the garment, completing the darts, gathers, pleats, or ease stitching according to the design of the garment.

Step 1

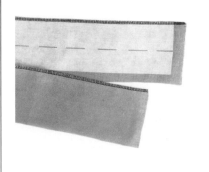

---

2. Check the size of the pattern waistband against the needed cut length using the formula below.

3. Adjust the waistband pattern if needed, then cut the waistband according to the measurements. Note: Waistbands are traditionally cut on the lengthwise grain of the fabric for stability but cutting on the cross grain offers a slight bit of "give" that can make the band more comfortable. Interfacing is especially important if cutting on the cross grain.

4. Cut fusible or sew-in interfacing to match the waistband; trim the seam allowances first if using fusible.

5. Fuse or sew the interfacing to the wrong side of the waistband.

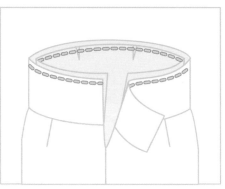

Step 9

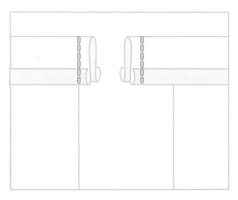

Step 12

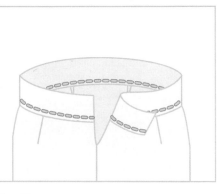

Step 15

Trim interfacing seam allowances next to the stitching if using a sew-in type.

6. Finish one long edge (will go inside the garment) using a 3-thread overlock stitch or bias binding.

7. Divide the garment edge into quarters (center front and back, sides) and mark with straight pins.

8. Overlap the ends of the waistband, as it will be worn and pin, forming a circle; divide into quarters (center front and back, sides) and mark with straight pins.

9. Pin the waistband to the garment edge with right sides together, matching the quarter marks.

10. Stitch the band to the garment, making sure darts and seams are positioned correctly.

11. Grade the waistline seam if needed by trimming the garment to ⅛" and the waistband to ¼"; press the seam allowances up.

12. Fold the waistband right sides together and stitch the seams at each end.

13. Turn the waistband to the right side and press. The finished edge should extend down into the garment slightly covering the garment seam allowances.

14. To finish the lower edge of the underlap, turn the seam allowance to the inside and slipstitch closed.

15. From the right side of the garment, stitch-in-the-ditch through all layers to secure the band.

Elastic pulled through a stitched casing is an easy way to fit a waistline.

ELASTIC CASING

Feed elastic through a channel to gather a waistline to fit your body. The casing can be cut as an extension of the garment, or it may be a separate piece of fabric stitched onto the garment. Try these methods to find your favorite.

WIDTH OF ELASTIC

The width of the elastic you select is a personal choice you make according to comfort and style, although heavier fabrics generally need wider elastic for more support. Using 1"–1½" wide elastic simulates the look of a standard waistband.

HOW SNUG IS SNUG?

The length of elastic you use varies, depending on the type of elastic you have and the degree of snugness you like. Take a length of elastic and wrap it around your waist, pinning where it is comfortable. Spend a couple of minutes moving around (bending, sitting, walking, etc.) to judge the comfort and the stableness of the elastic. It should feel snug but not tight, and it should stay at or near your waistline even when moving.

JOINING THE ENDS

Once you have decided the needed length, cut the elastic exactly that size with no overlap. Join the ends by cutting a small piece of ribbon or fabric and placing it under the cut ends. Using a zigzag stitch, sew the two ends to the fabric, positioning the center of the presser foot where the ends meet. If your machine has a sewn-out or 3-step zigzag stitch, use it as it has more give to it and will be more compatible with the elastic. The elastic may be joined at the beginning of the technique or at the end, depending on the method.

FLAT INSERTION

One of the easiest ways to make an elastic casing is to sew the casing first and insert a length of elastic.

1. Finish the upper edge of the pants or skirt by serging or overcasting the raw edge.

2. Measure the width of the elastic plus ⅛" from the finished edge to find the fold line. Fold on this line to the inside of the garment; pin.

3. Stitch along the finished edge to secure the fabric, leaving a 2"–3" opening at one side of the garment.

4. Using a bodkin, feed the elastic through the casing, pinning the free end to the garment to keep it from pulling out.

5. Join the two ends of the elastic as directed above.

6. Complete the line of stitching to close the opening.

Pull the elastic through the casing and adjust to fit.

CIRCULAR INSERTION

A little trickier, this method results in a flatter, more fitted elastic waistline.

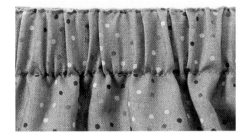

Using a free arm sewing machine makes it easy to sew this circular technique.

1. Join the two ends of the elastic.

2. Finish the upper edge of the pants or skirt by serging or overcasting the raw edge.

3. Fold the upper edge of the garment to the inside; edgestitch the folded edge.

4. Place the circular elastic band into the garment, positioning it against the stitched fold; pin at the front and back centers and at the side seams.

5. Using a zipper foot or an edgestitch foot, stitch through the fabric layers, next to (but not through) the elastic. Sew for 3"–4" and stop with the needle in the fabric.

6. Smooth out the fabric (it will gather or "bunch" as you sew), lower the foot and continue to stitch, stopping as needed to adjust the fabric. Overlap the beginning and ending by a few stitches to secure.

Edgestitching the upper folded edge of the waistline helps to sharpen the edge and neaten the look.

SLEEVES

The sleeves not only finish the armholes of a garment but also add style and warmth. They can be made in any length in several variations: set-in, raglan, and kimono.

SET-IN SLEEVES

The most common type, the cap of the sleeve may be rounded or full. In either case, the measurement of the sleevecap is longer than the measurement of the armhole. Ease the rounded cap into the opening with no gathers or pleats, leaving a smooth finish. The full cap can be gathered or pleated, adding to the design of the garment.

Smooth set-in sleeve

SMOOTH EASED SLEEVE

Use this one-piece sleeve in dresses, blouses, shirts, and jackets. A two-piece version is often used in tailored jackets.

1. Cut out the sleeve and transfer all markings from the pattern to the fabric.

2. Using a stitch length of 4mm–5mm, sew two rows of ease stitching in the seam allowance of the cap, around the top (most patterns mark the area with a dot on the front and one on the back and the ease stitching goes between the dots).

3. Using a regular stitch length of 2.5mm, sew the underarm seam of the sleeve.

4. Stitch the shoulder and side seam of the garment.

5. Place the sleeve into the armhole with right sides together; pin at the underarm seam and at the beginning points of the ease stitching.

6. Pull the easing threads to adjust the sleeve cap to fit the sleeve opening. Pin in place, matching markings and notches and distributing the extra fabric smoothly with no pleats or gathers.

7. Turn the garment to the right side and check your work. Make any adjustments needed.

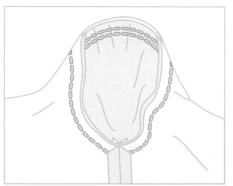

Step 5

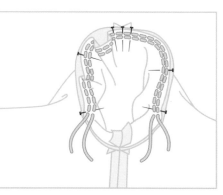

Step 8

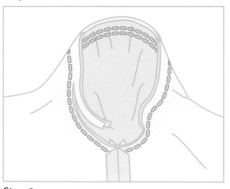

Step 9

8. When the sleeve cap has the desired look, stitch the seam, starting and ending at the underarm. Work with the garment against the machine and the needle on the inside of the sleeve.

9. Trim the underarm seam allowance between the notches. Serge, zigzag or bind the seam allowances for a finished look.

10. Press the seam allowances only of the sleeve using a sleeve board and/or a pressing mitt.

Gathered set-in sleeve

PUFFED SLEEVE

This softer version of the set-in sleeve, found in dresses, tops, and children's clothing requires light to medium weight fabric. The cap is full, allowing you to gather, pleat, or tuck the sleeve as desired. The directions below are for gathering; stitch pleats or tuck into the cap if desired and then ease any excess as needed.

This type of sleeve is sewn in the same manner as the smooth eased sleeve, except the edge between the notches is gathered to ease. When the sleeve is stitched to the garment, you want the sleeve cap to be gathered and full, not smooth.

SLEEVE TIPS

- For set-in sleeves: Once the pinned sleeve looks correct (Step 6), unpin the sleeve, leaving the ease stitching gathered as needed. Using a pressing ham, steam the sleeve cap to shape and "shrink" it, removing as much of the puckers as possible before continuing.

- For kimono sleeves: For reinforcement, shorten the stitch length for the curved underarm seam.

FLAT EASED SLEEVE

Often used on shirts, children's clothing, and casual sportswear, this type of set-in sleeve is the easiest to sew. The cap of the sleeve is less rounded, giving less fabric to ease into the body of the shirt.

1. Cut out the sleeve and transfer all markings from the pattern to the fabric.

2. Using a stitch length of 4mm–5mm, sew two rows of ease stitching in the seam allowance of the cap, around the top (most patterns mark the area with a dot on the front and one on the back; the ease stitching goes between the dots).

3. Using a regular stitch length of 2.5mm, sew the shoulder seam of the garment; press.

4. Place the garment flat, right side up. Lay the sleeve right side down, matching notches and markings.

5. Place the garment under the needle with the sleeve on the bed and the garment facing up. Using a regular stitch length of 2.5mm, sew the sleeve to the garment.

6. Serge or zigzag seam allowances together and press toward the sleeve.

7. With right sides together, fold the garment and pin the underarm seam from the lower edge of the sleeve to the lower edge of the garment.

8. Sew the pinned seam in one continuous seam, starting at the lower edge of the garment.

RAGLAN SLEEVE

This simple sleeve has a dart for shaping and is stitched to the garment with diagonal seams running from the underarm to the neckline.

1. Cut out the sleeve and transfer all markings from the pattern to the fabric.

2. Fold the sleeve right sides together along the dart markings; stitch. Press the dart, slashing it open if needed.

3. Fold the sleeve right sides together, and stitch the underarm seam.

4. Stitch the side seam of the garment, finishing the seam allowances as desired.

5. Pin the sleeve to the garment, right sides together, matching the underarm seams and all markings.

6. Working with the garment on the machine and the sleeve facing up, stitch the seam.

7. Add a second row of stitching between the notches under the arm. Trim the underarm seam allowance between the notches and press the seam open above the notches. Serge, zigzag or bind the seam allowances for a finished look.

Raglan sleeve Steps 2 and 3.

KIMONO SLEEVE

An extension of the garment, the kimono sleeve does not require a separate sleeve pattern. Reinforced under the arm, it may be loose or close fitting which requires a gusset for a comfortable fit.

1. Place the front and back of the garment right sides together at the shoulder seams; pin.

2. Using a regular stitch length of 2.5mm, stitch the shoulder seams, starting at the neckline and ending at the lower edge of the "sleeve."

3. Press the shoulder seam open and finish the edges as desired.

4. Pin the underarm seam and position a 4"–5" length of seam binding or stay tape over the back curve of the seam line.

5. Using a regular stitch length of 2.5mm, stitch the underarm seam, sewing through the tape.

6. Clip the seam allowance (but not the tape) along the curve.

7. Using a seam roll, press the seam open.

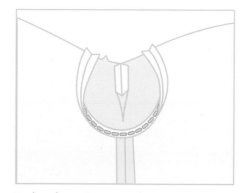

Raglan sleeve Steps 6 and 7.

CUFFS

Cuffs offer a way to finish the lower edge of sleeves. Along with the cuff, there is usually an opening in the sleeve to make it easy to slide it onto your arm. This opening can be finished in one of several ways. Shown are three of the most common openings with a typical faced cuff, closed with a single button. Also shown is a simple banded cuff and a French cuff.

CUFF OPENINGS

HEMMED SEAM OPENING

1. Stitch the sleeve seam, stopping about 2"–3" from the lower edge of the sleeve.

2. Clip the seam allowance above the opening and press the seam open.

3. Turn the raw edges of the opening (seam allowances) under to create a double folded narrow hem.

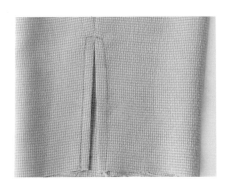

Hemmed seam opening

CONTINUOUS LINE PLACKET

1. Make a slit at the bottom of the sleeve, positioning it according to the pattern instructions.

2. Straighten the slit and bind the raw edge.

3. Fold the sleeve right sides together, aligning the bound edges.

4. Stitch a tiny dart (diagonal line) at the folded edge of the opening.

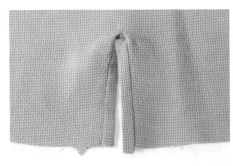

Continuous line placket

BUTTONED CUFF

1. Cut a piece of interfacing the size of the finished cuff (remove seam allowances). Fuse the interfacing to the upper cuff.

2. Press the seam allowance of the interfaced edge to the wrong side.

3. Fold cuff right sides together and stitch the ends. Trim and grade the seam allowances as needed; press. Turn cuff to the right side.

4. Pin the cuff to the wrong side of the sleeve with the ends even with the placket or opening.

5. Stitch the cuff to the sleeve; turn the cuff to the right side.

6. Edgestitch the upper edge of the cuff to secure; topstitch the sides and lower edge as desired.

7. Add button and buttonhole, positioning them as the pattern indicates.

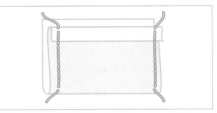

Step 3

Steps 4 and 5

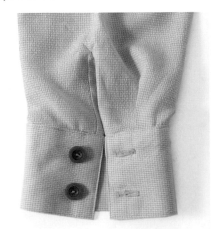

Buttoned cuff

FRENCH CUFF

A French cuff is a double cuff folded back on itself. The edges do not overlap but are "stacked" on top of each other and held together with cufflinks.

1. Cut a piece of interfacing the size of the finished cuff (remove seam allowances). Fuse the interfacing to the upper cuff.

2. Press the seam allowance of the interfaced edge to the wrong side.

3. Fold cuff right sides together and stitch the ends. Trim and grade the seam allowances as needed; press. Turn cuff to the right side.

4. Fold the inside of the placket back toward the shirt; pin the cuff to the wrong side of the sleeve.

5. Stitch the cuff to the sleeve; turn the cuff to the right side.

6. Edgestitch the upper edge of the cuff to secure; topstitch the sides and lower edge as desired.

7. Make four buttonholes as shown in the illustration. Another option is to fold the cuff back and make a buttonhole through the double cuff layer on each side.

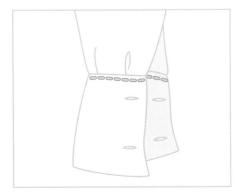

Steps 6 and 7

French cuff

MACHINE STITCHED HEMS

One of the last tasks to complete when making a garment or other project is the hem. Three of the most often used hems are turned, faced, and serged; the choice depends on the project, fabric, and finished look you want.

TURNING A HEM

The depth of a turned hem allowance depends on the style of the garment and the type of fabric selected. Use these figures as guidelines but your goal should be a flat, even, uniform hem: Straight, 2½"–3"; A-line, 1½"–2"; Full ½"–1". Soft sheer fabrics and soft knits require narrow hems so the hemline doesn't sag; curved edges also require a narrow hem allowance.

SHIRTTAIL HEM

This narrow, simple hem works best on light to medium weight fabric; it's good for straight or slightly curved edges.

1. Sew a line of straight stitching ³⁄₁₆" from the lower edge of the un-hemmed shirt (you are sewing on a single layer of fabric).

2. Fold and press the edge of the fabric along the line of stitching to the wrong side.

3. Fold it again ¼" and press to ease in any fullness. Pin or baste if needed.

4. Using a regular straight stitch (about 2.5mm), topstitch the hem to secure.

Shirttail hem

KNIT HEM, DOUBLE NEEDLE

When hemming knits, make sure you use a technique that stretches with the fabric, or you'll find the stitches popping as the fabric is stretched. This easy sewing machine method is a great way to do exactly that.

1. Fold the hem allowance (1¼"–1½" in depth) to the wrong side of the garment; pin or baste in place.

2. Insert a double needle in the machine and thread the machine accordingly.

3. From the right side of the fabric, topstitch the hem in place, about ½"–1" from the lower finished edge.

4. Trim the excess hem allowance above the double line of stitching on the inside of the garment.

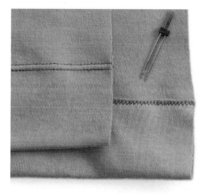

Double needle hem

NARROW HEM

Perfect for lightweight and soft, sheer fabrics, this narrow hem is inconspicuous and adds a little weight to the edge to make a nice drape.

1. Fold ½" to the wrong side of the garment; press.

2. Using a regular straight stitch (about 2.5mm), sew close to the fold.

3. Trim the hem allowance close to the stitching.

4. Turn the hem ⅛" to the wrong side and topstitch in place.

Narrow hem

FACED HEM

Hem bulky fabrics or garments with little hem allowance using a bias strip of lightweight fabric as a facing.

1. Cut the strip the width of the hem allowance plus ½" times the length needed to fit the garment edge plus two seam allowances.

2. Stitch the short ends of the bias strip together to form a circle; press seams open.

3. Place the bias strip right side down on the garment, matching one raw edge to the lower unfinished edge of the garment.

4. Sew the strip to the garment edge using a ¼" seam allowance and a regular straight stitch (about 2.5mm).

5. Fold the bias hem to the inside of the garment. Press and pin in place.

6. Fold the upper edge of the bias strip ¼" to the wrong side. Stitch the hem by hand using instructions on page 65 for a blind stitched or slip-stitched hem.

Faced hem

III

Buttons are available in a myriad of shapes and colors.

CLOSURES

Usually a way to hold a garment together, closures can also add style and interest to your clothing. Even the most practical closure should be well done and nicely stitched, so it doesn't detract from the quality look you want for your garments.

BUTTONS

Wood, plastic, bone, clay, pearl, leather, or metal, no matter what buttons are made of, they usually serve a practical purpose—holding something together. They can also be decorative, adding charm and style to a variety of projects including all types of garments, purses, book covers, pillows, etc.

SEWING ON BUTTONS

Many machines have a special foot designed to hold the button in place while it is being stitched. This technique works for 2-hole and 4-hole flat buttons.

1. Attach the button foot to the machine. If the foot has an adjustable shank setting, set it as needed (high shank for thick fabrics and low shank for medium to lightweight fabrics). If the buttons are for decoration only and will not be buttoned, stitch them to the fabric without creating a thread shank.

2. Position the button as needed on the fabric. Temporarily hold the button in place for stitching using a glue stick if desired.

3. Lower or cover the feed dog of the machine.

4. Make your stitch selection. Some machines have a special function or program for sewing on buttons. A simple zigzag stitch can also be used.

5. Using the handwheel, make sure the width of the stitch is appropriate for the spacing of the holes. Once this is established, sew the button on using 8–10 zigzag stitches or the full sew-on program.

6. When the stitching is complete, remove the fabric from under the needle and clip the thread, leaving several inches. Pull the thread tails to the back and tie, then trim.

HOOKS, EYES, SNAPS

These fasteners are sewn to the fabric in the same way that buttons are. If the foot does not sit properly on these odd-shaped findings, stitch them without using a presser foot. Note: Even though you sew without a presser foot, the presser foot lever must be in the "down" position to engage the thread tension.

BUTTON SEW ON TIPS

- Use the above directions for a 2-hole button; for 4-hole, stitch the front holes first, then slide to the back holes and complete.
- Put a dot of seam sealant on the back of the button for more security.
- When sewing 4-hole buttons in place, plan the path you will take: Make an "X," a square, an arrow, or the dashes that result from the directions above.

The fastest and most secure way to sew on a button is by machine.

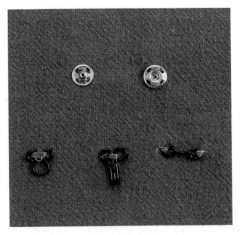

Hooks, eyes, and snaps are sewn on by hand or in the same manner as buttons by machine.

Buttonholes

BUTTONHOLES

Most sewing machines today have functions or programs that automatically stitch buttonholes. Some have memories that will repeat the same size buttonhole over and over again, which is especially helpful on garments such as shirts and jackets that have multiple buttons of the same size. There are also machines that offer several different types of buttonholes, designed for specific sewing situations.

On women's garments, the buttonholes are on the right and the buttons on the left for a front closure. For men's garments, it is the opposite—buttons on the left and buttonholes on the right.

VERTICAL OR HORIZONTAL?

The orientation of your buttonholes depends on the placement and project involved. Horizontal buttonholes are usually more secure because when the garment is pulled due to wear, stress is placed on the button, which then pulls against the buttonhole. With vertical buttonholes, the stress is placed on the buttonhole, causing it to gap, potentially making the garment come unbuttoned. Vertical buttonholes are used on plackets or banded openings such as on men's shirts.

Vertical buttonholes are stitched on the center line of the garment, parallel to the garment edge. Horizontal buttonholes are stitched perpendicular to the center line, starting ⅛" beyond the center toward the garment edge.

DETERMINING BUTTONHOLE SIZE

Some of the newer computerized machines have methods of measuring the selected button and automatically determining the size buttonhole needed. There are also models that have a special presser foot that controls the size of the buttonhole depending on the size button placed in the holder of the foot. Check your manual for specifics on how to use these features if your machine is equipped with one or both.

To determine the buttonhole size manually, measure your selected button using the directions below:

FLAT BUTTON: Measure the diameter and add ⅛". If it is a thick button (⅛" or more), also add the thickness.

BALL OR ROUND BUTTON: Measure around the button; take half the measurement and add ⅛".

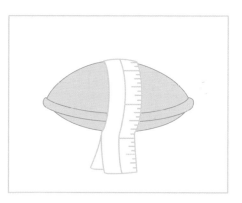

Measure your buttons to determine the correct buttonhole size.

🌸
COMMON BUTTONHOLE TYPES

STANDARD OR REGULAR BUTTONHOLE: The most commonly used type, this buttonhole is made of two lines of parallel close zigzag stitching (called beads) with a bartack at each end.

DELICATE OR HEIRLOOM BUTTONHOLE: Similar to a regular buttonhole but it is less dense and has narrower beads; good for heirloom sewing, baby clothes, and sheer fabrics.

STRETCH BUTTONHOLE: Uses a stitch that has stretch so the buttonhole has some "give" to it; good for knit fabric.

KEYHOLE BUTTONHOLE: Made with an open zigzag stitch, this buttonhole has a round opening or "keyhole" at the end that is closest to the garment edge. It's perfect for coats and jackets that have shank buttons, because the shank fits into the keyhole.

Mark the center (opening) and the two endpoints of the buttonhole.

MARKING BUTTONHOLES

In most cases, commercial patterns have markings that should be transferred to the garment. If no changes have been made to the pattern, you can use the markings as printed. If the pattern has been altered, the buttonhole placement should be changed accordingly. To determine the placement of buttons down the front of a garment, mark the neck, waist, and fullest part of the bust (the point with the most stress). The remaining buttons should be evenly spaced between these, commonly 2"–3½" apart.

The traditional way to mark buttonhole placement is to draw a line for the button opening and one at each end to form an "H." If marking a series of buttonholes down the front of a garment, the markings form a ladder. Use chalk, marker, basting stitches, or tailor's tacks to mark the buttonholes.

STITCHING BUTTONHOLES

Since each machine has its own method of making buttonholes, you should follow the instructions in your manual, keeping the following tips in mind:

- To confirm correct sizing and test the project materials, always make a sample buttonhole.
- Use the required presser foot for best results. Buttonholes can usually be made with an all-purpose foot but because the sole of the foot is flat, it drags on the thread build-up resulting from the buttonholes. The finished buttonhole may be adequate but not as beautiful and full as it is when the correct foot is used. Some buttonhole feet have two tunnels or grooves on the sole to allow the thread to pass under it easily; others have a slider sole for easy feeding.
- Be sure the buttonhole area is interfaced, so it can support the extra stitches. If extra support is needed, place a layer of water-soluble stabilizer behind the stitching area. Once the buttonhole is stitched, remove the stabilizer.
- If your machine allows it, play with the stitch length of the buttonhole to make sure you have the look you want. Heavier threads require a longer stitch length and fine threads, a shorter one.
- For added security, squeeze a line of seam sealant on the wrong side of the center of the buttonhole after it is stitched. Let dry before cutting the buttonhole open.
- If stitching a buttonhole in a part of the project that has uneven areas such as seam allowances down the front of a jacket, it may inhibit the feed of the presser foot, making it virtually impossible to sew a beautiful buttonhole. Use a compensation plate (check with your sewing machine dealer) to even the fabric surface.

CORDED BUTTONHOLE

To reinforce the buttonhole and make it stronger, stitch it over a cord such as embroidery floss, topstitching thread, or perle cotton. Cording a buttonhole is also a good way to stabilize the opening, keeping it from stretching out of shape (especially useful on knit fabric). Many buttonhole feet will hold the cord in place, so the needle can stitch over it as the buttonhole is formed.

Once the buttonhole is stitched, pull the cord tails tight until the buttonhole is slightly "crumpled." Trim the cord tails and smooth the buttonhole, causing the ends of the cord to pull up into the buttonhole. The finished buttonhole is strong, stable, and has a full round look.

Corded buttonholes are strong and stable and especially good for heavy fabrics and knits.

114

🌿 BUTTONHOLE TIPS

- Make a test buttonhole size, layer a swatch of project fabric, with interfacing, facing material and/or lining as needed to simulate the layers of the garment. Cut a slit the size of the buttonhole opening and check the button to see if it fits.
- Cut your buttons open with a buttonhole cutter instead of scissors or a seam ripper. The beveled edge helps avoid cutting through the beads and also keeps you from cutting through the bar tacks at the ends of the buttonhole.

Use turned tubes for ties or as loops in place of buttonholes.

TIES, TABS, AND LOOPS

Useful in a wide variety of sewing situations, including garments, curtains, and kids' clothing, these ties, tabs, and loops are easy to make.

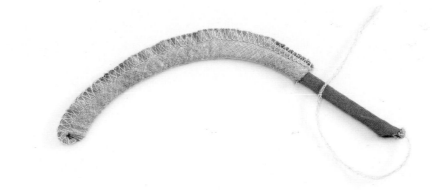

Turning narrow tubes of fabric is easy when using the serger.

Fold and stitch a strip of fabric to eliminate the need to turn a tube when making tabs.

TIES

Use these narrow "strings" for ties, button loops, and frogs. They also make good straps, often referred to as "spaghetti straps."

1. Cut a bias strip of fabric about 1" by the desired finished length. Fold right sides together in half lengthwise.

2. Using an all-purpose presser foot or a quarter-inch and a slightly shortened stitch length (about 2mm), stitch a ¼" seam. Optional: Stitch a second time next to the first in the seam allowance for added strength.

3. Using a narrow tube turner or bodkin, turn the tube to the right side. Note: Do not trim the seam allowance before turning, as it fills the tube to give it shape and form.

SERGER VERSION

1. Set the serger for a narrow 3-thread overlock stitch.

2. Serge a chain of thread twice the length of the fabric strip plus an extra 3"–4". Pull it around to the front of the foot without cutting it away from the serger.

3. Fold the bias strip right sides together around the serger chain and position it under the foot for stitching.

4. Serge down the raw edges of the folded strip, taking care not to stitch into the serger chain.

5. When the stitching is complete, remove the tube from the serger. Gently pull on the chain to turn the tube to the right side.

TABS

Make tabs the same way as ties using a wider strip of fabric and stitching across one end before turning.

Here is an alternate method that does not require turning the fabric. A narrow version of this method makes tailored belt loops for pants and skirts; a wider version makes good straps or handles. Note: These tabs are not finished on either end; they work for applications where the ends are inserted into a seam or are turned under and then topstitched in place.

1. Cut a strip of fabric two times the size of the finished width plus two seam allowances. Make the length as desired.

2. Fold the seam allowance on one short edge to the wrong side; press.

3. Fold the seam allowance on each long edge to the wrong side; press.

4. Fold in half lengthwise wrong sides together, matching the folded edges; press.

5. Edgestitch along the folded edges through all layers; stitch a second time about ¼" in from the edge if desired.

Tabs are a stylish way to create closures with buttons.

Zippers come in several styles for different applications.

ZIPPERS

Mostly practical but sometimes decorative, zippers are available in several types and styles for a wide variety of applications. Using the correct one in your project and the correct application gives a professional look to your sewing.

TYPES OF ZIPPERS

CONVENTIONAL ZIPPER: Used mainly in the side and back seams of skirts and pants, at the back neckline and front opening of tops and dresses, or in the side seams of close-fitting dresses, conventional zippers are made with polyester coils or metal teeth. The polyester zipper is a good all-purpose zipper that is lightweight, heat-resistant, and flexible; it works well in most garments and home decorating projects. The metal zipper is also an all-purpose zipper designed for heavier fabrics and projects such as sportswear, outerwear, and heavy home dec projects.

TROUSER ZIPPER: With extra wide tapes and heavy-duty metal teeth, this zipper is available in 9" and 11" lengths. One type of a trou-ser zipper is the jeans zipper, which is designed to be used with medium to heavyweight denim and has blue tapes and brass teeth. It is available in 5" and 9" lengths.

SEPARATING ZIPPER: Available in several styles, separating zippers come apart at the teeth into two separate pieces, making them perfect for jacket and sweater front openings. Separating zippers with metal teeth are heavy-duty and good for coats, jackets, home dec, and sturdy garment and travel bags. Separating zippers with plastic molded teeth are lightweight, strong, and add a decorative look to outer wear such as ski jackets. Separating zippers with polyester coils look more like conventional zippers and are good for lighter garments such as sweaters and lightweight jackets. There are options when buying separating zippers—most have one slider that starts at the bottom and pulls up, some have two-way sliders that allow the zipper to be opened from the top or the bottom, and others are reversible separating zippers with sliders that flip from one side of the zipper to the other (front to back).

INVISIBLE ZIPPER: One of the easiest types of zippers to install, the invisible zipper requires a special foot that will hold the polyester coils out of the way so the needle can stitch the zipper on the seam line of the garment. Once the zipper is closed, the only part that is visible is the teardrop tab. This zipper is often used in high-end and couture garments because it does not spoil the line or design of the finished garment.

ZIPPERS OF ANY LENGTH: Ideal for purses, bags, outerwear, and home dec projects, this type of zipper is sold by the yard with detached sliders/tabs that you attach. This allows you to have the perfect length for any project.

DECORATIVE ZIPPERS

Add some dash to a project using zippers with colored teeth or rhinestone coils. These unique closures usually become a focal point of the garment, purse, or other project in which they are sewn.

ZIPPER COMPONENTS

Even though everyone is familiar with zippers, using them daily in a variety of ways, most people have probably never stopped to look at the parts and understand the unique function of each. In order to know exactly how versatile a zipper can be, you should become intimately familiar with its makeup.

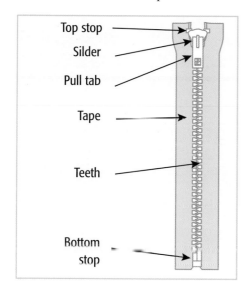

COILS OR TEETH: These interlock together to close the zipper and can be made of metal, nylon, or polyester.

TAPE: The part of the zipper sewn to fabric and to which the coils or teeth are attached.

SLIDER: Moves up and down the zipper to lock and unlock the coils.

PULL TAB: Connected to the slider, this is how you move the slider up and down the coils.

TOP AND BOTTOM STOPS: Brackets, one on each tape at the top of the zipper that keep the slider and pull tab from running off the tape. Conventional zippers have one bracket at the bottom to stop the slider when unzipping and separating zippers have a split one at the bottom so the tapes can be separated.

CENTER INSERTION

Often used at back and front neck edges, this application is inserted in a seam and is one of the simplest to learn.

1. With fabric right sides together, place the zipper along the edge and mark the position of the bottom tab stop.

2. Sew the seam together using a regular stitch length (about 2.5mm) below the mark and a basting stitch length (4mm–5mm) above it.

3. Press the seam open. Place the zipper face down on the opened seam and pin or glue in place.

4. Attach the zipper foot to the machine. Adjust the foot or the needle position as needed (see your manual) to sew next to the coils. Note: This zipper is stitched from the right side of the fabric.

5. Starting at the center seam at the bottom of the zipper, topstitch across about ¼", then pivot and stitch to the upper edge of the fabric on both sides of the zipper.

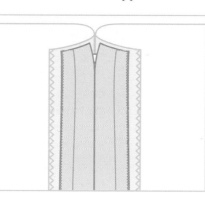

Step 3

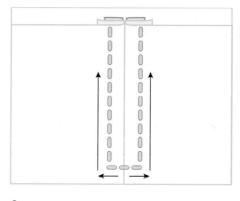

Using a zipper longer than the opening simplifies the insertion process.

Step 5

ZIPPER TIPS

- Finish raw edges of fabric if needed before starting the zipper application.
- Stitch both sides of the zipper in the same direction, from the bottom of the zipper to the top.
- Consult your machine manual about the zipper foot for your machine. Some feet are stationary, and the needle position is moved from one side to the other as needed. Other zipper feet use a center needle position, and the foot slides from side to side as needed.
- Most zippers come in lengths from 7"–22". To shorten a conventional zipper, create a new bottom stop by zigzagging in place across the coils at the new desired length. Trim excess zipper tape below the stitching.
- Use zippers that are 3"–4" longer than needed so the ends extend beyond the fabric. Slide the pull-tab to the top so it doesn't interfere with the stitching. Once the zipper is stitched, unzip the zipper and trim the excess tape. Note: Take care not to slide the tab up and off the tape before the upper edge of the fabric is finished with a facing, waistband, or hem.

LAPPED INSERTION

Usually inserted in the side seam of skirts and pants, it's best to use a pressing ham or mitt to accommodate the shape of the hipline when pressing.

A lapped insertion zipper has one side stitched close to the coils.

1. With fabric right sides together, place the zipper along the edge and mark the position of the bottom tab stop.

2. Sew the seam together using a regular stitch length (about 2.5mm) below the mark and a basting stitch length (4mm–5mm) above it.

3. Press the seam open. Unzip the zipper and place one side face down on the right seam allowance (as you look at the right side of the fabric). Position with the coils on the seamline and pin or glue-baste in place.

4. Attach the zipper foot to the machine. Adjust the foot or the needle position as needed (see your manual) to sew next to the coils.

5. Set the machine for a basting stitch length (4mm–5mm) and, starting at the bottom of the zipper, sew the tape to the seam allowance only.

6. Close the zipper and fold the fabric away from the zipper, forming a narrow strip of fabric between the coil and the basted seam. Using a regular stitch length (about 2.5mm) and starting at the bottom of the zipper, sew through the folded seam allowance and zipper tape.

7. Place the zipper flat on the seam allowances and baste the remaining tape to the remaining seam allowance only.

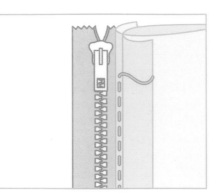

Step 6

8. From the right side of the garment, topstitch from the bottom of the zipper; starting at the seam, sew ½" out, pivot and stitch to the upper edge of the fabric.

9. Remove the basting stitches from the seam and press using a press cloth.

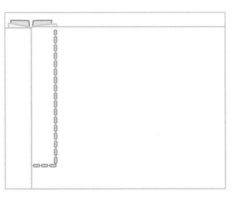

Step 8

EXPOSED ZIPPER

With an exposed zipper, the coils or teeth become part of the design of the garment. Large coil or plastic teeth zippers work well for this application.

An exposed zipper application shows the coils of the zipper.

1. Mark the fabric. Make the length 1" longer than the zipper and the width wide enough to show the coils or teeth of the zipper.

2. Using a regular stitch length (about 2.5mm), sew along the drawn lines, shortening the stitch length at the corners for reinforcement.

3. Cut down the center and slash into the corners of the opening. Fold the edges to the inside and press.

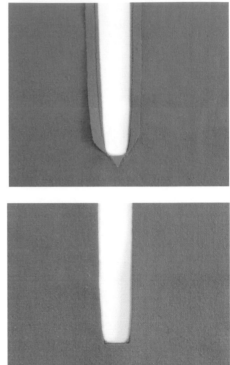

Wrong side and right side of opening

4. Position the zipper behind the opening and pin in place.

5. Attach the zipper foot to the machine. Adjust the foot or the needle position as needed (see your manual) to sew next to the coils.

6. Set the machine for a regular stitch length (about 2.5mm) and, starting at the bottom of the zipper, topstitch close to the opening along one side.

7. Stitch across the bottom and up the remaining side.

INVISIBLE ZIPPER

This zipper application requires a special zipper and a specific zipper foot. The zipper looks like a seam line when finished, and the only part that shows is the tab.

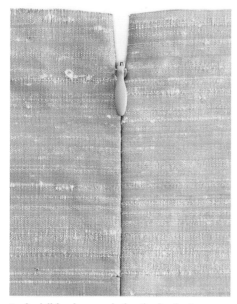

An invisible zipper mimics the look of a seam when closed.

1. Attach the appropriate zipper foot on the machine. Your machine may have an invisible zipper foot, or you may be able to use a "generic" version.

2. Unzip the zipper; press the zipper flat using a low setting on the iron to avoid melting the coils.

3. Position the coils of one side of the zipper right side down on the seam line (right side of fabric). Note: The seam that the zipper is being sewn into is not stitched at this time; you should be working with two separate pieces of fabric. Tip: Use chalk or fabric marker to mark the seam line.

4. Position the zipper under the foot with the coil in the groove of the foot; pin if needed. The purpose of the foot is to hold the coils up so the needle can stitch close to them.

5. Using a regular stitch length (about 2.5mm), sew the zipper starting at the top and continuing down until you cannot move forward (the foot will come to the tab).

Step 5

6. Repeat Steps 4 and 5 on the opposite tape and the second piece of fabric.

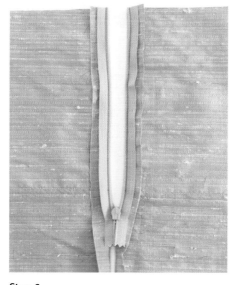

Step 6

7. Close the zipper. Using a regular zipper foot, stitch the remainder of the seam below the zipper, overlapping the seam stitching with the zipper stitching about ¼".

SEPARATING ZIPPER

Used on edges that come apart such as on jackets, sleeping bags, and backpacks, separating zippers are easy to install. They are usually inserted in the seam between a project piece and facing.

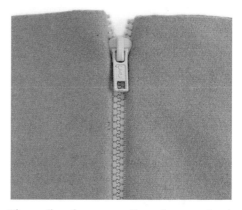

The coils of a separating zipper extend beyond the edges of the zipper opening.

1. Separate the zipper and position each piece separately on the appropriate side of the project. Mark the position of the bottom of the zipper on both pieces of the project fabric.

2. Place one tape right side down on the appropriate side, with the teeth or coils of the zipper facing away from the raw edge of the project. Take care to position the bottom of the zipper with the mark previously made.

3. Place the facing right side down on the project piece. Pin the layers together.

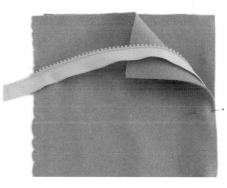

Step 3

4. Using a zipper foot and a straight stitch, sew next to the coils, adjusting the needle position or the zipper foot as needed.

5. Fold the facing to the inside of the project; press.

6. Optional: From the front, top-stitch one or two rows of stitching next to the zipper.

7. Repeat with the remaining side of the zipper.

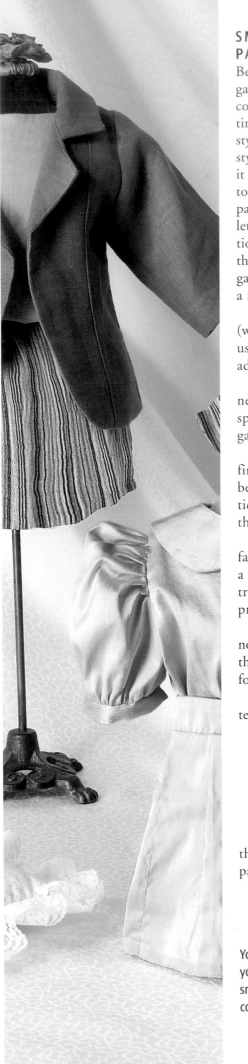

SMALL SCALE PRACTICE PATTERNS

Becoming proficient at making garments requires learning multiple construction techniques and then putting them all together to make the style of garments you desire. Different styles require various techniques, so it seems there are always new ones to practice and learn. The next few pages offer small-scale patterns that let you try many of the basic construction techniques discussed earlier in this chapter, so you can expand your garment-making knowledge base with a minimum of time and effort.

Similar to making doll clothes (where many of us started sewing), using small scale patterns has several advantages.

1. It's quick. You can practice a new technique without having to spend time completing an entire garment.

2. You don't have any of the finishing steps unless you choose, because, in most cases, you are practicing just the fundamental steps of the technique you are learning.

3. Small-scale patterns take little fabric so the monetary risk of making a mistake is not as great as when trying a new technique on a full-size project.

4. Practicing a technique in a no-stress way makes it easier to try new things and builds your confidence for making the actual garment.

The patterns included in this chapter are for the following garments:

1. Raglan top
2. Kimono top
3. Jacket
4. Puffed sleeve blouse
5. Pleated skirt
6. Pull-on skirt

Before using the patterns, read the following instructions for preparing, cutting, and stitching.

You can create a mini-wardrobe for your favorite 18" doll while using these small-scale patterns to practice clothing construction techniques.

PREPARING THE PATTERNS

The patterns shown on the next few pages are sized to fit the page. They may be used in this size but since their small size may be difficult to manage they are designed to be photocopied at 200%, making them large enough to handle easily.

Once the patterns are enlarged, cut them out along the outer solid lines of each piece.

CUTTING THE PATTERN PIECES

Pin the paper pattern pieces to your fabric, placing them along the lengthwise grain unless otherwise indicated. Note: When possible, use a fabric that is appropriate for the type of garment you are making (e.g., lightweight silk for the top, medium weight linen for the jacket, etc.). An exception to this is the use of heavy fabrics such as thick wool or sturdy denim. These are not recommended for the small-scale patterns as the bulk of these types of fabrics will be difficult to manage because of the reduced size of the seam allowances and garment openings.

Cut out the pieces needed for the techniques you want to practice (see patterns for specific techniques). For instance, if you want to practice a set-in sleeve, you will need only the jacket back, one jacket front, one side front, and one sleeve.

STITCHING THE PATTERNS

Unless otherwise noted, seam allowances are approximately ½".

Once the pieces are cut, transfer all markings to the fabric before removing the paper pattern pieces.

Referring to the directions on the indicated pages, complete the portion of the garment that addresses the technique you want to learn.

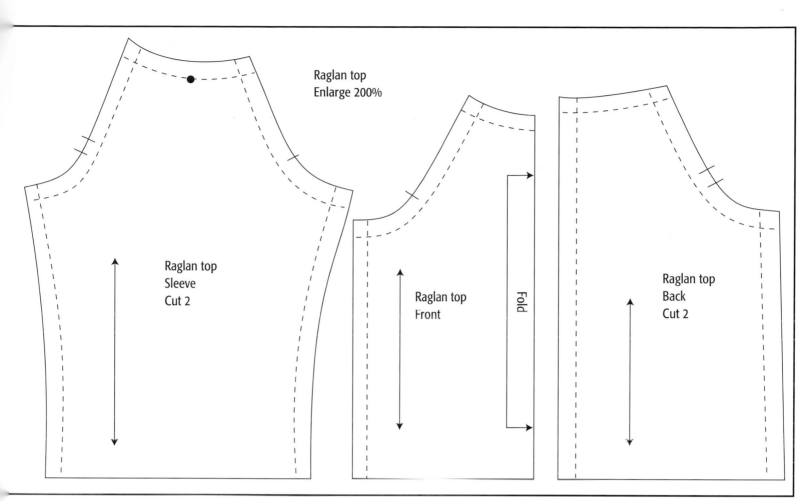

Raglan top
Enlarge 200%

Raglan top
Sleeve
Cut 2

Raglan top
Front

Fold

Raglan top
Back
Cut 2

Kimono top
Enlarge 200%

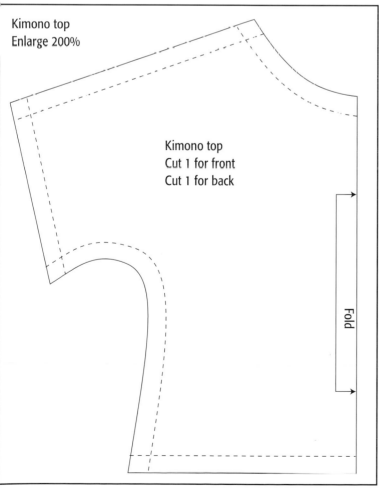

Kimono top
Cut 1 for front
Cut 1 for back

Fold

Raglan top techniques: Raglan sleeve, page 109; shirttail hem, page 111; bias facing, page 103. For an 18" doll, leave the back seam open, hem the edges and add snaps or hook-and-loop-tape for easy dressing and undressing.

Kimono top techniques: Kimono sleeve, page 109; shirttail hem, page 111; Bias facing, page 103. For an 18" doll, leave one shoulder seam open, hem the edges and add a snap.

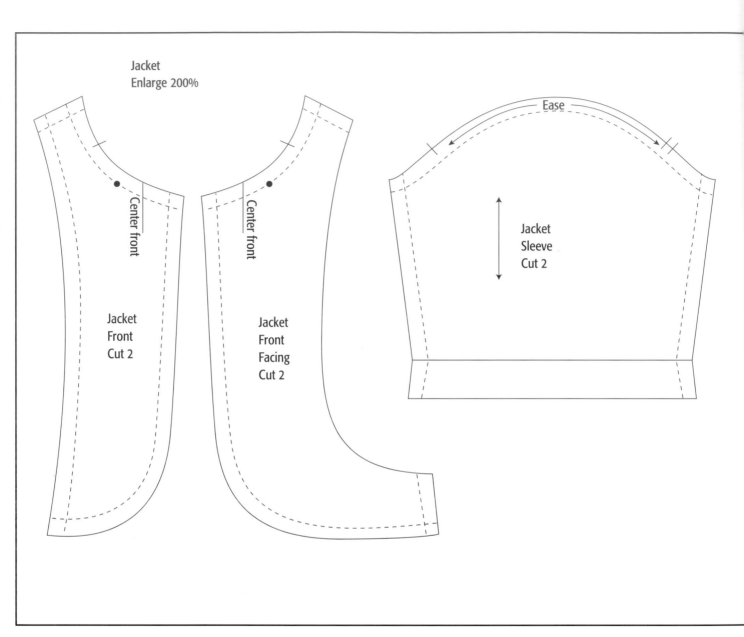

Jacket
Enlarge 200%

Ease

Center front

Center front

Jacket
Front
Cut 2

Jacket
Front
Facing
Cut 2

Jacket
Sleeve
Cut 2

Jacket techniques: Shaped facing, page 102; rolled collar, page 105; smooth set-in sleeve, page 108.

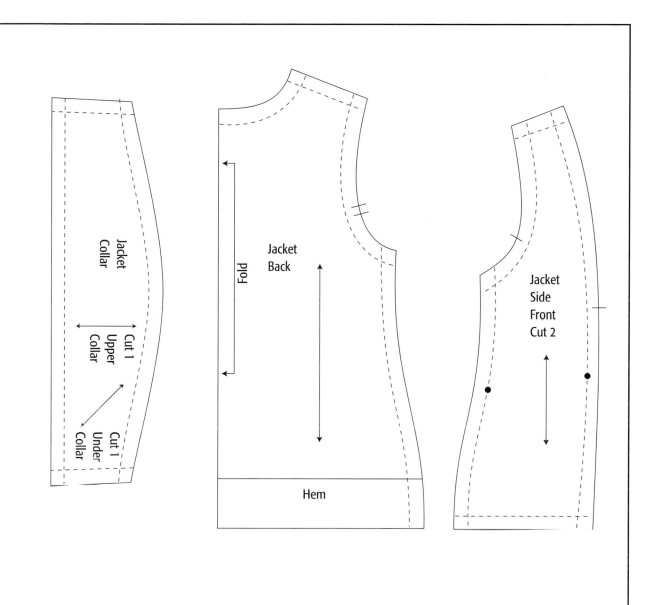

Jacket Collar

Cut 1 Upper Collar

Cut 1 Under Collar

Fold

Jacket Back

Hem

Jacket Side Front Cut 2

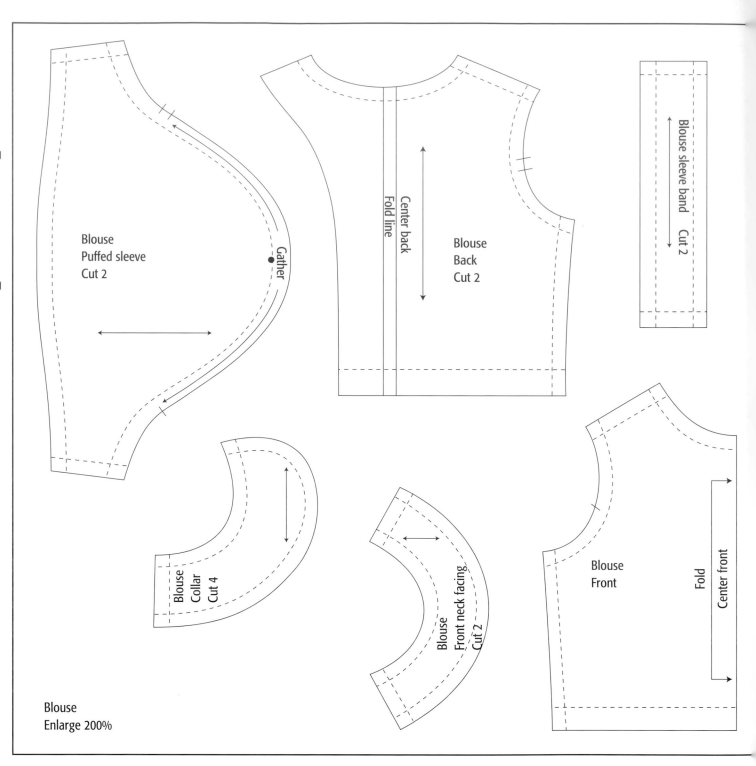

Blouse
Puffed sleeve
Cut 2

Gather

Blouse
Back
Cut 2

Center back
Fold line

Blouse sleeve band   Cut 2

Blouse
Collar
Cut 4

Blouse
Front neck facing
Cut 2

Blouse
Front

Fold

Center front

Blouse
Enlarge 200%

Blouse techniques: Cut-on facing, page 102; flat collar, page 104; puffed sleeve, page 108; narrow hem, page 111.

Pleated skirt
Enlarge 200%

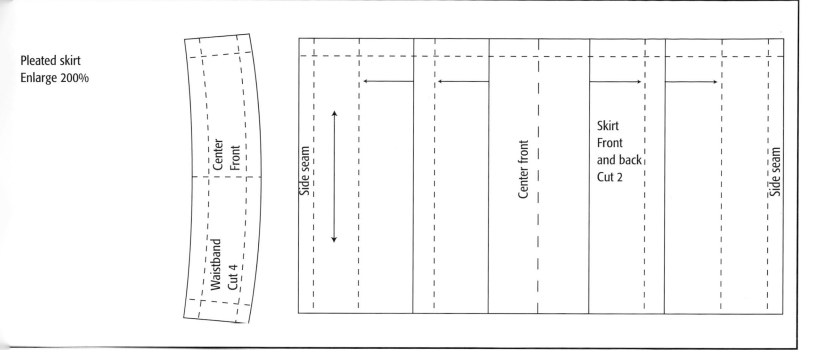

Waistband
Cut 4

Center
Front

Side seam

Center front

Skirt
Front
and back
Cut 2

Side seam

Pull-on skirt
Enlarge 200%

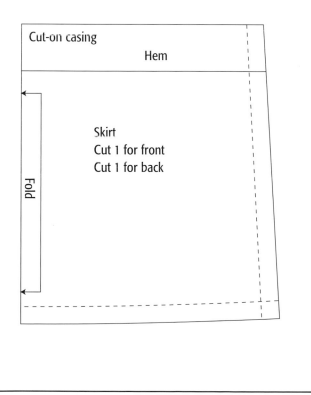

Cut-on casing

Hem

Skirt
Cut 1 for front
Cut 1 for back

Fold

Pleated skirt techniques: Box pleats, page 137; knife pleats, page 137; Narrow hem, page 111. For an 18" doll, leave one side seam open about 2"–3" and finish the waistband along that side. This opening will aid in easy dressing and undressing.

Pull-on skirt techniques: In-seam pockets, page 101; elastic casing, page 107; shirttail hem, page 111.

custom elements

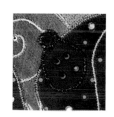

MANY PEOPLE LEARN TO SEW BECAUSE they want to have clothing and items for their homes that are unique and unusual—not the same as those owned by other people. Anyone can use the same pattern to make a blouse, or a pillow, or a curtain, but what makes the difference are the fabrics each person chooses and the decorative touches and embellishments they decide to add. The satisfaction of adding custom elements to clothing and other projects is a driving force behind learning new techniques.

This chapter divides custom elements into two categories: decorative details and embellishments. The decorative details involve methods that are used in the sewing and construction process. Techniques such as gathered ruffles, crisp pleats, and bound edges add interest and detail to otherwise plain projects. Embellishments are usually methods that add design and dimension to the surface of the fabric. Techniques such as beading, appliqué, quilting, and silk ribbon embroidery help to define the style and "flavor" of a project. These decorative applications are often applied to the flat fabric before a project is sewn or may be a part of the construction process.

The good news is that often there is a presser foot or nifty tool that makes many of these techniques almost as simple as sewing a straight stitch. So don't assume that custom details and embellishments are difficult to achieve—try them all, and soon you'll be incorporating them into your projects.

decorative details

Bound edges can add style and color with a professional-looking finish to almost any project.

BOUND EDGES

Often used as a finish for quilt edges, binding is also excellent for trimming the edges of other projects such as purses, pillows, placemats, and tablecloths. Use this technique in garment sewing to finish seam allowances, replace facings, and trim jackets—great for making reversible clothing.

Binding starts as a strip of fabric. Bias-cut strips offer the most flexibility and "give" and are necessary for binding curved or shaped edges. Cross-grain strips have a small amount of stretch and will work for binding straight edges while strips cut on the lengthwise grain should not be used for binding edges.

JOINING SINGLE STRIPS

When joining individual strips, a diagonal seam will be the most inconspicuous on the finished bound edge. To get this diagonal seam, place two strips right sides together at right angles. Stitch a ¼" seam and press the seam open; trim dog ears if necessary. Continue this method until you have a strip long enough for your purpose.

Diagonal seams are the most inconspicuous when joining bias strips.

A diagonal edge is the most inconspicuous way to end bias binding.

CONTINUOUS BIAS STRIPS

To eliminate the need to stitch short strips together, try this method of cutting continuous bias.

1. Cut a square of fabric in half diagonally.

2. With right sides together, sew the triangles back together along a straight side using a ¼" seam; press open.

3. On the wrong side of the fabric, draw lines as shown, spacing them the desired width of the strips.

4. Pin the short diagonal edges with right sides together, forming a tube, offsetting the drawn lines by one strip.

5. Stitch the pinned edges using a ¼" seam allowance; press open.

6. With scissors, cut along continuously drawn line, creating one strip.

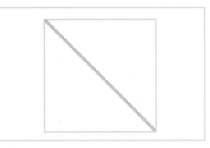

Step 1

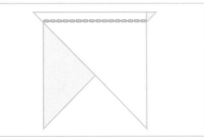

Step 2

Step 3

Steps 4, 5, and 6

SPECIAL ACCESSORY

Some machines have special attachments that will fold the fabric strips and hold them in place, so the needle can stitch along the edge—folding, wrapping, and stitching all in one operation!

128

SINGLE BINDING

This method starts with a flat strip of bias cut four times the desired finished width plus ¼" to allow it to wrap around the edge of the project. Stitch the flat strip to the edge of the project using a ¼" seam allowance. Fold the strip around the project edge, turn under, and slip stitch in place by hand.

Sew a single layer of bias to the fabric for single binding.

SINGLE BINDING TIP

Before stitching a binding to the edge of a project, use a Clover Bias Tape Maker to fold the edges in for pressing. Unfold the pressed edges before applying.

DOUBLE BINDING

Sometimes called French Binding, this method is a smart finish for sheer fabrics and is often used for quilt edges. The finished look is very similar to single binding but double binding is stronger and withstands more wear and tear. Cut the bias strip six times the desired finished width plus ¼" to allow it to wrap around the edge of the project. Fold the bias strip in half lengthwise and press. Position the folded strip on the project edge, matching the raw edges. Stitch the folded strip to the edge of the project using a ¼" seam allowance. Fold the strip around the project edge, turn it under; sew to secure the binding by machine or slip stitch it in place by hand.

Stitch a folded strip to the edge for double binding.

FINISHING A BOUND EDGE

Stop sewing about 2"–3" before coming to the starting point. Fold the upper fabric (ending) under about ½" at a diagonal and pin in place. Resume stitching the binding in place, overlapping the beginning with a few stitches.

A diagonal join in the least conspicuous.

MITERED CORNERS

To miter the corners of double binding, sew the binding to one edge of your project, stopping the distance of one seam allowance away from the corner; backstitch and clip the threads. Fold the binding strip up, away from the project. Fold the binding strip down so the fold is even with the top of the project and the raw edges of the binding are aligned with the raw edges of the project. Starting at the upper edge of the project, stitch the next side, repeating the previous steps at each corner. When the stitched binding is wrapped around the edge, the corner will form a miter.

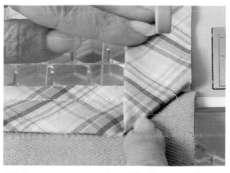

Stitch one side, then fold binding straight up.

Fold binding straight down and stitch next side.

The bias forms a miter when wrapped around the fabric edge.

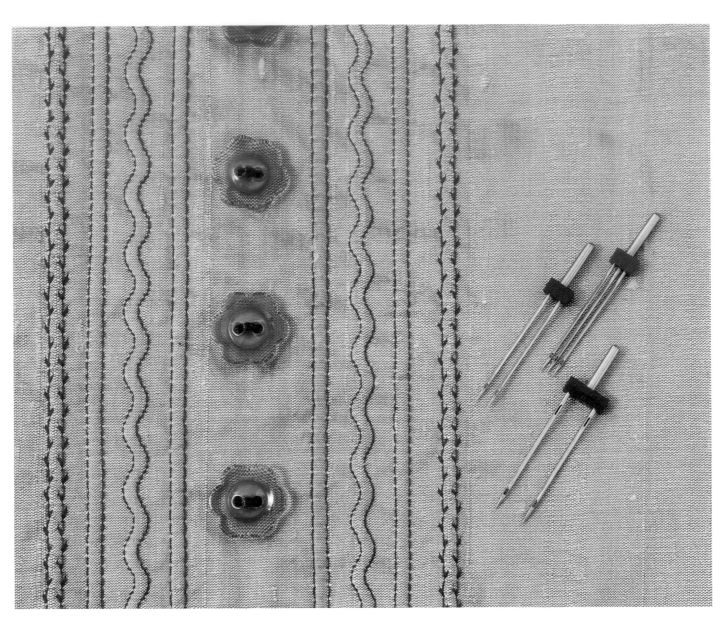

Even simple stitching becomes special when using multiple needles.

130

MAXIMUM WIDTH

Use this formula to determine the maximum stitch width you can use on your machine for double/triple needles:

$$A - B = C$$

A = Widest stitch width the machine can make
B = Width of needle
C = Widest stitch width allowed before needle strikes the presser foot

---

DOUBLE AND TRIPLE NEEDLE STITCHING

Note: For information on specific double and triple needles, see page 74.

One of the easiest special effects to sew is almost identical to regular sewing but uses multiple needles. The biggest difference is in setting up the machine. Double and triple needles are mounted onto one shank and go into the machine exactly the same way as a single needle. Once you have the needle inserted, you need two or three spools of thread for the machine. Tip: For the second and/or third spool, wind a bobbin and use it as a spool.

This eliminates purchasing multiple spools of the same thread, if you don't need them.

Place the spools on the spool pins of the machine. Most machines today have two pins and some have three. If yours doesn't have enough, you can set a thread stand behind the machine and pull the thread from there, or you can place a plastic drinking straw on a spool pin and stack spools and bobbins on the same pin. Position the spool so that the thread moves off in different directions; this helps avoid tangling as the thread moves along the thread path.

Continue threading the machine as

Place thread on each side of the tension disc.

Bypass the thread guide with one of the threads.

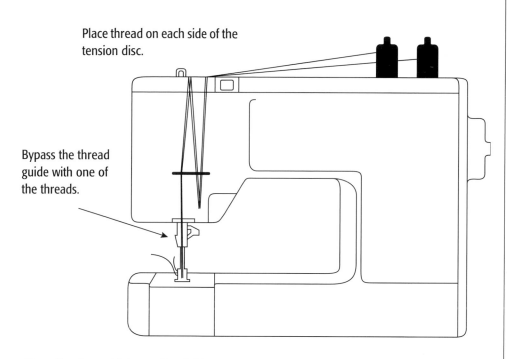

Threading for multiple needle stitching.

MULTIPLE NEEDLE TIPS

- Sew at a slower speed than usual, engaging the half-speed function if available on your machine.
- Use different colored threads in the needle for an interesting effect.

usual, consulting your owner's manual for specifics. You can generally treat the threads as one and thread the machine as usual. If you have trouble with the threads tangling, separate them at the tension disc, placing one on the left side of the disc and one or two on the right. You can also

separate the threads at the seam guide just before the needle, placing one in it and bypassing the guide with the remaining thread or threads.

When selecting your stitch, keep in mind that some stitches are not suitable for double or triple stitching. Intricate patterns may not track well and many stitches are just not pretty with a reduced stitch width. Some machines may have security features that automatically restrict the width of the stitch so the double needle doesn't hit the foot and break. If your machine doesn't, be sure to carefully check your settings. Use your handwheel to "walk" the machine through the process of forming the stitch to make sure the width you have selected will work with the multiple needles.

Once you have the machine threaded, sew as usual using almost any stitch you choose. Sew rows of sample stitches to decide what is best for your project. If your goal is to add texture to the fabric, select a straight stitch and a lightweight fabric with no stabilizer. Stitch closely spaced rows across the fabric, forming tiny tucks that add texture to the surface of the fabric.

- Use a metallic thread in one of the needles to add a bit of sparkle to your stitching.
- A double needle straight stitch provides an easy way to stitch narrow ribbon in place. Select a ribbon that is slightly wider than the distance between the two needles. Place the ribbon on the fabric and position the needles over the center so each one stitches close to the corresponding outer edge. Stitch along the length of the ribbon, securing both edges in one pass.

Texturize fabric with double and triple needle stitching.

131

Use a long straight stitch and two lines of stitching for simple gathering.

GATHERING

Used as a way to stitch a longer piece of fabric to a shorter one, gathering results in a soft, full look used for waistlines, puffed sleeves, and lingerie. The ratio of gathering is usually two to one but can be three or four to one if very lightweight or sheer fabric is used. Experiment with your fabric to determine what works best for your project.

SIMPLE GATHERING

This gathering method works for light to medium weight fabrics. Using a long straight stitch (4mm–5mm), sew a line of stitching about ⅜" from the raw edge. Sew a second line a scant ¼" away, placing it just inside the seam allowance. Secure the threads at one end of the fabric by winding them around a straight pin. Pull both threads from the other end to gather the fabric, adjusting the gathers evenly across the fabric. Tip: Loosening the needle tension slightly for stitching will make the threads easier to pull when gathering the fabric.

GATHERING OVER CORD

Good for heavier fabrics such as denim and corduroy, this gathering method utilizes a zigzag stitch and a narrow cord such as perle cotton or topstitching thread. Set the machine for a medium zigzag stitch (width and length, about 2.5mm). Sew over the cord without stitching into it. Tie a knot into one end of the cord; pull the cord from the other end, gathering the fabric and adjusting the gathers evenly across the fabric. Once the fabric is stitched into a seam, the cord can be removed if desired.

Gathering over cord works well with heavy fabrics.

132

Stitching over clear elastic is an easy way to gather a flat edge.

GATHERING WITH ELASTIC THREAD

This is a stretchy form of gathering that works for light to medium weight fabric and is usually sewn in multiple parallel rows of stitching to create a shirred effect. Wind elastic thread onto a bobbin by hand and thread the needle with regular thread. Select the straight stitch; adjust the stitch length to 4mm and sew several evenly spaced parallel rows of stitching. Secure each line of stitching at one end by tying the threads together. Pull the elastic threads from the other end to gather the fabric, holding them together and adjusting the shirring evenly across the fabric. Once the fabric is shirred, secure each end by a vertical line of stitching in the seam allowance using regular thread in the needle and bobbin with an average stitch length (2.5mm).

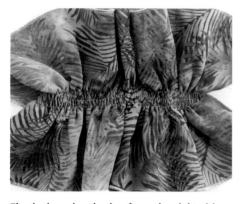

Elastic thread gathering from the right side.

SPECIAL ACCESSORY

Some machines have gathering feet that will gather the fabric with one pass of the needle and may gather fabric and attach it to flat fabric in one operation. These can be a real timesaver for certain projects but usually produce gathers that are not as adjustable as other methods.

GATHERING WITH CLEAR ELASTIC

This method is an easy way to evenly gather a long edge to a shorter one such as when gathering a skirt to a jumper bodice. It's also an easy way to finish the bottom of a little girl's sleeve by stitching along the wrist, creating a ruffled edge. Cut a piece of narrow clear elastic the length of the finished edge and anchor it to one edge of the fabric with a few stitches. Using a zigzag, sewn-out zigzag or running stitch, sew down the center of the elastic while stretching it to fit the fabric. This works best for light to medium weight fabrics.

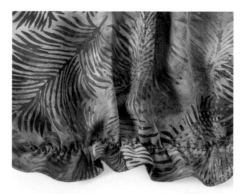

Clear elastic gives even gathers that are not adjustable.

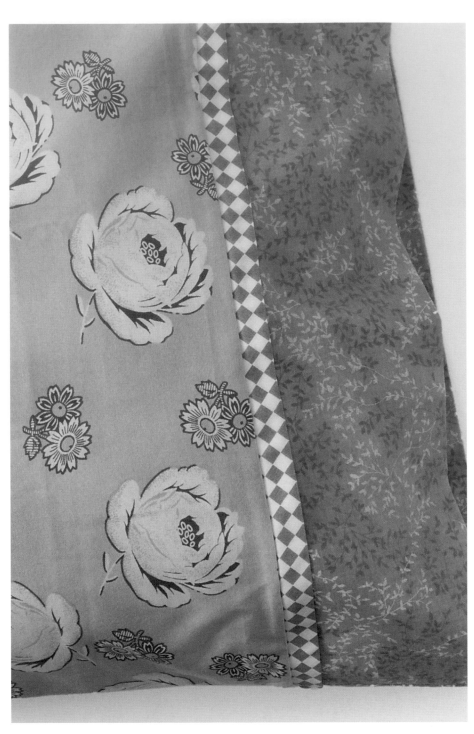

seam allowances. For instance, if the finished size is ¼" and the seam allowance is ⅝", the strip should be cut 1¾" (¼" + ¼" + ⅝" + ⅝"). Usually stitched on straight edges, this type of piping can be cut on any grain (direction) of the fabric. Handle a bias-cut strip carefully to avoid stretching it.

TECHNIQUE
Once the strip is cut, fold it in half lengthwise and press. To insert it into a seam, simply place it on the edge of the fabric, matching the raw edges, then pin or baste in place. Position a second piece of fabric right side down; stitch the seam through all layers. Open the fabric and press the seam with the seam allowances folded to one side; the piping will face the opposite side.

CORDED PIPING
Single corded piping is similar to cordless piping, however it has a filler cord to give it more definition. This cord can vary in size to suit the project. For instance, use a narrow cord to make mini piping for a baby garment, a large cord to make jumbo piping for a floor pillow, or any size between these for other projects.

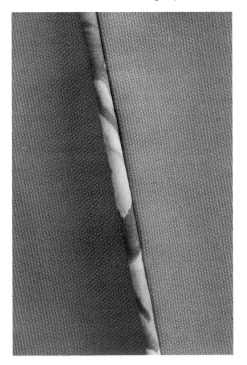

Define edges and seams of a project with piping made of contrasting fabric.

A contrasting strip of cordless piping is a great accent for a pillowcase

PIPING
A classic technique, piping sharpens and defines edges, especially when stitched in a contrasting color. It can be used on almost any type of project from children's clothing to designer suits to soft jumpers. Prepared piping can be purchased ready for stitching into a seam or along an edge. Custom piping can also be created using filler cord and any medium weight fabric you choose.

CORDLESS PIPING
Sometimes called a flange, cordless piping is simply a strip of folded fabric inserted into a seam as an accent on almost any type of project. Used mainly on interior seams rather than edges, this method is often seen as an inner border accent on pieced quilts.

FABRIC
Usually created from a contrasting fabric, the strip should be cut twice the desired finished size plus two

FABRIC

Cut fabric strips the diameter of the filler cord plus two seam allowances. Cord that is about ¼" in diameter is one of the most common size cords used on pillow edges and jacket openings; the strips cut for this size cord are 2¼"–2½". The fabric strips can be cut on the lengthwise or crosswise grain if being used on straight edges only. If the edge to be piped is curved or goes around corners as on a pillow, cut the strips on the bias for more flexibility. Strips are often also cut on the bias when using a print or striped fabric to create a diagonal accent.

PRESSER FOOT

A common method of making piping uses a zipper foot which allows you to stitch close to the cord. This works but doesn't offer the best control; the foot sits only on the edge of the seam allowances, and you must keep the cord in position. A better choice is a piping or cording foot if your sewing machine has one available. This type of foot has a tunnel or groove on the bottom of the sole that hugs the cord and keeps it in position for stitching. You generally adjust the needle position to place it close to the cord.

TECHNIQUE

Wrap the fabric strip around the filler cord. Straight stitch next to the cord, adjusting the needle position (if your machine allows it). Get close to the cord but stay at least one needle position away, so you can adjust it when you attach the piping; this will ensure that your original stitching does not show on the finished project. Once the cord is covered, position it on the fabric with the raw edges even. The stitching on the piping should be just inside the seamline. Position a second piece of fabric right side down; adjust the needle position one step closer to the seamline and stitch

For best results, use a special presser foot to hold the cord as you cover it.

CORDED EDGE

Similar to a piped edge, this method works by applying decorative cord to a finished edge such as a cuff or collar. The cord does not have a seam allowance and is usually about ¼" in diameter.

Thread the machine (needle and bobbin) with monofilament thread or with thread that blends with the cord being attached. Select a zigzag stitch and set it for a width that is slightly wider than the chosen cord; adjust the length to 2mm–3mm. Simply place the decorative cord next to a finished edge and under the piping foot, which should straddle the edge of the fabric. Attach the cord, letting the stitch go into the edge of the fabric, then over the cord and into the air (off the edge of fabric).

135

the piping in place. Open the fabric and press the seam open or with the seam allowances folded to one side as desired. For stitching shaped edges, use the following steps:

CURVED EDGE: Cover the cord as directed above. Clip the seam allowance every ½"–¾", up to the stitching. Position the piping on the curved edge and spread it as needed to fit, making more clips if necessary.

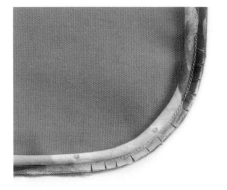

Clip the piping seam allowance for smooth curves.

CORNER: Stitch the piping to the first side following the technique directions above. Stop with the needle down in the fabric at the point where the two seamlines intersect. Lift the presser foot; using sharp scissors, clip the seam allowances at the intersection. Pivot the fabric and turn the piping, bringing it around to the second side, placing it next to the seamline. Continue sewing, attaching the remainder of the piping.

Clip the piping seam allowance to turn corners.

ENDS THAT MEET: Cut the ends of the cord (not the bias strip) so they meet. Fold one end of the bias under about ¼" and overlap with the raw edge of the other bias strip (the folded edge is on the outside). This method gives a smooth, unbroken look to the finished edge.

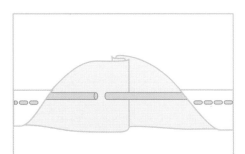

Finishing a piped edge.

DOUBLE PIPING

A stronger accent, double piping is popular for home dec items and is sometimes used in contrasting colors so each cord is covered with a different fabric. Referring to the directions above, cover one cord using a ⅞" seam allowance and another one with a ⅝" seam allowance. Stitch the first cord to the fabric, matching the seam allowances. Position the second cord on top of the first with seam allowances even and stitch in place. Proceed as directed above to insert the piping in a seam.

Layer contrasting colors of piping for a strong accent.

Insert double piping into a seam or place it along an edge.

PLEATS

Stitched pleats control fullness and can be soft or sharp depending on the crispness of the fabric selected and/or the finished look desired. Skirts are common places to find pleats, including knife, box, and inverted types. Pleats can also be used on jacket backs and shirts.

KNIFE PLEATS

Use a fabric marker to mark the fold and placement lines; different colors of markers or different methods of marking for each type make it easier to fold and place the pleats. Once the fabric is folded on the foldline, position the folded edge on the placement line and baste in place. Press the pleats, steaming sharp pleats from both sides to set them or steaming them slightly for soft ones. Topstitch the upper area of the pleats, sewing through all layers. If desired, pleats can be edgestitched the entire length of the fold, starting at the lower edge and stitching to the top.

Knife pleats

BOX PLEATS

Working from the right side of the fabric, mark, fold, and stitch the pleats as indicated on your pattern. At this point, they look similar to extra-wide knife pleats, but, instead of pressing the pleats to the side, flatten the fabric so the foldline is on top of the stitched line, then press. Baste the pleats in place. Topstitch the side edges of the upper area of the pleat, sewing through all layers.

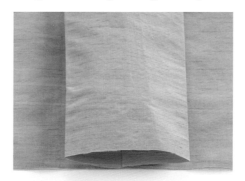

Box pleat

INVERTED PLEATS

This pleat is stitched in the same manner as the box pleat but is worked from the wrong side of the fabric. A separate underlay can be added as a contrast by stitching a panel of fabric to the pleat extensions. Topstitch pleats on both sides of the seam, starting at the lower point of the stitching and sewing to the top through all layers.

Inverted pleat

For style and wearing comfort, add an inverted pleat to the back of a jacket or shirt.

🌼 MARKING PLEATS

When marking pleats, use one color fabric marker for fold lines and another color for stitch lines. Another way to quickly mark pleats is to snip the seam allowance at the ends of the lines, using one snip for fold lines and two for placement lines.

Gathered ruffles add a soft look to the edges of this bib apron. Courtesy of Donna Lang.

allowance and one hem allowance. Hem one long edge by turning under twice and stitching, serging a rolled hem, or using a hemmer foot. Gather the opposite long edge using one of the gathering methods described earlier in this chapter on page 132. Adjust the gathers so they are even and the length of the ruffle matches the fabric to which it is being sewn. Pin in place and proceed to seam or hem the fabric as desired. Note: Create a double layer ruffle by cutting the fabric strip twice the finished width and adding two seam allowances. Fold the strip in half wrong sides together and gather the raw edges, treating them as one layer.

For a double-edged ruffle, cut the fabric strip the finished width plus two hem allowances; hem both long edges as desired. Gather down the center using one of the gathering methods described earlier in this chapter on page 132. Adjust the gathers so they are even, and the length of the ruffle matches the fabric to which it is being sewn. Pin in place and stitch down the center using a straight or decorative stitch.

RUFFLES

Ruffles are decorative fabric pieces that are gathered, pleated, or otherwise fuller than the fabric to which they are being attached. Single-layer ruffles have one edge attached or sewn into a seam with the opposite edge free. Ruffles can be a single layer or double layer of fabric. Double-edged ruffles have two finished edges and are gathered or pleated down the center then applied to the surface of the fabric.

GATHERED RUFFLES

This popular detail uses a gathered strip of fabric as a trim for clothing, pillows, and window treatments. Cut the fabric strip from light to medium weight fabric, twice as long as the desired finished ruffle. For a single ruffle, the width should be cut the finished width plus one seam

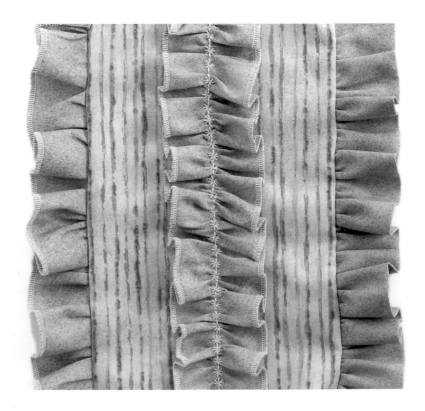

Single-layer ruffle with rolled edge, double-edged ruffle, double-layer ruffle.

CIRCULAR RUFFLES

Sometimes called flounces, these ruffles add softness to an edge while offering less fullness than gathered ruffles. Cut from a circle, the strip is straightened to match a fabric edge to which it will be attached. Create a pattern by drawing a circle which has a circumference that matches the edge you are trimming with a 1:1 ratio—no fullness. Cut out the center of this circle, one seam allowance inside the drawn line. Note: You may need to make two or more circles and stitch them together to match the length of the edge to which you are attaching the ruffle.

Decide how wide you want the ruffle to be. The wider the flounce, the fuller it will be and the lighter weight the fabric should be. Measure that distance from the original drawn circle and create a second circle around the first. Add a seam allowance to this edge. You should now have a doughnut with seam allowances on the inside and the outside edges. Slice from the outer edge to the inner edge and straighten to create a strip.

Staystitch just inside the inner seam allowance and clip the seam allowance about every ½". Hem the outer edge of the ruffle using a hemmer foot or serger rolled hem, taking care not to stretch the edge. Straighten the clipped edge and position it on the project; pin or baste in place. Stitch the ruffle to the project and proceed as needed.

A circular ruffle results in a soft flounce that can finish the edges of a variety of projects.

Circular ruffles start with a circle of fabric.

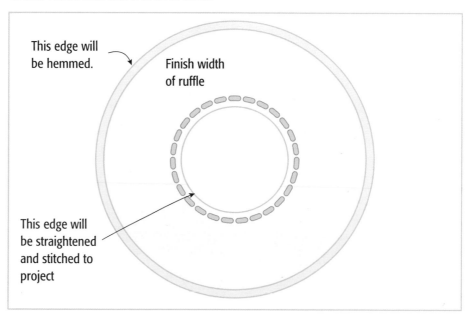

This edge will be hemmed.

Finish width of ruffle

This edge will be straightened and stitched to project

139

Define edges and seams with topstitching.

lapel of a jacket) and useful (such as in a hem). It usually follows the lines of the project, stitched parallel to a finished edge, and may be stitched in multiple lines or a single row. Edgestitching is a form of topstitching that is close to the edge, flattening, sharpening, and defining it.

FABRIC, NEEDLE, AND THREAD

Topstitching can be sewn on any weight of fabric, light to heavy. The thread can be almost any type in a weight that is appropriate for the fabric; use a suitable needle for the fabric and thread. Buttonhole Twist and topstitching thread are heavy threads that can be used with a topstitching needle when topstitching on heavy suiting or coating.

TECHNIQUE

Thread the machine with the desired thread and the appropriate needle. Adjust the stitch length to be slightly longer than normal (about 3mm–4mm)—the heavier the thread, the longer the stitch length. To make sure the stitching is parallel to the edge, use a seam guide and set it for the desired distance from the needle. As you stitch, keep the edge next to the guide so the stitching is parallel to the edge. Double and triple needles can be used for perfectly spaced multiple rows of stitching.

TOPSTITCHING TIPS

- For the most precise straight stitching, use a straight stitch presser foot with a straight stitch plate to focus the penetration of the needle.
- Change to a new needle when you begin topstitching. It's often one of the last steps in the project, so chances are the needle you have been using has lost its precision point.
- Shorten the stitch length as you maneuver curves to get a smooth look to your stitching.
- Do not backstitch; pull the threads to the back and tie off the tails, burying them between the layers of fabric.
- Prepare a test swatch, layering fabric, interfacings, and lining the same as your project and do a trial run to see if your needle, thread, and stitch settings give you the results you want.
- For a unique look to your topstitching, use two contrasting colors of thread in a topstitching needle.

TOPSTITCHING

Stitching that shows on the right side of a garment or project, topstitching can be both decorative (such as on the

Edgestitching is a form of topstitching.

Use a seam guide or edge of the presser foot to sew straight topstitching; adjust the needle position for exact placement of stitching.

TUCKS

SINGLE NEEDLE TUCKS

Simple to make, single needle tucks are made by folding fabric on the grain (lengthwise or crosswise) and stitching next to it. These can be stitched on all but the thickest fabrics and are often seen on blouses, skirts, and children's clothing.

Mark the fold lines for the tucks, then fold and press the fabric; pin the tucks if needed. Stitch parallel to the folded edge using an edgestitch foot for narrow tucks. For wider tucks, use a seam guide attached to the foot or one attached to the bed of the machine. The width of the tuck depends on the fabric, the project, and the look you want. After stitching the tuck, press it to one side, away from the center of the project for vertical tucks and downward for horizontal tucks.

CROSS-TUCKS: Stitch a series of evenly-spaced vertical tucks following the directions above; press. Stitch evenly spaced cross tucks taking care to keep the vertical tucks flat.

TWISTED TUCKS: Stitch a series of evenly spaced vertical tucks; press. Stitch across the tucks with a straight or decorative stitch, sewing over the flat tucks. Sew a second line of stitching parallel to the first from the opposite direction, flipping the tucks. Continue stitching across the tucks, alternating directions. Tip: Use a seam guide attached to the presser foot to evenly space the lines of cross-stitching.

RELEASE TUCKS: These tucks are open at one or both ends and are used to control fullness or add shape to a garment, such as at a waist or neckline.

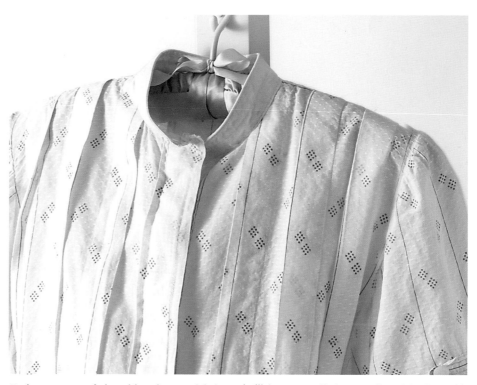

Tucks are one of the oldest known fabric embellishments, offering a tailored look to this vintage shirtwaist blouse (c. 1900). Private collection.

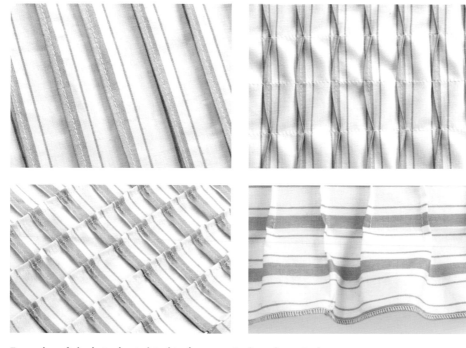

Examples of single tucks, twisted tucks, cross tucks, release tucks.

SINGLE NEEDLE TUCK TIPS

• Tucks can be stitched on the lengthwise or crosswise grainline; most fabrics will produce a slightly different look on each grain. Be sure to test each direction to see which is best for your project. For best results, spray starch the fabric before stitching the tucks.

• Vary the size of your tucks, depending on the fabric and the project. For instance, stitch narrow tucks close to the fold on fine batiste but go for wider, bolder tucks on linen suiting. Add "growth tucks" to children's clothing so the garment can grow with the child. Waistline, sleeve, and hem tucks can be unstitched to lengthen the garment as needed.

• For tucks that follow the grainline exactly, mark the first one by pulling a thread from the fabric (near the side edge). Fold on the drawn thread and use it as reference for the remaining tucks.

Bold patterns with simple shapes make great appliqué designs. Courtesy of Belinda Gibson.

FABRICS

Background fabric should be sturdy enough (may be interfaced) to support the appliqué shapes even after stabilizer is removed. The fabric for the shape can be almost anything from medium weight cotton to fake fur to lamé. Use tear-away stabilizer on the wrong side of the background fabric to keep the fabric from tunneling and puckering.

APPLIQUÉ SHAPES

Shapes should be simple, so it is possible to stitch around the edges. Intricate designs with multiple curves, corners, and contours are more difficult. Details can be added with decorative stitches, beading, and thread painting.

APPLYING SHAPES

Most methods of appliqué are easily stitched if you fuse the shapes to the background using paper-backed fusible web. Fuse the paper-backed web to the wrong side of a swatch of fabric selected for the shape, cut out the shape, peel the paper from the back and position the shape on the background fabric, and fuse. Note: This method requires that the shape be drawn in reverse on the back of the paper-backed web. This is especially important when working with letters or words.

FUSED APPLIQUÉ: SATIN, DECORATIVE, AND BLANKET STITCH

From the French, appliqué means "to apply." In sewing, it is a method of embellishment that involves cutting decorative shapes of coordinating fabrics and stitching them to a background fabric. Often used on children's clothing, appliqué is also seen on adult clothing, decorator pillows, and purses, among other projects. There are several types of appliqué, often named for the look of the edges of the finished shapes.

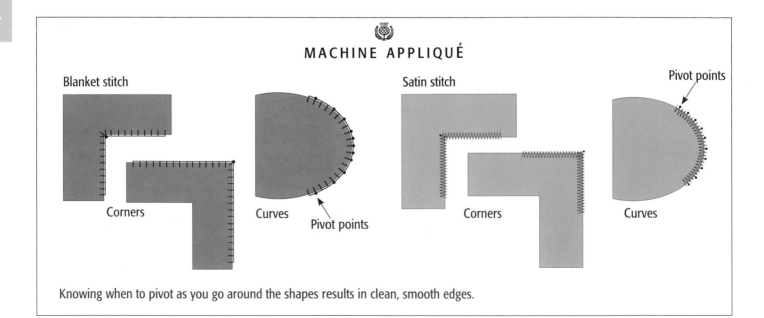

MACHINE APPLIQUÉ

Blanket stitch

Corners

Curves

Pivot points

Satin stitch

Pivot points

Corners

Curves

Knowing when to pivot as you go around the shapes results in clean, smooth edges.

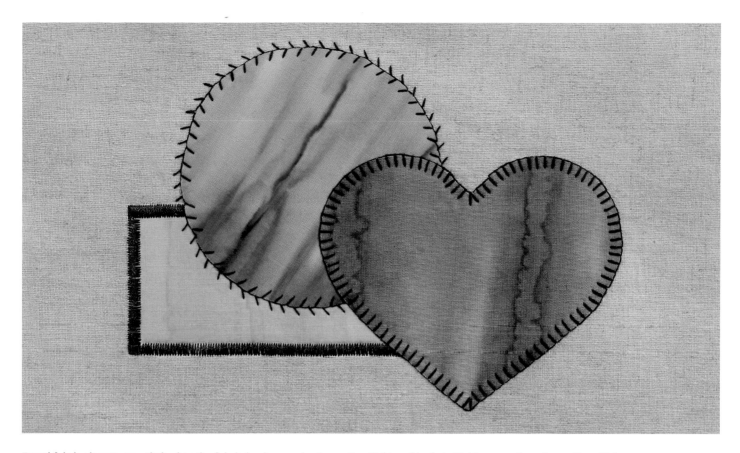

Fused fabric shapes are stitched to the fabric background using satin stitching, blanket stitching, or other decorative stitches.

PRESSER FOOT

Select a presser foot that works best for the type of stitching you plan to do. For example, satin stitching requires a presser foot that has an indentation on the sole to allow it to ride over heavy stitching, and open decorative stitching requires a foot that can easily move over the fabric as it goes back and forth to form the stitch. Visibility is important so look for a clear foot or one that is open in the center, so you can see exactly where the needle is stitching. Many sewing machine brands offer a foot designed for appliqué.

STITCHING

The stitch you select for the edge of your appliqué shape has a lot to do with the finished look you want. Blanket stitching in a contrasting thread (often black) has a primitive feel to it, reminiscent of hand-stitched samplers. Satin stitching has a bolder, heavier look and can blend with the fabric shapes, giving a strong, defined border or it can contrast, resulting in a look that resembles coloring book art. Other decorative stitches offer unlimited options from fun to whimsical to elegant, depending on the stitch you choose.

Stitch along the edge of the appliqué shape to secure it to the background. Learning to maneuver smoothly around various shapes such as rectangles, circles, and triangles is the key to becoming an expert at appliqué. Knowing when to pivot as you go around the shapes results in clean, smooth edges.

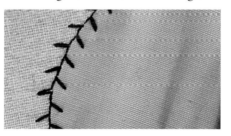

Side-to-side decorative stitches should be centered on the edge of the appliqué shapes.

Blanket stitching should be sewn just outside of the appliqué shape with the "fingers" of the stitch falling on the shape.

FUSED APPLIQUÉ TIPS

- Position the inner toe of the foot along the outer edge of the appliqué shape. Adjust the needle position, so it lands just outside the shape. If you guide the edge of the shape along the inner toe of the foot, your stitch will fall mainly on the appliqué shape.
- If the appliqué design is multi-layered, start with the pieces in the background first, stitching them in place before adding the next layer (stitch only the edges that will not be covered by another appliqué shape).
- To protect your iron and ironing surface from the fusible web, use a Teflon® pressing sheet when fusing.

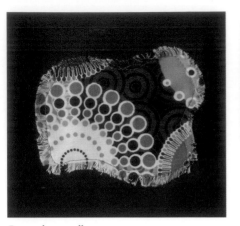

Raw edge applique

Invisible or hand-look applique

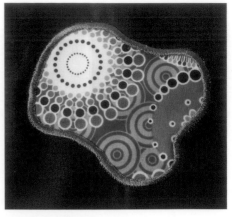

Reverse applique

NON-FUSED APPLIQUÉ: RAW EDGE, INVISIBLE, AND REVERSE

Raw edge, invisible, and reverse are additional types of appliqué but they are not fused to a background fabric. From the easy and casual raw-edge appliqué to the more involved invisible and reverse techniques, there is a way to appliqué for every situation.

FABRICS

Background fabric should be a sturdy medium to heavyweight fabric. Use tear-away stabilizer on the wrong side of the background fabric to keep the fabric from tunneling and puckering. After stitching is complete, remove the stabilizer. Note: It is sometimes easier to remove if you use two or more layers of lightweight stabilizer and remove them one layer at a time.

PRESSER FOOT

Select a presser foot that works best for the type of stitching you plan to do. For example, satin stitching requires a presser foot that has an indentation on the sole to allow it to ride over heavy stitching, and open decorative stitching requires a foot that can easily move over the fabric as it goes back and forth to form the stitch. Visibility is important, so look for a clear foot or one that is open in the center, so you can see exactly where the needle is stitching. Many sewing machine brands offer a foot designed for appliqué.

Experiment with a variety of threads including variegated and metallic to give a custom look to your appliqués.

144

NON-FUSED APPLIQUÉ TIPS

- To fray the edges of the raw-edge appliqué shapes, clip the edge about every ¼" and then brush the edge with a soft toothbrush.
- For trimming layers from reverse appliqué, try appliqué or duckbill scissors. Hold them flat as you cut, and they will protect the lower layer from accidentally being snipped.

RAW EDGE: Use light to medium weight fabric that ravels easily. Cut the shape as desired and stitch in place using a straight or open zigzag stitch placed ¼"–½" in from the edge. After stitching, fray the edges. Most fabrics will soften and fray more as they are laundered.

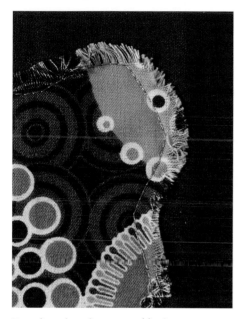

Fray the edges for a casual look.

INVISIBLE: Place the appliqué fabric right sides together with a lightweight stabilizer. If you do not want the stabilizer to remain in the finished project, choose a water-soluble "paper-type" of stabilizer that will dissolve as the item is washed. Trace the shape onto the fabric. Using a construction thread, stitch along the drawn line, overlapping the stitching to secure. Trim the excess fabric away along the outside of the stitching. Trim the seam allowances close to the stitching. Tip: Use pinking shears to trim, eliminating the need to clip and notch for a smooth turn. Make a slit in the stabilizer only and turn the shape to the right side; press and stitch to the background using the following instructions.

Thread the machine with monofilament thread and select a hand-look appliqué stitch or a blindstitch with a narrow width. Position the shape under the needle so the straight part of the stitch sews along the side of the shape and the wide part bites into the shape slightly.

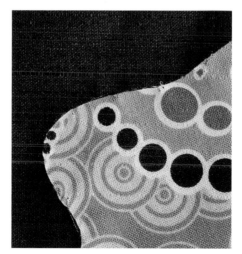

Using a blindstitch and monofilament thread gives a look similar to hand appliqué stitching.

REVERSE: Draw or trace the shape onto the background fabric. Layer the fabric for the shape right side up behind the background fabric (stabilizer goes behind the bottom layer of fabric); pin in place. Sew a straight stitch on all lines of the shape through all layers. Using sharp trimming scissors, trim the background fabric only from inside the shape next to the stitching, exposing the bottom fabric. Select a satin stitch or a decorative stitch of your choice and sew over the straight stitching, covering the raw edge of the shape.

Stitch the design through two layers of fabric.

Snip in the top layer of fabric only.

Trim the upper fabric from inside the design to show the lower fabric.

145

Beads can be added to fabric individually or by the strand using simple machine stitching.

146

BEADING

Add sparkle, color, and texture to any project by stitching strands or clusters of beads in selected areas. Couch down strands of beads or sew on single beads one at a time.

FABRIC

Any type of fabric can be beaded, but you should consider the weight of the bead and the fabric; tiny glass seed beads work well on sheer fabrics and heavier wooden beads are great for wool. Using smaller beads on heavy fabric is not a problem, but heavy beads will drag down a light fabric and spoil the line of the garment.

NEEDLE

For couching strands of beads, use the appropriate needle for the selected fabric. For attaching single beads, use a size 60 needle. Note: When sewing single beads, the needle must fit into the hole of the bead; smaller beads should be sewn on by hand.

THREAD

Use a lightweight thread (60-weight) that matches or blends with the fabric and/or beads you are attaching, or use a monofilament thread for the least visibility.

PRESSER FOOT

For applying strands of beads, you'll need a presser foot that has a groove or tunnel on the bottom of the sole, so it can ride smoothly over the beads. The strand of beads should fit into the groove. For attaching single beads, you will not use a presser foot, but will sew with a "bare needle."

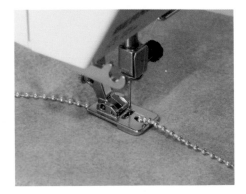

Couch strands of beads to fabric using a presser foot that feeds the beads smoothly.

COUCHING STRANDS OF BEADS

This is done in the same manner as couching a cord, using a foot that accommodates the beads. Your fabric should be interfaced and/or stabilized to support the beads. Select a zigzag, blind hem, or universal stitch. Adjust the stitch length to about the same as the bead size (2mm, 3mm, etc.); this will place the cross thread between the beads, making the stitching almost invisible. Straight and curved lines are easy to stitch with this technique but designs with tight curls and intricate areas cannot be beaded in this way. You can also attach a strand of beads to the finished edge of a project using this technique.

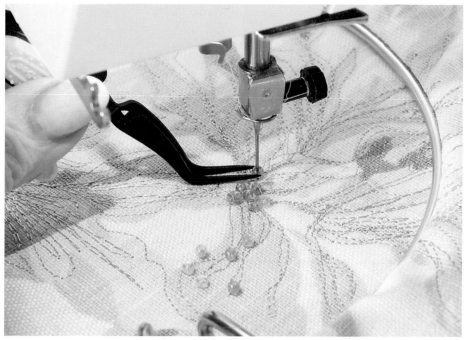

Hold each bead with tweezer as you take one stitch into the bead and then into the fabric beside the bead.

Accent finished edges by adding strands of beads as the final step.

Sew clusters of beads by attaching the beads individually using monofilament thread.

147

BEADING TIPS

- Reverse-action tweezers (squeezing opens the tweezers) are easier to manage and make your hand less tired.
- Pour a few beads into the hoop; the hoop will keep them handy, and it'll be easy to pick up the next one as you move through your beading project.

SINGLE BEADS

When sewing on single beads, the fabric should be hooped using a wooden embroidery hoop or a spring hoop. The feed dog is down and the needle is bare (no presser foot). Pull the bobbin thread up to the surface, take a few small tie-off stitches, and clip the thread tails. Using long tweezers, hold a bead with the hole facing up. Place the tip of the needle into the hole by turning the handwheel of the machine. Lower the needle into the fabric through the hole, and then raise it. Note: Some machines will take ½ stitch (lower or raise the needle) by pushing a button or by tapping the foot control. Take a tiny stitch next to the bead; the bead will roll to its side, showing its beauty rather than the hole. Travel (stitch) to the next bead location; continue this method until the final bead is attached, and then take a few stitches to tie-off.

Stitch free-motion designs with novelty yarn on the bobbin.

Sew decorative stitches upside down with heavy threads on the bobbin.

BOBBINWORK TIPS

- If your machine is equipped with a separate bobbin case, consider purchasing an extra one for bobbinwork. That saves you from the frustration of readjusting it for regular sewing.
- If you have a pattern or design to follow, draw it on stabilizer and adhere it to the wrong side of the fabric with temporary spray adhesive. When sewing upside down, the drawn pattern will be on top and easy to follow.
- Hold your bobbin case over a bowl when loosening the tiny screw. If it drops out, it can be hard to find.

BOBBINWORK

Bobbinwork is a type of stitching where the thread from the bobbin is displayed on the right side of the fabric and the needle thread is on the wrong side. Because this is a decorative technique, the thread used on the bobbin is a heavy decorative thread, narrow ribbon, or small yarn; a regular sewing weight thread is used on the needle. The bobbin tension must be loosened to allow stitches to form and the project is worked from the wrong side. This technique is used in crazypatch, silk ribbon embroidery, or as a stand-alone type of embroidery.

BOBBIN SYSTEM

If your machine has a separate bobbin case, it is easy to adjust the tension by turning the screw. Make very small adjustments, stitching a sample until you get the look you desire. If your bobbin is a drop-in bobbin, consult your manual or check with your sewing machine store for adjustment specifics.

DECORATIVE CORDS

Heavy decorative thread, perle cotton, narrow ribbon, and small yarn are all good choices for this technique. The selected cord has to fit into the bobbin case and move through it easily when the tension is loosened.

WINDING THE BOBBIN

The bobbin can be wound using the machine, winding at a slow speed (if possible) to avoid stretching the decorative thread/cord. It can also be wound by hand, which goes quickly because of the size of the decorative thread/cord.

FABRIC

Almost any type of fabric can be used for bobbinwork but it must be adequately interfaced and/or stabilized to support the heavy stitches. The fabric may also be hooped to make it stable enough for stitching.

STITCHES

Select machine-fed decorative stitches or free-motion designs for this technique. When using decorative stitches, adjust the length and width settings until you have the desired look. Experiment with your stitches to select what is needed for your project. To start stitching, use the handwheel of your machine to take one stitch, pulling the bobbin thread to the surface; you may need to "tug" on the needle thread to bring the heavy bobbin thread through the fabric.

PRESSER FOOT

For decorative stitching, select a presser foot that is designed for appliqué or embroidery. It should have a wide and/or deep indentation on the bottom of the sole to allow the decorative threads/cords to feed smoothly.

SEWING UPSIDE DOWN

Don't forget to flip your project and sew from the wrong side. Stop occasionally to check the right side of the fabric to see if the results are satisfactory.

Add texture to fabric by stitching closely-spaced double needle tucks across the surface.

DOUBLE NEEDLE TUCKS

Also called pintucks, double needle tucks are usually corded and can be stitched in several sizes. This type of tuck requires a special pintuck foot that has a series of grooves on the bottom of the sole. The groove indicates the finished size of the pintuck and the double needle should correspond with the size of the groove.

Insert a double needle into your machine and thread the machine with two spools of thread (see page 131). Use a narrow cord such as perle cotton, placing it under the fabric so that the needles straddle it. Some machines have a hole or a guide to feed the cord under the needles (see your manual).

Stitch the first tuck in the desired position (mark the fabric if needed). Stitch parallel tucks by placing the stitched tuck in a groove next to the needle; this places the tucks next to each other with no space between them. To add space between pintucks, position the first pintuck in an outside groove, use the side of the foot or an attached seam guide.

Check the double needle tucks' spacing and the groove spacing on the sole of the presser foot.

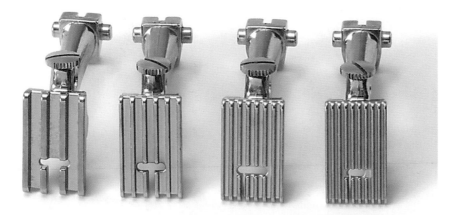

The size of the groove on the sole of the presser foot determines the size of the finished pintuck.

PINTUCK TIPS

- If stitching tucks down the front of a blouse or across the body of a skirt, stitch them on flat fabric before cutting out the pattern pieces.
- To make the tucks more prominent, tighten the needle tension slightly.
- To turn corners while sewing a pintuck, stitch to the corner and stop with the needle points just above the surface of the fabric. Lift the foot and pivot 45°. Take one stitch, lift the foot, and pivot 45° again, which should align the needle with the next side; continue sewing.

149

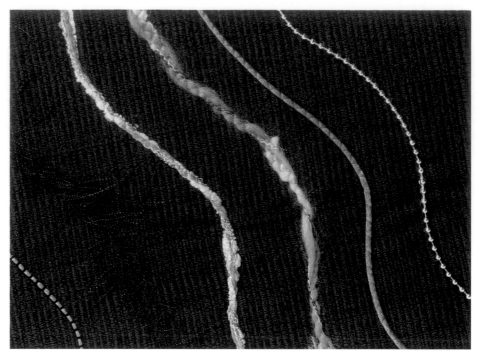

Couch yarns, cords, and beads to fabric to add color and texture.

COUCHING

Couching, a term borrowed from hand embroidery, means "to stitch a cord to the surface." It is used to add color and texture to fabric and can also be used to define an edge such as the outer edge of an appliqué shape. When couching with the sewing machine, the end result can be extremely varied depending on the stitch, the cord, and the thread you use. Each combination alters the look and offers a new feel to your project.

STITCH

Almost any side-to-side stitch will work for couching. An open stitch lets the cord show through while a heavy one covers it, simply adding texture to the fabric. Using a blind stitch is the most inconspicuous way of attaching the cord to the fabric. A straight stitch will work in some cases but the presser foot needs to be designed to hold the cord in the right spot so that the stitch will penetrate it.

CORD

Soft yarns will be flattened by the stitches, which may be fine depending on the look you want; heavier cords will be more prominent. Several yarns, cords, and/or decorative threads can be twisted together for a blended or spiral look. Whatever you choose, it must fit through the presser foot you have selected to use. Yarns and threads that have slubs, causing thick and thin areas, will work for couching, but you need to make sure they feed through the foot easily.

THREAD

Almost any type of machine sewing thread can be used but the color will make quite a difference in the finished look. A color that matches the fabric (with a cord that contrasts) makes the cord look woven into the background; matching the colors of the fabric, cord, and thread gives a textured look to the fabric; using a cord and thread of the same color will make the cord more prominent; using monofilament or "invisible" thread (usually with a blind stitch) makes the cord appear to be floating on the surface of the fabric.

FABRIC

Most medium to heavyweight fabrics are suited for couching but must be adequately interfaced and/or stabilized to support the added cords and stitches.

PRESSER FOOT

Machine couching is almost impossible to do without a foot designed to hold the cord in place for stitching. Check with your sewing machine store to see what is available for your machine—some brands have several options. A couching foot usually has a hole or groove in the top of the sole that you feed the cord through, going under the sole and out the back. The foot may hold one or several cords, depending on its design.

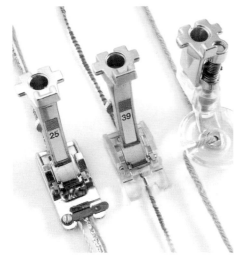

Many sewing machines have a variety of presser feet made for couching.

Free motion couching allows you to stitch cord in any pattern or direction you choose.

Twist multiple strands of cord or yarn together for a multi-colored effect.

151

COUCHING TIPS

- If you are having trouble threading the cord though the hole in the foot, use a serger looper threader or a dental floss threader (found at your local drugstore) to make it easier.
- Play with different thread, stitch, and cord combinations; stitch a sampler of ideas until you find what's best.
- If using a yarn, cord, or heavy decorative thread from a spool or skein, lay it in your lap as you sew, making sure you stop and unwind a length from time to time as you stitch to keep it feeding evenly.
- Create custom cord using the serger by stitching without fabric, creating a thread chain. Wrap the chain around a card for storage and use as you would any other cord when couching.

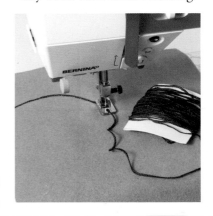

Crazypatch piecing with embellishment is an old form of creative expression dating back to the Victorian era.

CRAZY PATCH

A form of piecing that starts with a foundation fabric and small scraps of fabric, crazy patch is heavily embellished with decorative stitching, beading, and embroidery. This technique was highly popular as a hand technique during the Victorian era and is sometimes called crazy quilting even though it is traditionally worked without batting. This richly stitched embellishment can be used on almost any type of project.

FABRIC

The foundation should be a light to medium weight, firmly woven fabric such as muslin or broadcloth. The patches for the surface can be just about anything but are usually rich fabrics such as moiré, taffeta, velvet, velveteen, etc. No scrap is too small, so you can start a crazy patch basket to collect any and all pieces that you want to incorporate.

THREAD

Use regular construction thread for piecing and decorative threads, such as rayon or polyester embroidery thread, for decorative stitching and embellishment. Heavier decorative threads also work well for bobbinwork embellishment.

PRESSER FEET

Use an all-purpose foot for the piecing process. When the embellishment process begins, use a foot appropriate to the technique you have selected (decorative stitching, couching, bobbinwork, etc.).

STABILIZER

Stabilizer may or may not be needed, depending on the sturdiness of your foundation fabric. If needed, use a tear-away stabilizer and remove it after the piecing is complete. If it is also needed for the embellishment phase of this technique, place fresh tear-away behind the pieced fabric for each embellishment; remove it before moving on to another embellishment. Embellishing multiple seamlines before removing the stabilizer will make it almost impossible to remove.

PIECING

The goal of crazy patch piecing is to create a random, "patched-together" look, but it actually follows a plan and a process. Start with a five-sided scrap of fabric, placed near the center of the foundation fabric; pin in place. Position a second piece of fabric face down along one edge of the first swatch; stitch. Flip the second swatch to the right side and press, trimming the seam allowance to about ¼" if needed. Place a third swatch face down on another edge, then sew and flip. Continue this process, moving around the original piece and building out until the entire foundation is covered.

EMBELLISHMENTS

Embellish the seams of the pieced fabric using decorative stitches or bobbinwork (for more pronounced stitching). Machine embroidered designs can be added as part of the embellishment along with couching, beading, and adding 3-D items such as buttons, trinkets, and charms.

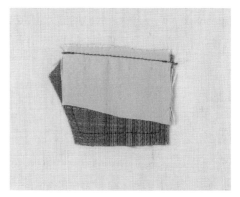

Add irregular shaped patches in a "stitch and flip" method to cover the foundation fabric.

DECORATIVE STITCHING

All sewing machines today come equipped with at least a handful of decorative stitches, although most have a wide selection at your disposal. These stitches can often be manipulated to expand their uses, making the creative possibilities almost limitless. Decorative stitches can be used in many ways on almost any type of project.

FABRIC

Decorative stitches can be added to almost any type of fabric as long as it is adequately interfaced and/or stabilized to support the stitching.

THREAD

Look for threads that will add to the beauty of the stitching—polyester, embroidery, and rayon threads offer a high sheen for a beautiful look. The polyester is a stronger thread that is colorfast, so if you plan to launder your project, it's a good choice. Metallic thread adds sparkle; multi-colored and variegated threads can add interest and depth to the stitching with no extra effort on your part. Use a heavier thread (30-weight) for a stronger look and a lighter one (50-weight) for a more delicate look. More and more machines offer wide decorative stitch options (7mm–9mm), so play with your choices and decide what works best for your project.

PRESSER FEET

Use the presser foot recommened in your manual for the stitch you have selected. Heavier stitches need a foot that has an indentation on the bottom of the sole for easy feeding. Clear or open feet offer better visibility when trying to align rows or match patterns.

PATTERNS

Decorative stitches can be used in rows, as borders or edgings for collars, cuffs, hems, tablecloths, pillows, etc., but you can also manipulate and/or combine the stitches in a variety of ways to provide embellishment for almost any project. Try these methods with the decorative stitches on your sewing machine.

STITCH LINES: Sew rows of decorative stitching next to one another, using functions such as mirror image and elongation, if desired. Sew lines of selected stitches to create all-over patterns, borders, and focal points for your project. Use the side of the presser foot or an attached guide for spacing the rows. Use multiple colors of thread for added interest or variegated thread to add depth without the bother of changing threads. Add buttons, charms, or trinkets as desired to enhance the stitching.

COMBINED STITCHES: If your sewing machine is equipped with a memory function, select several decorative stitches and program them into memory. The machine will see the combination as one pattern that you can repeat over and over again if you want. The memory also gives you the capability of programming letters (if your machine has preprogrammed alphabets) for monogramming or for writing words.

ROTATING STITCHES: A fun way to manipulate decorative stitches is to stitch one pattern, stopping with the needle in the fabric; rotate or pivot 90°, then stitch the second half of the pattern. Continue stitching and rotating as desired.

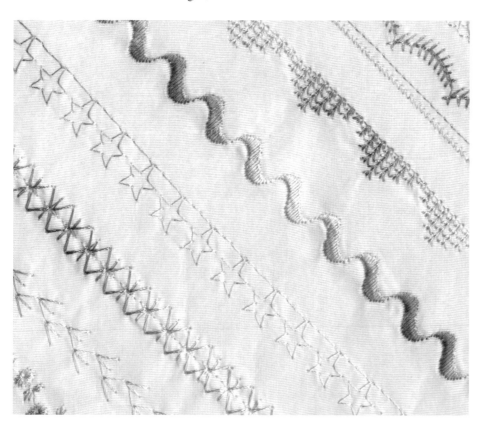

Decorative stitching can add interest and "flavor" to any type of project.

DECORATIVE STITCHING TIP

- If using tear-away stabilizer for added support, it may be easier to remove if you use two or more layers of light-weight rather than one layer of medium or heavyweight.
- If stitching parallel lines, use a seam guide that attaches to the presser foot for straight guiding.

Felted fibers add color and design to fabric.

NEEDLE PUNCH

Machine needle punch, sometimes called felting, is similar to hand felting where loose fibers are pushed or punched with sharp, barbed needles through a base fabric to add color and create designs. It requires a special machine or attachment, so check with your sewing machine store to see if one is available for your machine. All types of projects from pillows to purses, and jackets to rugs can be embellished with needle punching.

BACKGROUND FABRIC

Often worked on wool, other sturdy fabrics such as denim or felt also make good backgrounds for needle-punched designs. Lighter fabrics such as silk noil may be used if care is taken not to "over-punch" them.

FIBERS

A wide variety of fibers can be punched into the fabric including the most commonly used wool roving (wool that has been carded and combed, ready to be spun); silk and cotton are also available as roving. Yarn works well for punching, although some yarns have netting that needs to be removed before you can pull the fibers apart. Fabric, such as silk, cut into small "confetti-like" pieces, can also be used.

DESIGNS

Fibers can be punched in a free-form design to add color and texture or may be worked into specific shapes such as flowers, hearts, or geometric designs. You can mark the design on the fabric using chalk or fabric marker or create it as you punch.

PUNCHING

This technique is the easiest type of free-motion stitching you will ever do because you are not using thread; there is no bobbin and the needles have no eyes. Note: The barbed needles are very sharp, and you should never punch without the presser foot/needle guard on the machine. After you have loosely placed the fibers on the fabric, quickly move the fabric and punch over the entire surface to "baste" the fibers to the background. Next, go back and work each area from the front, then turn over and punch from the back. Finish the punching process with one more pass on the right side of the fabric. Add layers of fiber as needed and continue the punching process until the desired finished look is achieved.

Needle punching is a free-motion technique that anyone can do.

EXTRA EMBELLISHMENTS

Combine needle punching with other techniques such as free-motion quilting, beading, and couching. An easy way to create a punched design is to stitch a digitized outline design on the embroidery machine and then fill in the areas with needle punched fibers. You can also punch soft backgrounds on which you can sew decorative stitches or machine embroidery designs.

NEEDLE PUNCH TIPS

- Use a stiletto or a chopstick to hold fibers down as you punch.
- Start with light wisps of roving, building color and detail the same as an artist uses layers of paint.
- Use a multi-colored or variegated yarn to add depth and dimension to the felted fabric.

Wool fabrics and fibers are traditional felting materials.

QUILTING

One of the oldest fabric embellishment techniques, quilting is also one of the easiest. Stitching through layers of fabric and batting adds texture and dimension to almost any type of project. There are several options when quilting; some make use of straight lines using the machine to feed the fabric, and others are stitched in any direction while you control the path of the needle.

FABRIC

Quilting fabric is usually 100% cotton and comes in a multitude of colors and prints. In most cases, several colors and/or prints are cut into shapes and pieced together to form a patchwork pattern, although whole cloth quilting uses a single fabric that has batting and a backing behind it.

BATTING

Needle punched cotton batting is easy to handle and easy to sew through. Polyester battings usually have more loft or puffiness but may be harder to manage.

NEEDLE AND THREAD

Almost any type of thread can be used but a common choice is a quilting needle and 100% cotton thread, 40- or 50-weight. Use monofilament thread when you want emphasis on the design rather than the stitches.

PRESSER FEET

The presser foot used for quilting depends on the type of quilting you've selected. The best presser foot to use for machine-fed quilting is a walking foot or even-feed foot. This type of foot will feed the multiple layers of the quilt as one without shifting. An all-purpose foot may work for small quilting projects such as purses or placemats but a walking foot is recommended for a quilt.

If you choose to use free-motion stitching on your quilt, you'll need to select a foot that works without the feed dog of your machine. Some brands have several from which to

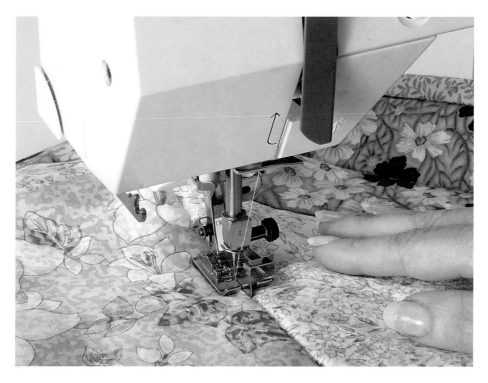

Stitching-in-the-ditch is a simple technique that follows the seamlines of the project.

choose including open and/or clear styles, which are good for following marked designs. Some machines are also equipped with stitch regulators, which allow you to move where you want but still have even, consistent stitches. Remember, with free-motion stitching you control the movement of the fabric and the length of the stitch, so if you are new to this technique, you'll avoid hours of practice by using a stitch regulator.

PATTERNS/DESIGNS

Quilting designs can be hand-drawn, preprinted on tracing paper, or taken from stencils. They can also be created as you stitch with more of a free-form or random technique.

PREPARATION

Prepare a "sandwich" of backing, batting, and top by stacking and basting the layers together using safety pins or temporary spray adhesive. Place the batting in the middle and the fabrics right sides out and smooth from the center out to the edges. If using a pattern, mark it on the quilt using your favorite method. Quilt the layers using any or all of the following quilting methods.

MACHINE-FED QUILTING

STITCH-IN-THE-DITCH: This method requires no marking as it follows the seams of the pieced quilt top. Using a foot that is open in the front with a center needle position, sew in the "ditch" that is formed when two pieces of fabric are seamed together. Quilts are often stitched with this technique to invisibly hold the layers together, and then other more decorative techniques are used to complete the quilting.

CHANNEL: Straight parallel lines forming channels are simple to stitch. Mark the first line in the desired position and decide on the spacing you want. The easiest way to stitch parallel lines is to use a guide that attaches to the presser foot; most sewing machines have some version of this. Position the guide the desired distance from the needle. After stitching the first marked line, sew the second line with the guide following the stitched line. Continue sewing rows, positioning the guide to follow the previously stitched row. If a guide is not available, use the edge of the presser foot as a guide or mark each line for consistent spacing and straight sewing. A variation of channel quilting uses randomly curved lines that are not evenly spaced. This creates interesting texture and pattern across the surface of the fabric.

GRID: Create a stitched grid by first sewing channels on the fabric using the instructions above. Complete the grid by sewing a second set of channels across the first at a 90° angle. Grids can be stitched on the lengthwise and crosswise grain, creating squares, or on the bias grain, creating diamonds.

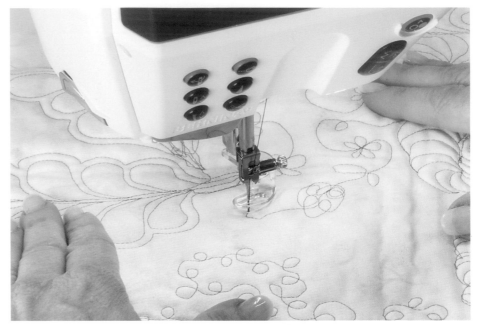

Free-motion stitching offers the freedom of stitching any design or pattern because you can move the fabric in any direction.

Grid quilting can be stitched in straight lines or on the diagonal.

FREE-MOTION QUILTING

STARTING AND ENDING TECHNIQUE: As you start your quilting, use the handwheel of your machine to pull the bobbin thread up to the surface of your work. Take several tiny stitches to secure your stitching, and do the same to end the stitching once you have completed your chosen design.

As a beginner, it will take practice to gain control of moving the fabric. The shape you stitch is not important, but if you have a specific shape in mind, you'll know when you have gained the control you need to execute it.

CONTINUOUS LINE: As the name implies, this style of quilting uses designs sewn without stopping and starting multiple times. This is not only quicker, it eliminates the need to tie-off threads and gives a smoother look to your quilting stitches. Sew these designs with the feed dog disengaged (covered or lowered, depending on your machine) and with you moving the fabric. Similar to learning to write

---

QUILTING TIPS

- Always start with a new quilting needle, specially designed to go through multiple layers of fabric and batting.
- If quilting a large project such as a bed quilt, place tables behind and to the left of your sewing machine to support the weight of the quilt, avoiding distorted stitches.
- When stitching, do not watch the needle, or you'll lose track of your design. Pay attention to where you are going and you'll stay on track.

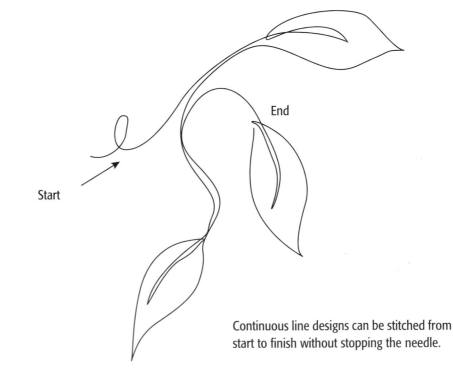

Continuous line designs can be stitched from start to finish without stopping the needle.

or draw, this technique requires some study but is easily mastered with a little practice.

STIPPLING: A type of "fill" stitch, this technique is also sewn with the feed dog disengaged and is used to fill large areas, adding texture and interest to the surface of the quilt. The closely spaced (about ¼" apart), randomly placed stipple stitches are like little "puzzle pieces" that have rounded edges and don't cross each other. Often used to quilt around a pieced or stitched item, such as an appliqué or embroidery design, this stitching flattens the background, making the decorative item stand out. Micro stippling is a tiny version of this technique with the stitches placed about ⅛" apart.

Stipple quilting is a fill stitch that adds texture.

FREE-MOTION STITCHING TIPS

- Use pen and paper to practice your "stitching." It helps to get the feel of the design and keep you on track when using needle and thread.
- Make a quilt sandwich and practice various shapes and designs as shown. Aim for a rounded, fluid look to your shapes.
- Try writing your name. You already know how to do this using pencil and paper so you are already on your way to learning to "write" on fabric using the needle as your pencil.
- For the best results, run your machine motor at a fast speed and move your fabric at a moderate pace.

RIBBONWORK

Ribbons add color, shape, and texture to fabric projects. Use them flat to form patterns such as stripes and plaids or stitch ribbons edge-to-edge and use as a piece of fabric.

RIBBON

For flat ribbonwork and creating yardage, use almost any type of fabric ribbon. Match the care of the ribbon to the other materials in the project (machine washable, dry cleanable, etc.). Silk ribbons in 4mm–7mm widths are used for the elements of silk ribbon embroidery.

FABRIC

Almost any type of fabric, even sheers, can be used for ribbonwork, but it must be adequately interfaced and/or stabilized to support the stitching. When working with sheer fabric, select a type of stabilizer that can be removed after the ribbon is applied.

THREAD

Almost any type of machine sewing thread (polyester, rayon, cotton, etc.) can be used. When edgestitching ribbon in place, the stitching will show but can be minimized, if desired, by matching the colors or using monofilament thread.

STITCHING

When sewing ribbon in place, it is best to edgestitch along each side. Using an edgestitch foot makes this easy and also helps to ensure that the stitching

Use ribbons to create plaids, stripes, and patterns on a base fabric.

is parallel to the edge. An alternative method is to use a twin or double needle to sew both edges at once. The width of the ribbon should be slightly wider (no more than ⅛") than the distance between the two needles.

CREATING RIBBON FABRIC

Place two pieces of ribbon edge-to-edge. Using monofilament thread and a side-to-side stitch such as a zigzag or featherstitch, sew the ribbons together. Continue adding ribbons until the "fabric" is the desired size.

Stitch ribbons side by side to create "fabric."

RIBBONWORK TIPS

- Use a fabric gluestick to hold narrow ribbon in place on the fabric for stitching.
- Create a border and finish both sides of a straight edge by folding ¼" to the right side, placing ½" wide ribbon even with the fold and edge-stitching in place — great for table toppers and jacket openings.

Silk ribbon embroidery can be a combination of techniques as shown above. Bobbinwork was used for the vine and surface techniques for the flowers and buds.

SILK RIBBON EMBROIDERY

Silk ribbon embroidery by machine is a technique that bears a striking resemblance to hand-worked silk ribbon embroidery. There are two methods, one a form of bobbinwork (see page 148) and the other, employing couching techniques. The method described here is the surface technique where the ribbon is formed into shapes and tacked to the fabric. A great embellishment for garments such as blouses and jackets, this technique also looks good on home dec projects.

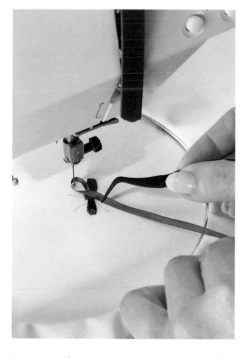

Reverse-action tweezers make shaping ribbon into flowers and leaves easy to manage.

FABRIC

Most light to medium weight fabrics can be used for silk ribbon embroidery as long as the fabric is stabilized properly to support the weight of the embroidery. Place water-soluble stabilizer behind the fabric with a second layer on top of the fabric. Hoop all layers in a wooden machine embroidery hoop or a plastic and metal spring hoop. Draw the design on the top piece of stabilizer.

THREAD

For an inconspicuous look, use clear monofilament thread in the needle and bobbin. Matching the color of thread to the silk ribbon will also work but will have you re-threading often.

RIBBON

Silk ribbon comes in different sizes. The most common for machine worked silk ribbon embroidery are 2mm, 4mm, and 7mm. Using a variety of widths makes the design interesting, with the wider widths creating fuller designs and the narrow ones offering a more delicate look.

STITCHING

Lower or cover the feed dog and select straight stitch. Pull the bobbin thread up to the top of the fabric; take a few tiny stitches to anchor the thread. Use the following directions to create flowers, leaves, and buds.

ROSES: Draw a spiral on the fabric where you want to place the rose. Tack the end of the ribbon at the center of the spiral. Shape the ribbon around the spiral, tacking the ribbon in two more places, forming a soft, rounded triangle. Continue in this manner, building the rose to the desired size. Tack the end of the ribbon under a portion of the rose and clip the excess.

DAISY: Draw four intersecting lines to form spokes. Tack the end of the ribbon in the center and stitch to the end of one spoke. Swing the ribbon to the needle and tack, leaving a little slack in the ribbon. Stitch back down to the center; swing the ribbon back to the center and tack. Repeat this process until all of the spokes are covered.

LEAVES/BUDS: Mark the desired length of the leaf. Using green ribbon, stitch a leaf by tacking the end of the ribbon at the bottom of the mark, stitch to the top of the mark. Swing the ribbon to the needle and tack, leaving a little slack in the ribbon. Stitch back down to the bottom; swing the ribbon back to the needle and tack in place. Clip the ribbon, leaving about a 4" tail. Using a large eye needle, feed the ribbon to the wrong side, tie-off, and clip the excess.

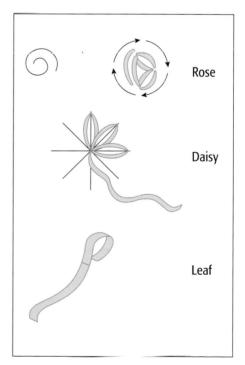

Rose

Daisy

Leaf

Use black embroidery thread to add depth and dimension to fused motifs.

THREAD SKETCHING

Thread sketching is exactly what the words imply—using threads to "sketch" a design or picture on fabric. Draw lines of stitching using your sewing machine to create a picture or design. This is a free-motion technique, so you move the fabric, using the needle to draw and fill in the parts of the design.

FABRIC

Almost any fabric can be used for thread sketching but it must be adequately interfaced and/or stabilized to support the added stitching. The fabric is also stabilized by placing it in a machine embroidery hoop (with or without stabilizer as needed). The hoop is useful as a way to handle the fabric as you move it to create your design.

NEEDLE AND THREAD

Look for decorative threads such as rayon and polyester embroidery thread. Use 40-weight for most designs but 30-weight can be used for bolder designs and 60-weight for more delicate sketches. Use an embroidery needle in the size suited to your fabric. The color of the thread can blend with the fabric for a subtle look or use a contrasting color for a striking look.

PRESSER FOOT

This is a free-motion technique, so you will need a foot designed to work with the feed dog disengaged. Some brands have several types including one open in the front. This offers more visibility for following a design. If your machine does not offer a free motion foot, you can use a spring needle, which helps to keep the fabric from "flagging" (traveling up the needle) as you sew.

DESIGNS

Trace or draw the design onto the right side of the fabric using a fabric marker.

STITCHING

Set the machine for a straight stitch. The feed dog of the machine should be lowered or covered. Using the handwheel, pull up the bobbin thread to the top of the work. Take a few tiny stitches to secure the thread and then clip the tails. Holding the hoop on each side, move the fabric back and forth and from side to side to trace over the drawn design as desired. Move the hoop smoothly and consistently and do not rotate the hoop as you stitch. Change thread colors as needed, stitching one color over another as desired for a shaded or blended effect. When the sketch is finished, take a few tiny stitches to secure the thread and then clip the tails. Remove the work from the hoop and remove the stabilizer if desired.

WING NEEDLEWORK

In most cases we try to avoid putting holes in fabric but in the case of wing needlework, the objective is make decorative patterns full of embroidered holes. The needle has flattened "wings" on each side that makes a hole as it penetrates the fabric. Combined with a certain type of decorative stitch, you end up with embroidered holes that can be a single line of simple embellishment or an overall pattern of texture.

FABRIC

Natural fiber fabrics such as linen and cotton work best for this type of stitching. Synthetics tend to "bounce back" and fill the hole once the needle comes out of it; natural fibers will stay out of the way, leaving a decorative hole in the fabric.

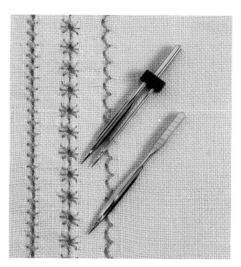

Create decorative holes in natural fabric using wing needles.

THREAD

Use a lightweight cotton thread (60-weight) in the same color as the fabric. Wing needlework falls into the heirloom sewing category and is often worked in white.

STITCH

Look for a multi-motion stitch that goes into the same hole multiple times. This will make the hole more pronounced and will embroider the edges more heavily. Some machines have stitches specifically made to work with wing needles so check your machine manual for specifics.

TECHNIQUE

Insert the wing needle into the machine and thread as usual. Select an appropriate stitch and sew a line of wing needle stitching. Continue stitching to cover as much area as desired.

Finish hems on table toppers, runners, and placemats using wing needle stitching.

WING NEEDLEWORK TIPS

- Press the fabric using spray starch before stitching for added body and better control of the stitching.
- Sew closely spaced rows of wing needle stitching across a swatch of linen and use it to cut a shape to appliqué onto a background fabric.

specialty sewing

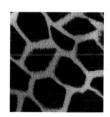 MOST PEOPLE WHO SEW USE GENERAL sewing techniques that work for a wide array of projects, but there are some particular types of sewing that often include specific tasks and special techniques. With all of the fabrics and materials available, you're sure to come across challenges now and then on your sewing adventure. This chapter addresses several types of atypical fabrics and materials, offering ideas and suggestions for working with them.

When you try an unusual new fabric or material, you ask the same questions as for any fabric, but the answers may be more specialized. The questions are:

1. Is there a special needle needed to penetrate or protect the surface?
2. What type of thread is best for this fabric?
3. What stitches work best?
4. What is the best method of seaming for this fabric?
5. Are there any special tools or notions that will make working with this fabric easier?

These questions come from problems that arise when using common sewing methods with uncommon fabrics and materials. If you don't find the answers in this chapter, try your local sewing store or experiment on your own to develop solutions to sewing with specialty fabrics.

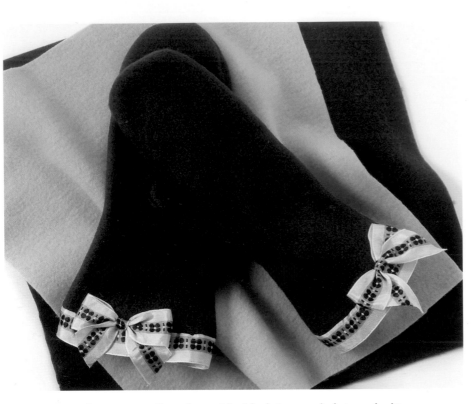

Toasty warm and easy to sew, fleece is great for blankets, caps, jackets, and mittens.

FLEECE

A fun fabric, fleece has some properties that make it perfect for beginning sewers. It doesn't wrinkle or ravel, and it can be used for a variety of projects including outerwear, hats, pillows, and bags. You don't have to interface or line it and, in most cases, added details such as collars and pockets are made with one layer of fabric, so they are faster and easier to finish.

Made of polyester or acrylic, most fleece fabrics do not shrink, but, if using a brand you haven't tried before, you may want to wash and dry it before cutting. Look for patterns that have simple lines with a minimum of detail. Many pattern companies have patterns specifically designed for fleece fabric.

TIPS AND TECHNIQUES

1. It's sometimes difficult to tell the difference between the right and wrong sides. To determine the right side, pull the selvage edge, and it will roll to the right side. It's a good idea to mark one side with chalk, so you can keep it straight.

2. Because of the pile of the fabric, always use the "with nap" layout,

Tip 1

placing the pattern pieces in the same direction to avoid getting different shades in your finished garment.

3. Pins tend to get lost in the "lushness" of fleece, so use long ones that have a prominent head such as flower-head pins.

4. Use a longer stitch length (about 3mm–4mm) when sewing with a straight stitch. A narrow zig-

Tip 3

zag (length and width of 1mm) gives a bit of stretch to the seam and a serged seam (3-thread overlock) is even more flexible.

5. Start with a new universal needle (size 80/12 or 90/14). Usually this will be fine, but if you are having trouble with skipped stitches, change to a ballpoint needle.

6. A strong polyester thread in a matching or blending color is the best choice for sewing fleece.

7. An all-purpose presser foot will usually work for sewing fleece, but if you are experiencing trouble with feeding the fabric, switch to a walking foot and/or lessen the foot pressure.

8. One area that requires a little care is the pressing of fleece. It will melt if high heat is applied, and, in most cases, it is best not to press it at all. Finger-press seams and top-stitch the seam allowances in place if curling is a problem. If you must press, use a press cloth and a dry iron.

9. If adding closures such as zippers or buttons, bond fusible interfacing to the wrong side of the area to add stability. For buttons and snaps, put a patch of the fleece over the interfacing and attach the closures through all layers.

10. Since fleece doesn't ravel, you don't have to finish the seam allowance. However, if you want a more finished look, an easy way to finish the edges without adding bulk is to bind the edges with tricot knit. Cut a strip about 1" wide; gently pull on the tricot, causing it to curl. Position it over the edge and secure with a narrow zigzag (stitch width and length, 2mm).

Tip 10

Once you know a few simple techniques, sewing fur and fake fur is easy with spectacular results.

FUR AND FAKE FUR

Sewing fur and fake fur is not difficult, but it requires a few special techniques and can be more time consuming than working with fabric. Part of the challenge of working with fur is its density. Even though they use the same techniques, longer pile fur is trickier than shorthair types. Look for fur coats at your local thrift stores, so you can practice fur-sewing techniques without cutting into your fur "fabric."

TIPS AND TECHNIQUES

1. Use a napped layout so all of your pattern pieces are facing the same direction. Place the fur right side down in a single layer and cut the pattern pieces out from the back.

2. Trace each pattern piece onto the backing. If the pattern piece has a fold line, flip it over and trace the entire pattern piece.

3. Cut along the drawn lines through the backing only using a craft knife or very sharp scissor tips.

4. Thread the machine with a strong polyester thread in both the needle and bobbin.

5. Use an 80–100 universal needle, depending on the weight of the backing and the density of the fur.

6. The best presser foot choice for sewing fur is a walking foot. It will help feed the bulk under the needle.

7. Sew fur and fake fur using a straight or a narrow zigzag stitch.

8. Turn the project to the right side and pull fur from the seams using a straight pin. A comb can also be useful; the fur should hide the seamline.

9. From the wrong side, trim the fur from the seam allowances using sharp scissors.

10. Clean your machine frequently as you sew with fur. Keep your vacuum cleaner handy, as the fur will cover almost every surface in your sewing area.

Tip 8

Tip 9

Tip 5

Similar techniques are used to successfully sew leather and suede.

LEATHER AND SUEDE

The natural look of leather and suede is perfect for a variety of projects that range from rustic and western to smooth and sophisticated. Sewing leather and suede requires a few special tools and some of the techniques are different than when working with fabric. Almost any type of project can be made from leather; clothing, pillows, and purses are just a few examples.

TIPS AND TECHNIQUES

The following tips work with natural leather and suede but not with imitations. Faux leather and suede are usually similar to fabric and use more "normal" sewing techniques.

1. Avoid using pins since once a hole is made, it is permanent. If you must use pins, put them in the seam allowances, so the holes will not show. Use weights instead of pins to hold pattern pieces in place.

2. Use paper clips or binder clips instead of pins to hold pieces of leather together for stitching.

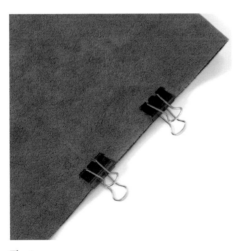

Tip 2

3. Leather and suede do not have a lot of "give" so projects with simple lines and straight pieces usually work best.

4. Sew with a straight stitch and lengthen the stitch to 3mm–4mm.

5. A leather needle is the best choice; it has a special "wedge" point that easily goes through the leather without cutting or tearing it. Use the smallest size that works for the thickness of leather and suede you are sewing.

6. Knot the threads on the back

of the project; do not backstitch as it is nearly impossible to do so without making extra holes in the leather.

7. Use a napped layout for suede as the surface will look different when brushed in different directions. Leather does not usually need a one-way layout.

8. Do not press leather! To flatten the seam allowances, apply contact cement to the wrong side of the leather and use a brayer to press them.

9. Steam can be used to raise and refresh the nap on natural suede. Hold a steam iron about 1" above the surface of the suede. Use the "burst-of-steam" feature of the iron and steam the surface well. Brush the nap of the suede with a soft rubber, bristle brush or a wire suede brush, and let the suede dry completely before handling.

10. A Teflon-coated presser foot moves over the leather easily without marking or scarring the surface. A roller foot also works well when sewing leather or suede.

Tip 10

Scrapbooking and cardmaking with sewing room scraps is a great example of reuse, reduce, and recycle.

PAPER

Scrapbooking, altered art, and fabric collage are all crafting trends that have been sweeping the nation for a number of years and appeal to crafters and non-crafters alike. Mixing fabric and paper to make art, greeting cards, or scrapbook pages adds a new dimension to your projects and opens an entirely new source for supplies and materials when planning your sewing projects.

TIPS AND TECHNIQUES

1. Use a straight, zigzag, or open decorative stitch to sew on paper.

2. When sewing with a straight stitch, use a longer than normal stitch length (3mm–4mm); a shorter stitch will perforate the paper.

3. If the paper is fragile, place stabilizer behind it for stitching.

4. Use the appropriate presser foot when stitching on paper. All the same rules apply: clear or open foot for the most visibility, couching foot for adding fibers, and free-motion foot for stitching in any direction.

5. If using a handmade or natural paper, be careful about natural elements such as leaves, twigs, and flowers that may be in the paper. Avoid sewing through them, if possible, to protect your needle.

6. Select the needle size to suit your project; a smaller needle sews finely for a delicate layout, and larger needles give a bolder or more primitive look to the stitching.

7. Be aware that stitching through paper dulls your needle. You may need to change several times, and you'll definitely need a new needle when you return to fabric.

8. If stitching an embroidery design or lettering, use embroidery software to adjust the density and remove the underlay stitching so the designs are not too heavy for the paper. The best way to know what works is to make the adjustments and then stitch a test design.

9. To embroider on paper, adhere two layers of cut-away stabilizer to each other using temporary spray adhesive. Hoop the stabilizer, then use spray adhesive to hold the paper in place on top of it. Once the stitching is complete, carefully un-hoop the stabilizer, then trim the stabilizer to match the paper.

10. Designs and lettering can be embroidered onto water-soluble stabilizer or organdy and added to the page using monofilament thread or fabric glue.

Learning to sew with plastics and vinyls increases the project possibilities available to you. This whimsical tote made from juice pouches is a great example.

PLASTIC AND VINYL

Sewing on plastic and vinyl is easy once you know a few tricks. Make purses, backpacks, rainwear, and out-door furnishings such as cushions and umbrellas for your patio using these durable, weather-resistant materials.

TIPS AND TECHNIQUES

1. A universal needle in the appropriate size is the best choice for sewing plastics. The thickness of the material determines the appropriate point size. If sewing thick vinyl, you may need a stronger, heavier needle such as a jeans or topstitching needle in a size 90 or 100.

2. Almost any type of thread works on plastic; all-purpose cotton or poly-ester thread is used most often.

3. Increase your stitch length, especially on thin plastics and vinyl.

Short stitch lengths can perforate soft or thin materials.

4. Trace pattern pieces directly onto the plastic using washable or air-soluble marker.

Tip 5

5. Feet with rollers or ones coated with Teflon® are good choices for presser feet that will move over the plastic without "sticking."

6. Pins make permanent holes in these materials so use tape or paper clips to hold pieces together for stitching.

7. If you are having trouble with the plastic sticking to the bed of the machine, place tear-away stabilizer behind the project before stitching, then remove it when the stitching is complete.

8. If sewing decorative stitches, select open ones that will not "over-stitch" the plastic.

9. Plastic and vinyl are usually not pressed with an iron. Finger press the seams open or to one side and top-stitch the seam allowances in place if desired. If you must press, use a dry iron, low temperature, and a press cloth. Heat will make plastic and vinyl soft, so be sure to let them cool before handling.

10. Waterproof items such as bags and tents can be made from plastic and vinyl, but you'll need to seal the holes made by the needle when stitching the seams. For complete waterproofing, seal the seam lines with silicone sealant available from marine supply stores.

11. You may want to mark seam lines with a fabric marker, so you will know exactly where to sew. Once a hole is in the vinyl or plastic mate-rial, it is there to stay and may show if you have sewn in the wrong place and had to remove stitches. If you do need to remove some stitching, you may be able to hide the holes using a warm hair dryer. Remove the thread, warm the holes and rub with your fingers to help seal them.

12. Since plastic and vinyl do not fray or ravel, the edges do not need to be stitched. However, for a more finished look, bind edges with fabric or vinyl strips or serge them for a decorative edging.

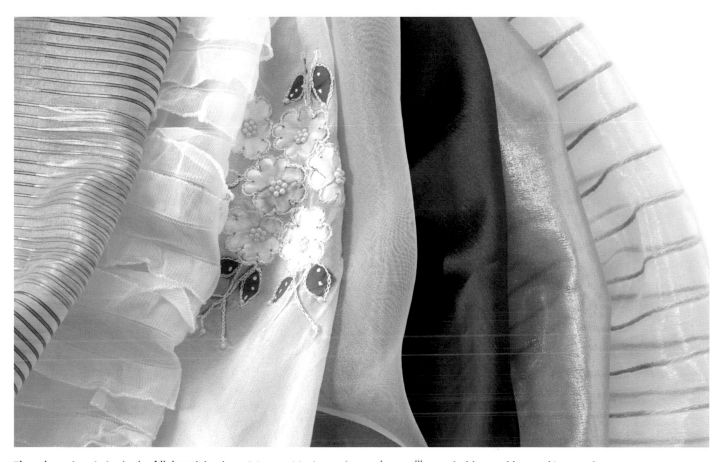

The ethereal and airy look of lightweight sheer fabrics adds dimension and versatility to clothing and home décor projects.

SHEER FABRICS

Organdy, handkerchief linen, organza, georgette, chiffon and voile are examples of beautiful elegant fabrics. Because of the sheerness of these fabrics, special techniques are required so that the results are stunning. Some sheer fabrics such as organdy are simple to work with, because they are crisp and easy to handle. Other sheers, such as chiffon are more of a challenge, because they are softer, more "fluid," and harder to control.

TIPS AND TECHNIQUES

1. The transparency of sheer fabric means that the inside of the project must look as good as the outside. A good choice for seaming is the French seam technique described on page 96.

2. Another option for seaming is the trimmed seam. Stitch on the seamline, then stitch a second line about ⅛" away. Trim the seam allowance next to the second row of stitching.

3. An effective edge finish is binding the edge in self-fabric. This continues the look of the fabric to the edge but adds another layer to sharpen and define it.

4. Use a small needle to minimize the size of the holes made by stitching.

5. The best presser foot is a straight stitch foot that focuses the needle penetration.

6. A straight stitch plate with a single hole works with the straight stitch foot to help keep the fabric from being pulled into the needle opening.

7. Try serrated shears for cutting the fabric; they grip the fabric and keep it from slipping as you cut.

8. Eliminate interfacing when making garments from sheer fabric, as it will be visible through the fabric. If you absolutely need interfacing for crispness and shape, use self-fabric for the most inconspicuous look.

9. Use a sharp, pointed needle such as a Microtex for the best stitching results on most sheer fabrics.

10. Sergers are great for use with sheer fabrics. A rolled edge and a 3-thread narrow seam are both good options for seaming and hemming.

Tips 5, 6, and 9

A walking foot is an indispensible tool for stitching plaid seams that match.

PLAID FABRICS

One sign of a well-made garment or quality home dec item is when the pattern of the fabric matches across seamlines; this is especially true when sewing plaids and stripes. Matching these patterns starts with the cutting process and goes smoothly if you keep the following points in mind.

TIPS AND TECHNIQUES

1. There are two types of plaids: balanced and unbalanced. Balanced are easier to match but unbalanced can be attractively sewn. If the pattern pieces are cut on the bias, use a balanced plaid as an unbalanced one will not match.

2. Use a napped layout so all pieces are cut in the same direction.

3. Extra fabric is needed to match plaids; measure the size of the pattern "repeat" to calculate the amount of extra fabric needed (see page 42).

4. For best results, cut all pieces in a single layer.

5. Don't expect the plaids to match at every seam; it is important to match at closures and major seams. Side seams, center fronts and center backs will meet. Sleeves should match the garment in the front from the notches down but the back generally doesn't match. Waistline seams, collars, and yokes should match where they connect to the bodice. Pockets should also match.

6. Woven patterns are easier to match than printed ones; if the printed plaid or pattern is off even slightly, it will be difficult to work with.

7. Lay out the pattern pieces, carefully placing the notches at the same part of the pattern. It can be helpful to pin the tissue paper pattern pieces together as they will be seamed, lay them over the plaid fabric and then trace the plaid pattern onto the paper using colored pencils. When you unpin the pieces, lay them on the fabric, matching the drawn pattern with the fabric.

8. Use a walking foot or even feed system to keep fabrics from shifting as you stitch.

9. Baste the pieces together to check the matching. If it is slightly off, you may be able to adjust the pieces to complete the matching.

Even plaid

Uneven plaid

sewing for children

Sewing for children can be fun and rewarding. The styles are often simple, the fabrics easy to sew, and the results small and cute! Techniques are the same as adult clothing, but keep in mind some special considerations when sewing for children.

Patterns made for babies and children are more than just miniature versions of adult clothing, and you'll find several categories to accommodate changing figures as they grow.

BABIES: Made for infants and babies that are not walking, this group of patterns is sized by height and weight.

TODDLERS: Designed for a figure that between a baby and a child, the size is determined by the chest measurement. Toddler pants are sized to fit over diapers.

CHILDREN: Sizes for children's, girls and boys clothes are determined by the chest and back waist length measurements and made for taller children with wider shoulders and back.

GIRLS: Designed for the young girl whose height ranges from 4'2" to 5'1", these patterns do not have bust darts as they are for the figure before bust development.

BOYS: Designed for boys whose height ranges from 4' to 4'10" that have outgrown smaller children's sizes.

When selecting fabrics for children's clothing, make sure they are durable and easy to launder. Cotton broadcloth, polyester blends, denim, fleece, and corduroy work well for children's clothes; knit fabrics are also good choices. Prewash and dry your fabric before cutting and sewing so you won't be surprised with shrinkage after the garment is laundered. If selecting prints, look for small scale designs that won't overwhelm the size of the wearer.

Look for soft fabrics that won't scratch or irritate young skin. If a stabilizer is required, use one that is

Small-scale coordinating prints are perfect for children's clothing such as the petaled skirt of this darling dress and hat. Courtesy of Donna Lang.

soft to the touch and becomes softer with washing.

You can also incorporate techniques that allow the clothes to grow with the child, such as adding to the length. Stitching growth tucks in a child's garment allows you to easily lengthen the garment as the child grows and can be added as a decorative feature such as on the lower, outside part of a skirt or can be hidden in the hem allowance. Allow for the tucks when cutting out the garment and stitch them in place with a longer than normal stitch length, so they can be easily removed.

Children's clothing needs to be durable, and here are a few areas that benefit from reinforcement:

KNEES AND ELBOWS: These areas take the most abuse and often

need patched and repaired before any other part of the garment. You can help avoid this by reinforcing them as you make the garment. Fuse lightweight interfacing on the wrong side of the knee and/or elbow areas. Make it wide enough to extend slightly into the seam allowance, so it will be stitched with the seams. Decorative patches can also be stitched on the right side of the garment in these areas for even more reinforcement.

POCKETS: Stitch the stress points (upper corners) of the pockets using a bar tack or short length of zigzag stitching.

SEAMS: Use flat-felled or welt seams for durability and strength. Simple topstitching of the seams also adds security to the garment.

171

sewing projects

SOMEONE ONCE SAID, "I DON'T LOVE TO sew, I love what I sew." That brings us back to the question, "Is it the process or the project that drives people to sew?" The answer is clearly both. At times, it's the process and, at other times, the project. This chapter offers twelve projects from talented designers that cover all types of sewing and a variety of techniques, both practical and decorative.

The Bohemian Bag is a simple shoulder tote that starts with fabric painting and ends with a fun and practical purse. The Tropical Table Runner is a great way to dress up your table with just two fabrics and a little bit of sewing. For a fashion forward look with unique embellishment, you'll want to make the Gypsy Shrug and the Let It Rain Yellow Slicker—a fun cover-up that will keep you dry.

If you're into quilts, you can choose from the Garden Party Lap Quilt and the Scrappy Cottage Quilt for a variety of techniques that result in warm and comfy covers. The baby in your life will love the Bugs in the Garden Book that gives him or her lots to do and lots to learn.

These are only a few of the projects you'll find in this chapter—just a taste of what you can accomplish with fabric, needle, and thread. From bags to books to quilts to clothing, there's no end to what you can sew with a few supplies and a little knowledge.

bohemian bag

Use oil paint sticks in your favorite colors with tinted vinyl shapes and decorative threads to express your creativity as you embellish fabric with spirals, stripes, circles and stars. This roomy tote has space to stash all of your essentials and is just the right size to carry a journal or sketchbook.

DESIGNED AND MADE BY JO LEICHTE
Skill level: Beginner
Finished size: 16" x 12" (excluding the strap)
Techniques: Fabric painting and simple construction
Seam allowances: ½"

MATERIALS

1¼ yards lightweight denim or medium weight chambray
1¼ yards lightweight cotton print for lining
Construction thread
Shiva Artist's Paintstiks® in desired colors
Clear tinted vinyl in desired colors
Decorative thread in desired color
Teflon-coated presser foot
Free-motion presser foot (optional)

GENERAL INSTRUCTIONS

Note: Refer to manufacturer's instructions for preparing fabric before applying Artist's Paintstiks.

1. Cut two 22" x 40" rectangles from main fabric. The fabric is your canvas—you will embellish the rectangles then use them for the outer pieces of your bag.

2. Using Artist's Paintstiks, and following manufacturer's instructions, draw spirals on one rectangle and straight lines on the other. If you like, use other simple shapes such as squiggles or triangles—it's your bag, and you can embellish it any way you want. Follow manufacturer's instructions to set paint.

3. Cut circles and long rectangles from the clear tinted vinyl. Stitch rectangles in place with a straight stitch down the center using a non-stick presser foot. Stitch circles in place using a free-motion presser

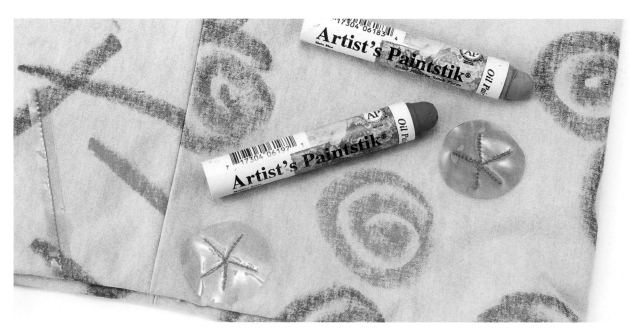

Steps 2 and 3

foot (a Teflon-coated foot may also be used). Other shapes such as triangles or squares can also be used. Stitch along the outer edges or from corner to corner to secure.

4. Fold each rectangle in half along the lengthwise grain. Photocopy and enlarge the pattern, then position on the folded fabric. Adjust the length of the strap as desired. Cut one piece on the fold for each side of the bag.

5. Cut two pieces on the fold for the lining.

6. Place the two lining pieces right sides together. Stitch the short sides of the bag together. Press seam allowances open. There is no need to finish the seam allowances, as all raw edges will be enclosed when the bag is finished.

7. Place the two embellished pieces right sides together. Stitch the short sides of the bag together. Press seam allowances open using a press cloth,

taking care not to melt any of the vinyl embellishments.

8. Turn lining right side out. Insert lining into bag, right sides together. Note: Bottoms of bag and lining are still open at this point. Stitch around the upper edge and handles of the bag. Grade and clip seam allowances. Notch curves at end of handles. Turn right side out. Press all edges using a press cloth, again taking care not to melt any of the vinyl embellishments.

9. Lay bag flat, lining inside, short seams at the center front and center back of the bag. Stitch across the lower edge of the bag, matching all seam allowances in the center of the bag. Trim seam allowance to ¼".

10. Turn bag inside out. Stitch across the lower edge with a half inch seam allowance.

11. Turn bag right side out.

12. Tie handles into a square knot.

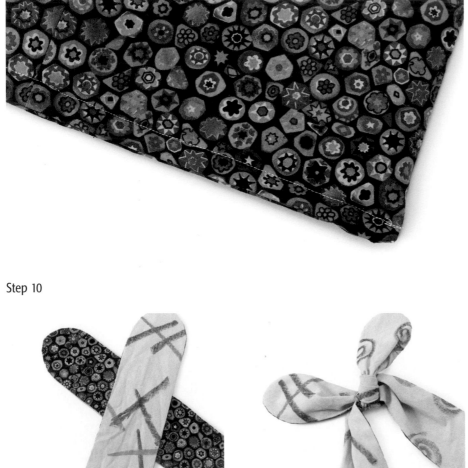

Step 10

Step 12

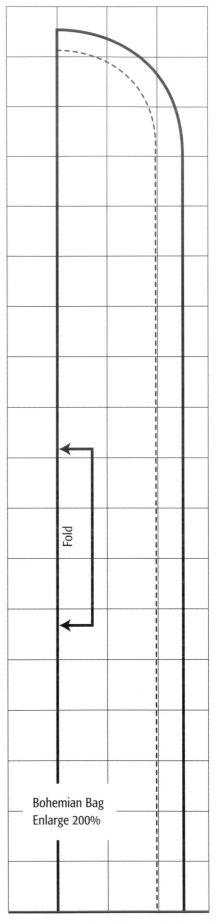

Fold

Bohemian Bag
Enlarge 200%

Adjust strap length as desired and join pattern pieces here.

176

Add strap piece here

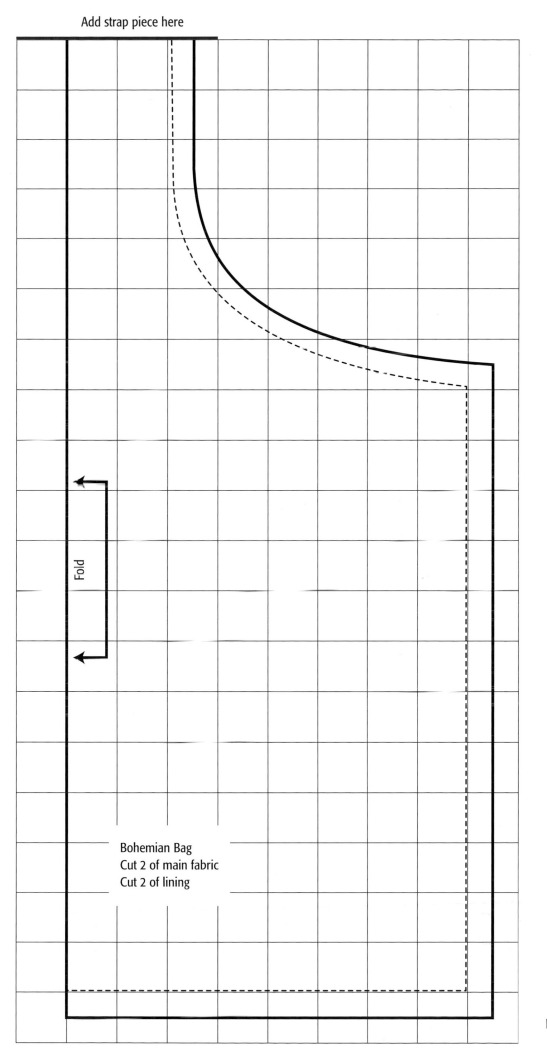

Fold

Bohemian Bag
Cut 2 of main fabric
Cut 2 of lining

Each box = 1 inch

singing canary pillow

Dress up your home with this cheery, appliquéd pillow. Use your "drawing" skills to add the finishing touches with thread sketching. It's easier than you may think, even if you are not an expert free-motion stitcher.

DESIGNED AND MADE BY SARAH GOODMAN

Skill level: Intermediate
Finished size: 20" x 20"
Techniques: Simple construction, piped edges, and thread sketching
Seam allowances: ½"

MATERIALS

Fabric:

Upper front (wallpaper) – 21" x 17"medium weight, sturdy fabric

Lower front (floor) – 21" x 5" medium weight, sturdy fabric

Back – two pieces, 14" x 21" each, medium weight, sturdy fabric

Bird appliqué – 8" x 8" cotton print

Eye appliqué – small solid scrap, 3" x 3"

2½ yards ¼" cording

2½ yards 1½" wide bias strips for piping (pieced to make one long strip)

1" decorative button for bird's eye

1 yard paper-backed fusible web

¾ yard tear-away stabilizer

Black quilting thread

Construction thread

20" x 20" pillow form

Basting spray

Fabric marker

PREPARATION

1. Bond the paper-backed fusible web to the wrong side of the appliqué fabrics. Cut out the bird and the eye using the pattern on page 181; set aside.

Note: Draw the bird in reverse on the paper, so when it is cut out and turned over, it will face the same direction as shown in the photo.

PILLOW FRONT

1. With right sides together, pin the "wallpaper" to the "floor" along one 21" side using a ½" seam allowance. Press the seam allowance down.

2. Position the appliqué shapes on the front of the pillow using the photo as a guide; fuse in place.

3. Place the stabilizer behind the pillow front, using basting spray to hold the layers together.

4. Using the illustration as a guide, draw the desired elements with a fabric marker on the pillow front.

5. Set your machine for free-motion

Thread sketching guide

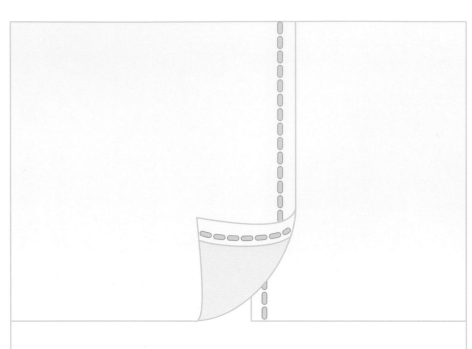

Pillow assembly – Step 2

stitching (feed dogs down) and thread with black quilting thread in the needle and bobbin. "Draw" with the black thread on the pillow front, outlining the bird and adding background elements as desired. Be as loose and free as you want, stitching the outlines multiple times (as shown) if desired. Tear-away the excess stabilizer from the back.

6. Sew the button for the bird's eye as shown.

PILLOW ASSEMBLY

1. Press the 21" edge of each piece of the pillow back under ½", twice; press. From the right side of the fabric, stitch the hem along the inside of the fold.

2. Overlap the back pillow pieces with right sides up and match to the pillow front. Baste the overlapped pieces together close to the edge.

3. Wrap the bias strip around the cording and stitch close to the cord using a zipper foot or piping (refer to pages 134–136).

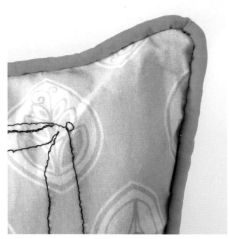

4. Position the piping along the seamline of the pillow front and stitch in place over the previous stitching.

5. Pin the pillow front to the pillow back, right sides together. Trim the back if needed, so it is the same size as the front. Stitch along all four sides. Tip: Move the needle position slightly closer to the cord to hide the previous stitching.

6. Turn the pillow right side out, using a point turner to push out the corners. Insert the pillow form through the back opening.

Singing Canary Pillow
Bird appliqué
Cut 1 of fused fabric

Singing Canary Pillow
Eye appliqué
Cut 1 of fused fabric

scrappy cottage quilt

This simple quilt uses alternating plain and 9-patch blocks set on point made from a low-contrast combination of fabrics. Because this is a scrappy quilt, you can select a variety of prints and mix and match them as desired when piecing the 9-patch blocks. The finishing touch is quilting the layers using an outline design and an embroidery machine.

DESIGNED AND MADE BY VICKY TRACY
Skill level: Intermediate
Finished size: 53½" x 61½"
Techniques: Piecing, quilting-in-the-hoop, and bound edges
Seam allowances: ¼"

MATERIALS

Note: The fabrics shown are from Kaye's Cottage Collection by Benartex.

Green whole blocks and outer border – 1¼ yard

Pink inner border – ½ yard

Light center blocks – ¼ yard

9-patch blocks – A variety of low-contrast coordinating prints to equal about 2 yards

Setting triangles – ½ yard

Binding – ½ yard

Quilting backing and batting, 54" x 62" each (piece to size if needed)

CUTTING

Green blocks and outer border
    Fourteen 6½" squares
    Five strips, 4½" across the width of the fabric

Inner border
    Four strips, 2½" across the width of the fabric

Inner blocks
    Six 6½" squares

9-patch blocks

Two hundred seventy 2½" squares: 150 pink and 120 green

Setting Triangles
    Nine 6⅞" blocks, each sub-cut diagonally into 2 triangles
    One 7¼" block, sub-cut diagonally into 4 triangles

Binding
    210" of 2½" wide bias strips, pieced together to create one long strip

PIECING

Create the 9-patch blocks by sewing

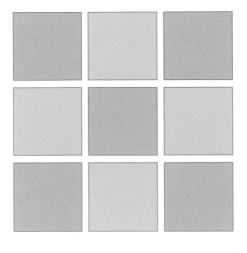

three squares together to create a row. Stitch three rows together to complete one block. Make 30 blocks.

PIECING TIPS

- For the greatest accuracy when piecing, use a presser foot specially designed for quarter inch piecing. Most sewing machines have one available that lets you align the edges of the fabric with the edge of the foot for consistent quarter inch seam allowances.

- To make sure your scrappy quilt has a random look to the patterns, place your pink squares in one paper bag and your green squares in another. Shake them up, then pull out the color you need as you go. Don't over think the process, and you'll love the finished look!

CONSTRUCTION

1. Arrange the 9-patch blocks with the whole blocks on a design wall (using the photo as a guide) until you are pleased with the placement.

2. Stitch the blocks together in rows, adding a triangle at each end.

3. Stitch the rows together and add the corner setting triangles to form the center of the quilt.

4. Add the inner border to the sides, cutting to fit. Add the inner border to the upper and lower edges, cutting to fit.

5. Add the outer border to the sides, cutting to fit. Add outer border to the upper and lower edges, cutting to fit.

Note: Refer to the expanded assembly diagram on the following page for these steps.

BASTING

Trim backing and batting to fit the pieced top. Layer the pieced top with batting. Smooth the layers, using basting spray to hold them together if desired. Pin baste the layers together, placing the pins about 3"–4" apart.

QUILTING

1. Starting in the center of the quilt, embroider the selected designs, following the directions for Quilting in the Hoop on page 186.

2. When stitching is complete, place the backing behind the batting and spray and/or pin baste in place.

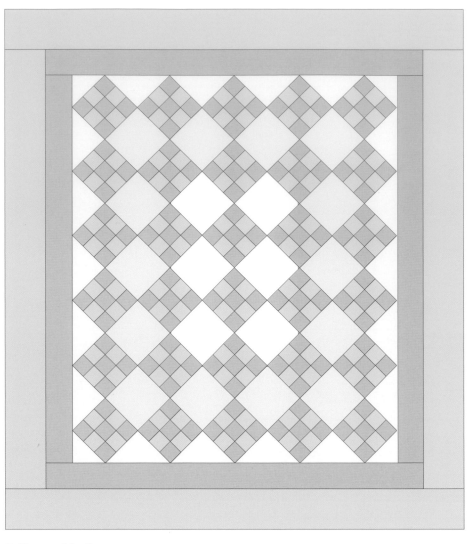

Quilt assembly diagram

3. After all desired areas of the quilt are embroidered, thread the sewing machine with 60-weight cotton thread in the needle and in the bobbin. Lower or cover the feed dog of the machine and stipple quilt the areas between the embroidered designs to make the density even between the designs.

BINDING

1. Fold the binding strip in half lengthwise and press. Starting along one side, stitch the folded binding to the edge of the quilt, matching the raw edges. Join the starting and ending points of the binding in a diagonal seam.

2. Wrap the binding to the back of the quilt and hand or machine sew it into place.

Using a striped fabric for bias binding adds an interesting finish for the edges of your quilt.

BORDER MEASURING TIP

- For side borders, measure down the pieced top at the center of the upper and lower edges. Cut your side borders this length.

- For upper and lower borders, measure across the pieced top at the center of the side edges. Cut your upper and lower borders this length.

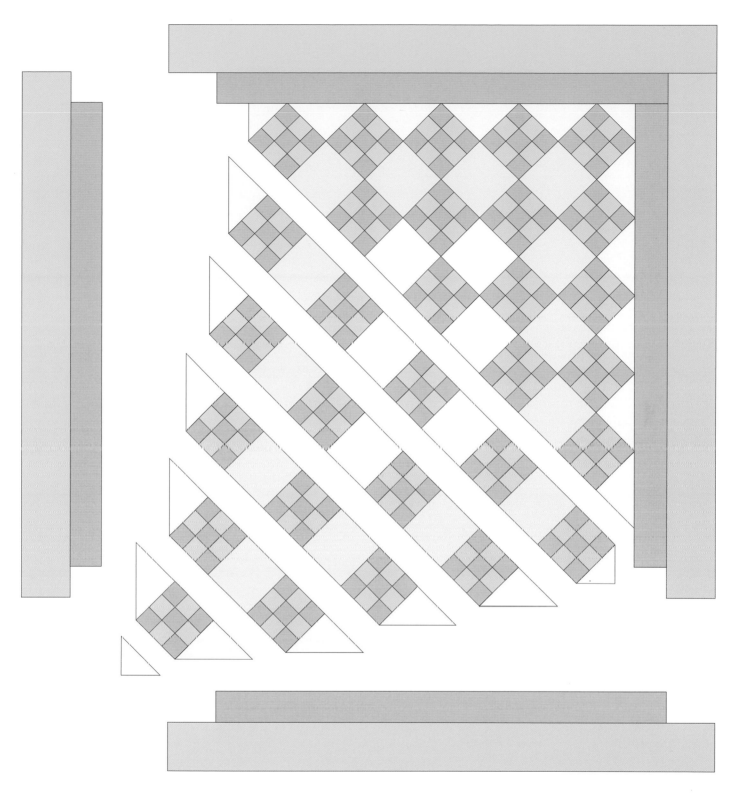

Expanded quilt assembly diagram

TIPS FOR QUILTING IN THE HOOP

- When basting the quilt layers together, do not include the backing. Put the pieced top and the batting together for quilting with the embroidery machine. After the designs are stitched, add the backing and finish the quilting process using the sewing machine.

- For best results when quilting with the embroidery machine, the project should be hooped and stabilized appropriately. Outline quilt designs are usually very light, making water-soluble stabilizer a good choice. The water-soluble stabilizer will rinse completely away, leaving your quilt soft and stabilizer-free.

- Embroidery designs are generally digitized for 40-weight embroidery thread. The nature of outline quilting designs often requires use of a heavier thread to prevent the designs from being lost in the fabric design. Heavier cotton quilting threads are absolutely beautiful for outline quilting motifs.

- Experiment with threads and consider using a variegated thread for the embroidered quilt designs. Another idea is to stitch the designs twice to make them more prominent.

- The easiest way to quilt with the embroidery machine is to repeat an outline design across the surface of the quilt, re-hooping as needed to randomly place the design, creating an all-over pattern. If you want to specifically place your design within the blocks of the quilt, photocopy your design templates and trim to fit the quilt block. Pin or adhere the paper template to the quilt top with double-sided tape for hooping. Be sure to use the plastic hoop templates to keep the design straight in the hoop. Use your machine's check function and adjust design position if necessary. Remove the templates and stitch the designs. Use the quilt block seam lines to help position design templates and as reference lines for the hoop template.

When quilting with the embroidery machine, you can place the stitched designs to work with the patchwork pattern, or you can simply embroider the design over the surface of the quilt, creating an all-over quilted effect.

Scrappy Cottage Quilt

deep pocket chef's apron

This two-layer, divided pocket apron is both functional and stylish. Make it using bright, cheerful coordinating prints, and you'll always have a happy cook!

DESIGNED AND MADE BY APRIL OLIVEIRA-WARD
Skill level: Beginner to Intermediate
Techniques: Darts, waistband, gathering, and binding
Seam allowances: ½"

MATERIALS
Fabric:
  Underskirt – ⅔ yard
  Over apron – ½ yard
  Waistband, ties, and bias trim for
    pockets – ⅞ yard
Fusible interfacing
Thread that blends with all three fabrics
Two buttons

CUTTING AND PREPARATION
1. Enlarge the patterns on pages 191–193 as directed and cut the following pieces from the selected fabrics:
    1 underskirt (see pattern)
    1 over apron (see pattern)
    1 pocket (see pattern)
    1 pocket facing (see pattern)
    2 ties, 4" x 30" each
    1 waistband, 4½" x 23"; fuse interfacing to wrong side
2. After cutting, transfer all markings to the fabric using a fabric marker.
3. Cut 2" wide bias strips and piece together to make one 60" long strip. Fold in half lengthwise and press.

INSTRUCTIONS
UNDERSKIRT

1. Mark and sew the darts; press to the sides, away from the apron center.

2. Finish the side edges by pressing ¼" to the wrong side, folding another ¼" and stitching the double fold in place.

3. Using a basting stitch (4mm–5mm), sew two rows of stitching between the dart and the hemmed edge along the top of the apron. Sew one row ⅜" from the edge and the second row ¼".

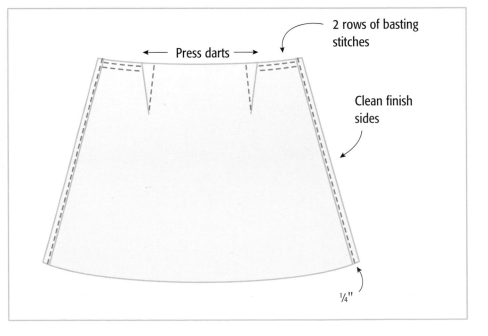

Press darts

2 rows of basting stitches

Clean finish sides

¼"

OVER APRON

1. Mark and sew the darts in the over apron the same as in the underskirt. Press darts toward the apron center.

POCKET

1. Finish the lower edge of the pocket facing using a zigzag or overcast stitch as desired. With wrong sides together, baste the upper edge of the pocket facing to the top of the pocket.

2. Cut a piece of the bias binding to fit the upper edge of the pocket. Position the raw edges of the folded strip on the wrong side of the upper edge of the pocket over the basted seam. Sew in place using a regular stitch length (2mm–3mm).

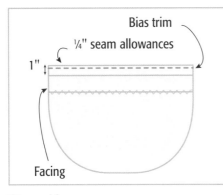

Wrong side

3. Wrap the folded edge of the bias strip over the upper edge to the front of the pocket. Sew closely along the edge of the bias to secure it to the pocket.

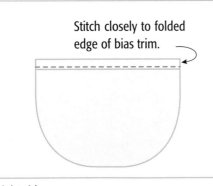

Right side

4. Position the pocket right side up on the right side of the under-skirt, matching the lower raw edge. Baste along the raw edge to hold it in place.

5. Sew a straight line as shown down the center of the pocket to form two pockets in the over apron. Reinforce the stress point of the pocket by backstitch-ing at the top on the bias trim.

6. Sew the remaining bias trim along the edges of the over apron and pocket using the same method as on the upper edge of the pocket.

7. Position the over apron on top of the under skirt, matching the center front edges and the seam lines of the darts (darts are pressed in opposite directions to eliminate bulk. Baste along the upper edge of the underskirt to hold it in place.

APRON TIES

1. Hem the long edges of the ties using the same method as for the side edges of the underskirt.

2. Baste along one short edge of each tie, ¼" from the edge, leaving 3"–4" of thread at each end.

3. Finish the remaining end on each tie by folding the tie right sides together and sewing a ⅜" seam. Turn right side out; press, forming a point as shown.

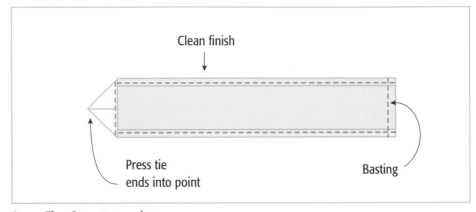

Clean finish

Press tie ends into point

Basting

Apron Ties, Steps 1, 2, and 3

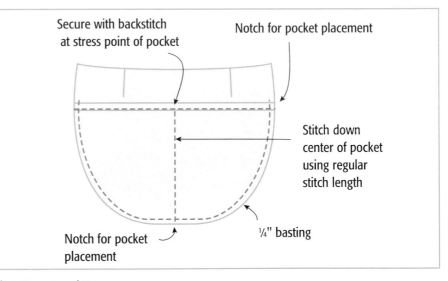

Secure with backstitch at stress point of pocket

Notch for pocket placement

Stitch down center of pocket using regular stitch length

Notch for pocket placement

¼" basting

Pocket, Steps 4 and 5

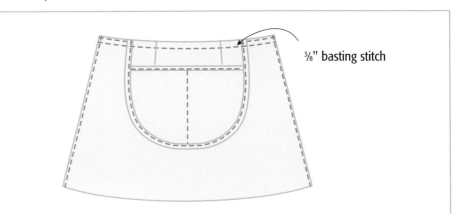

⅜" basting stitch

Pocket, Step 7

4. Pull the basting threads to slightly gather the end of each tie, taking care not to pull them out.

WAISTBAND

1. Press one long edge of waistband ½" to the wrong side.

2. Using a ⅜" seam allowance, sew the gathered ends of the ties to the short ends of the waistband, adjusting the stitches to fit between the center of the band and ⅜" from the cut edge as shown.

3. Fold the waistband right sides together as shown and sew the ends using a ½" seam allowance, stitching through the folded seam allowance and leaving the remaining seam allowance free to be sewn to the apron.

4. Turn the waistband right side out, trimming the end seam allowances as needed; press.

5. Position the waistband on the upper edge of the apron, adjusting the side gathering stitches on the underskirt to fit. Stitch the band to the apron.

6. Trim and/or grade the seam allowances of the waistband, over apron, and the underskirt to eliminate bulk inside the waistband.

7. To complete the waistband, sew close to the finished edge as shown.

FINISHING

1. Finish the lower edge of the apron using a zigzag or overcast stitch. Fold a 1½" hem to the wrong side and stitch by machine or hand to secure the hem.

2. Sew the decorative buttons to the pocket only, positioning each one in the middle of each pocket section, centered on the pocket facing.

Lower edge

Deep Pocket
Chef's Apron
One size
Pocket facing
Cut 1
Enlarge 200%

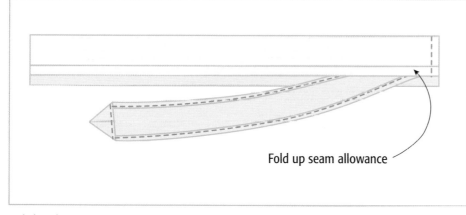

Fold up seam allowance

Waistband, Step 3

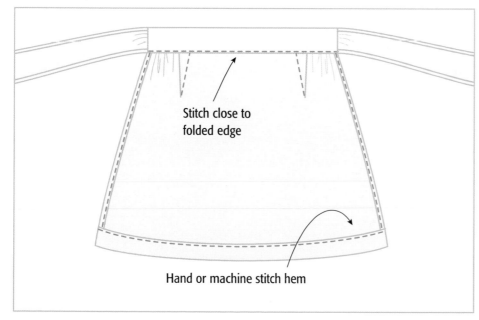

Stitch close to folded edge

Hand or machine stitch hem

Waistband, Step 5

191

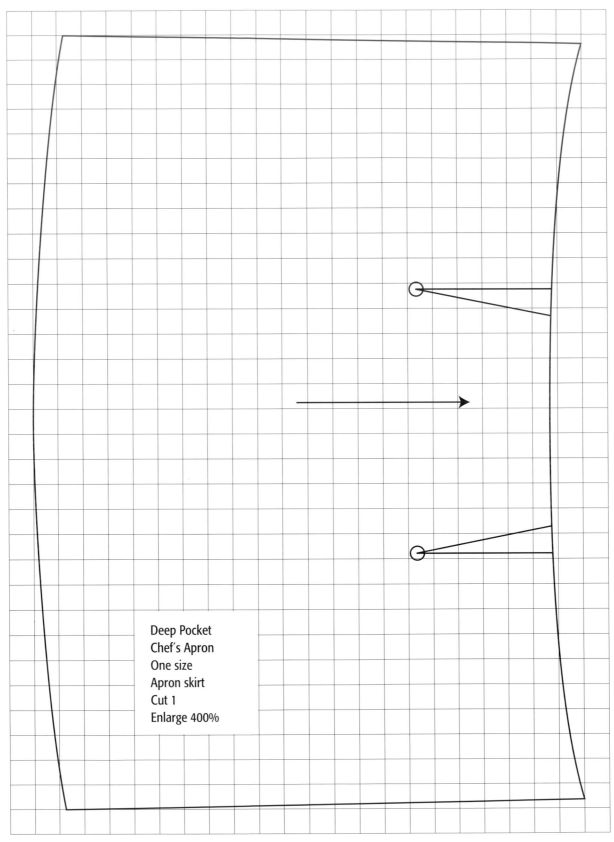

Deep Pocket
Chef's Apron
One size
Apron skirt
Cut 1
Enlarge 400%

Each box = 1 inch

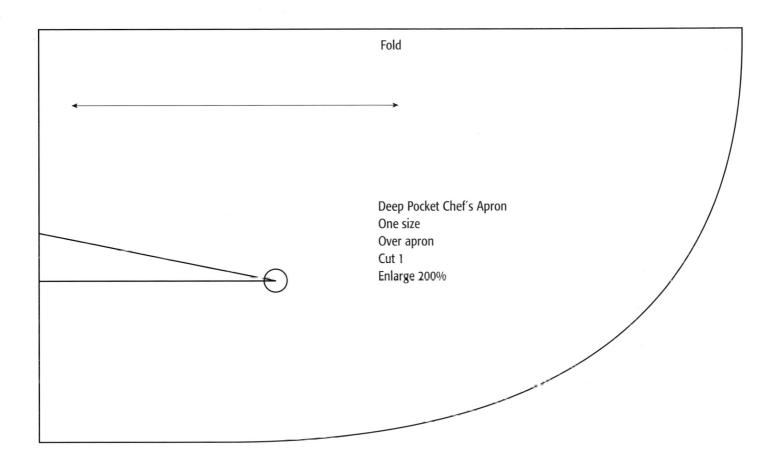

Fold

Deep Pocket Chef's Apron
One size
Over apron
Cut 1
Enlarge 200%

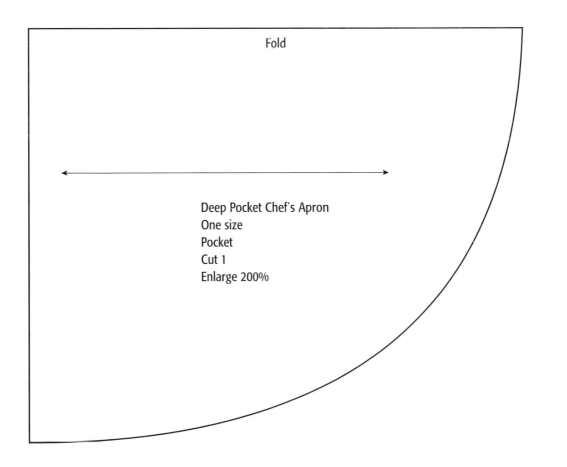

Fold

Deep Pocket Chef's Apron
One size
Pocket
Cut 1
Enlarge 200%

gypsy shrug

Wear this "one-size-fits-most" jacket with skirts, pants, and jeans. Enjoy the combination of vintage or "vintage-look" hankies and soft, draping fabric such as challis, georgette, or lawn.

DESIGNED AND MADE BY VICKI TRACY
Skill level: Intermediate
Finished size: One size fits most
Techniques: Simple draping, serger seaming, rolled heming, and applying trim
Seam allowances: ¼"

MATERIALS
3 yards soft fabric
4–6 vintage or new hankies
3 yards lace edging
Temporary spray adhesive
60 wt. cotton darning thread
Serger thread to match fabric
Assorted buttons

CUTTING AND CONSTRUCTION

1. Cut two fabric rectangles 3 yards long and 20" wide. You can adjust this width for a shorter (18") or longer (22") shrug.

2. Using the serger, roll hem one long edge on each fabric rectangle (these two edges will flow separately as the jacket is worn.)

3. Spray baste the two fabric rectangles *wrong* sides together, matching roll hemmed edges.

4. Serge both layers of the remaining three edges together with a balanced 4-thread stitch.

VINTAGE HANKIE COLLAR

1. This collar will cover the upper edge of the rectangle, adding color and visual texture to the shrug

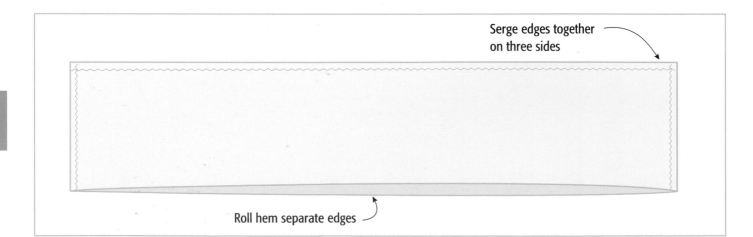

Serge edges together on three sides

Roll hem separate edges

Cutting and construction – Steps 1–4

opening. Cut 4–6 vintage hankies in half (collar should be as long as the upper edge of the rectangle).

2. Join the hankies using one of the following techniques:

a. Meet the short ends of the hankies without overlapping and stitch together using a medium zigzag stitch.

b. Seam the short ends together with a 1" seam. Press the seams open.

Note: Hankies may be different sizes. Position them so the raw edges are even. The lower hemmed edges of the hankies will be irregular and will add interest to the collar.

3. Finish the upper raw edge of the joined hankies using a zigzag overcast on the sewing machine or a rolled hem on the serger.

4. Stitch lace to raw edges of the hankies.

5. Stitch hankie collar to upper edge of the fabric rectangle. The lace will extend beyond the 4-thread serged edge.

FINAL ASSEMBLY

1. Find the middle of the 3-yard rectangle (the side with the hankie scarf). Measure 2½" from the middle on each side; mark with pins (this is the center back and back neck opening).

2. Bring both short edges to the marked neck opening, positioning them under the hankie collar. Topstitch, starting at the neck opening to create the shoulder seam and the sleeve opening.

3. Tack the lower edge of the hankie scarf in place using buttons and bar tacks to secure the loose edge to the shrug.

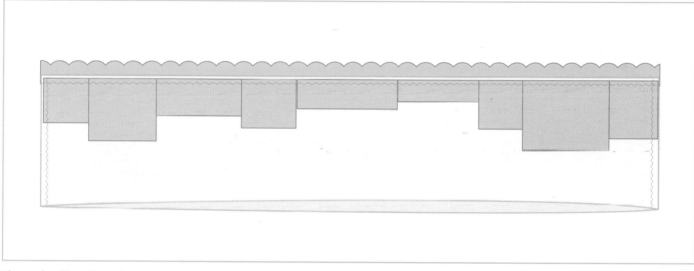

Vintage hankie collar – Step 5

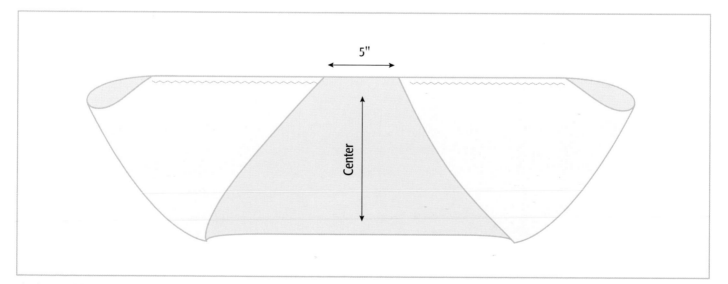

Final assembly – Step 2

tropical table runner

Give your table a fresh new look with this bordered table runner. The mitered frame offers tailored panache and lets you combine two fabrics for a coordinated style.

DESIGNED AND MADE BY SALLEY BOWMAN
Skill level: Beginner to Intermediate
Finished size: 14¾" x 50¾"
Techniques: Simple piecing, mitered corners, and "y" seams
Seam allowances: ½"

MATERIALS

Fabric #1 for center: ⅜ yard if cut cross-wise from 54" wide fabric;
  1¼ yard if cut lengthwise
Fabric #2 for border: ⅜ yard if cut cross-wise from 54" wide fabric;
  1⅜ yard if cut lengthwise
Fabric #3 for backing (can be the same as #1 or #2): ½ yard if cut crosswise from 54" wide fabric; no additional fabric if cut from center fabric or border fabric
Fusible interfacing (optional): same amount as backing
Construction thread

CUTTING AND PREPARATION

1. Using fabric #1, cut a 10" x 47" piece for the center.

2. Using fabric #2, cut two 3" x 15¾" strips for the end borders. Use the mitered corner template on page 201 to shape the ends. Transfer the markings from the template to the project.

3. Using fabric #2, cut two 3" x 53¾" strips for the side borders. Use the template to shape the ends.

4. Using fabric #3 or leftover fabric, cut a 16" x 54" piece for the backing. Note: This will be cut to size after runner is pieced.

5. Fuse interfacing to the wrong side of the backing (for more body and firmness), if desired.

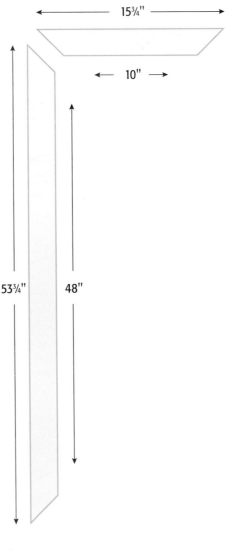

15¾"

10"

53¾"   48"

STITCHING THE BORDER

1. Stitch the long and short borders together as shown below to form a rectangular frame. Note: Start stitching each corner seam at the outer edge and stop stitching one seam allowance before reaching the inside edge. Press the seams open.

2. Pin the band to the edges of the center section, matching the corner border seams with the intersections of the seamlines (at each corner) on the center of the table runner.

3. Stitch the band to the center along all four edges; press.

FINISHING THE RUNNER

1. Trim the back to be the same size as the pieced runner.

2. Pin the back to the framed front with right sides together. Stitch the layers together, leaving an opening for turning.

3. Trim the corners and grade the seam allowances as needed. Turn the runner to the right side and press.

4. Edgestitch along all four sides of the runner, closing the opening.

Step 1

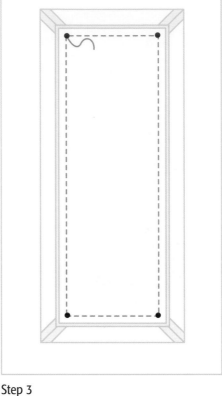

Step 3

PLACEMATS

Use the same techniques to make bordered placemats for your table. Simply cut the pieces as indicated and follow the directions that begin on page 198.

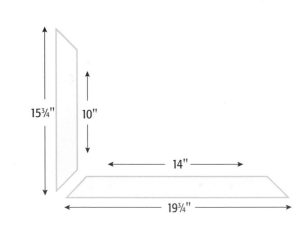

15¾"   10"   14"   19¾"

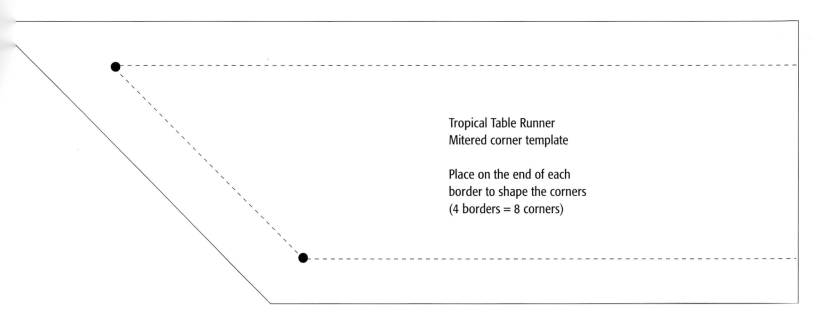

Tropical Table Runner
Mitered corner template

Place on the end of each
border to shape the corners
(4 borders = 8 corners)

berry pie pincushion

From strawberry to blueberry to raspberry, this multi-colored pincushion is as fun as it is functional. Easy to make from small scraps of fabric, the pattern can be resized from tiny to jumbo. You can never have too many pincushions!

DESIGNED AND MADE BY SUSAN BECK

Skill level: Beginner

Finished size: 5¼" circle

Techniques: Simple piecing, basic construction and stuffing, sewing on a button, and hand beading

Seam allowances: ¼"

MATERIALS

Six small pieces of firmly woven fabric in coordinating colors, at least 4" x 4"

One 8" square of felt or wool for base

Scraps of wool batting or felted wool sweaters for stuffing

Embroidery floss or perle cotton

Doll needle

Assorted beads

Hand beading needle

Construction thread

¾"–1 " flat button

CUTTING AND PIECING

1. Using the template on page 205 cut one triangle of each of the six colors of fabric.

2. Stitch three triangles right sides together using a ¼" seam.

3. Stitch the remaining three triangles together, again using a ¼" seam.

4. Stitch the two sets of triangles together with the points meeting in the center.

5. Place the pieced top right side down on the 8" square of base fabric; pin.

6. Cut out the paper circle template and pin it to the layered fabric, matching the centers. Tip: Fold the template in half twice to find the center.

7. Stitch through all layers, *just outside* the paper pattern, leaving a 2"–3" opening.

8. Trim about ⅛"–¼" outside the stitching; clip or notch the seam allowance so the turned curves will be smooth. Tip: Use pinking shears when trimming to eliminate the need for clipping the seam allowance.

Piecing – Step 7

STUFFING

1. Turn the pincushion to the right side. Press, smoothing out the curves.

2. Fill the pincushion with scraps of wool batting or felted wool sweaters. The lanolin in the wool will keep the pins sharpened.

3. Hand stitch the opening closed.

WRAPPING

1. Thread the doll needle with a double strand of floss or perle cotton. Insert the needle into the center of the base, coming up through the center of the top. Pull the thread through until only 3"–4" are extending; tie the thread tails together and trim.

2. Wrap the thread around the edge of the pincushion, positioning it over one of the seams; insert the needle into the base, coming up through the center again. Pull the floss snug enough to form the petal shape of the pincushion.

3. Repeat the previous step until all seams are covered with floss, coming up through the center of the pincushion each time. Take 2–3 small stitches to tie off the floss, leaving the needle and thread connected to the pincushion.

FINISHING

1. Using the floss, stitch a flat button in the center, ending on the back of the pincushion. Tie off the floss and clip the tails.

2. Using a hand beading needle, stitch beads (also known as "berries") along the seam of the pincushion. Use assorted sizes, shapes, and colors. The color, texture, and sparkle of the beading will remind you of the joy of sewing each time you see the pincushion.

Finishing – Step 2

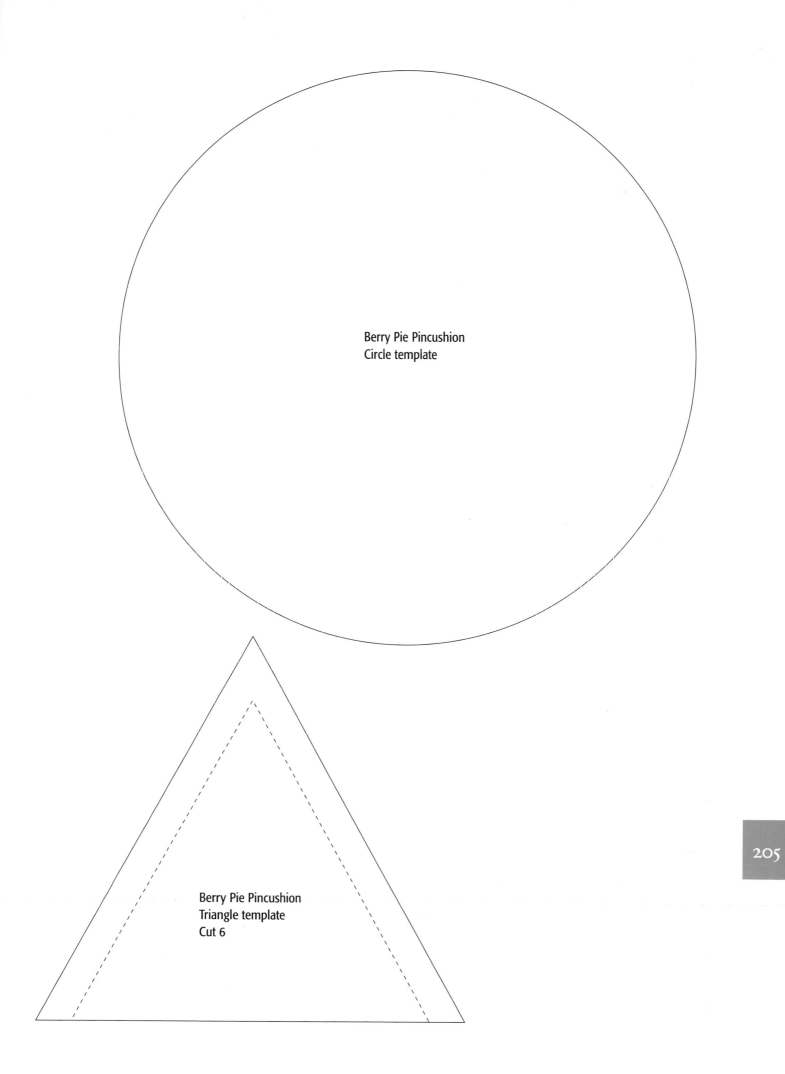

Berry Pie Pincushion
Circle template

Berry Pie Pincushion
Triangle template
Cut 6

bugs in the garden book

Every page of this soft fabric book has something to teach young toddlers. They'll have fun with the zipper, buttons, and snaps, and before long will be dressing themselves using their newfound skills.

DESIGNED AND MADE BY JO LEICHTE

Skill level: Beginner to Intermediate

Finished size: 9" x 10"

Techniques: Appliqué, zipper insertion, sewing on buttons and snaps, buttonholes, decorative serging

Seam allowances: ¼"

MATERIALS

Sturdy fabric such as lightweight denim or twill for pages, 8 pieces, 9" x 10" each

Tear-away stabilizer: place behind each page for appliqué and remove when stitching is complete

Scraps for appliqués: specific colors listed with each motif

Paper-backed fusible web such as Steam-A-Seam 2

Fabric marker

Fabric glue

Metal grommets (optional)

Colorful ribbon or shoelace

Construction thread

Serger

Three cones of serger thread for edging

Note: This book is not for infants. The buttons and snaps should be securely stitched. Supervision while playing with the book is encouraged.

ZIPPERED FLOWER

Yellow print fabric for center:
    two 5" x 8" rectangles and
    one 8" x 8" square
Blue fabric for petals
Yellow 7"–9" zipper
Yellow thread for center appliqué
Red or blue thread for petal appliqué

A zipper down the center of the flower makes a roomy pocket.

FLOWER CENTER

1. Stitch the two 5" x 8" rectangles of yellow fabric together with a straight stitch along one long side, adjusting your stitch length as follows to accommodate the zipper: 2" stitch length = 2mm, 4" stitch length = 5mm, 2" stitch length = 2mm. Press the seam open.

2. Position the zipper behind the seam; pin and baste in place. Using a zipper foot, stitch around the zipper opening as indicated on the pattern. Cut away excess zipper as needed.

"Unsew" the basting stitches. Open the zipper. (Refer to page 117.)

3. Using the pattern on page 210, cut a circle from the 8" x 8" square of yellow fabric. Place the circle wrong side down over the zippered rectangle, centering the zipper. Stitch around the outside edge of the circle, ¼" from raw edge, overlapping the starting and ending stitches. Trim excess fabric from the outer edge of the circle and notch curves. Tip: Use pinking shears to trim the outer edges and eliminate the need to notch.

4. Turn the circle right side out. You now have a zippered pouch.

FLOWER PETALS

1. Bond the fusible web to the wrong side of the blue print scrap fabric. Use the pattern to trace seven petals onto the paper of the fusible web.

2. Cut out the petals. Peel away the backing.

ASSEMBLING THE FLOWER

1. Position the petals and center of the flower on one 9" x 10" "page" of the book. Pin the petals then remove the center. Fuse the petals in place. Place tear-away stabilizer behind the fabric and appliqué the edges of the petals using a blanket stitch. (Refer to pages 142–143.)

2. Pin the center pouch in place; appliqué around the edge using a zigzag stitch. Remove the excess stabilizer from the wrong side of the page.

BUTTONED BEETLE

Brown print fabric for bug,
    2 pieces, 5" x 7" each
Thread for legs and appliqué
Two shank buttons for eyes

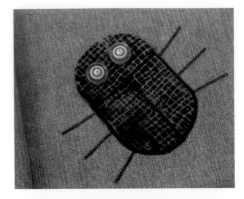

Decorative buttons make perfect eyes for this big brown bug.

1. Using the pattern, cut two beetle shapes from brown fabric. Place right sides together and stitch ¼" from all edges, leaving an opening on one side for turning. Notch curves and turn bug right side out; press.

2. Stitch two buttonholes in one end of the bug as marked on the pattern.

3. Stitch "wing" lines (indicated by dashed lines on the pattern) using a satin stitch.

4. Position the bug as desired on the fabric page. Draw the legs with a fabric marker using the photo as a guide.

5. Remove the bug and place tear-away stabilizer behind the fabric page; stitch the legs using a satin stitch.

6. Pin bug back in place over the legs. Stitch around *wings only* using a satin stitch (the "head" will remain unstitched). Remove excess stabilizer.

7. Sew buttons in place for eyes, positioning them under the "head" to correspond with the buttonholes. (Refer to page 112.)

A blanket stitch makes a fun finish for the edges of the zippered flower.

SNAPPED LADYBUG

Red print fabric for bug, two 6" x 6"
    squares
Thread for legs and appliqué
Two large snaps
Two large felt "googly" eyes

Snap the "googly" eyes in place on this
cheery lady bug.

1. Using the pattern cut two ovals
from red fabric. Place right sides
together and stitch ¼" from all edges,
leaving an opening on one side for
turning. Notch curves and turn bug
right side out; press.

2. Stitch "wing" lines (indicated
by dashed lines on the pattern) using
a satin stitch.

3. Stitch two snaps in one end of the
bug as indicated. (Refer to page 112.)

4. Position the bug as desired on the
fabric page. Draw the legs with a fabric
marker using the photo as a guide.

5. Remove the bug and place tear-
away stabilizer behind the fabric page;
stitch the legs using a satin stitch.

6. Pin bug back in place over the
legs. Stitch around wings only using
a satin stitch (the "head" will remain
unstitched).

7. Glue felt "googly" eyes in place
over snaps, hiding the snap stitching.

8. Stitch corresponding snap
pieces to the fabric page.

HOOK-AND-LOOP TAPE FLOWER

Red fabric for center, two 4" x 4" squares
Yellow print fabric for petals
½" square of hook-and-loop tape
Yellow or green thread for petal appliqué
Red thread for center appliqué

The center of this flower is easy to pull apart
and put back into place.

1. Using the pattern, cut two
circles from red fabric. Stitch around
the circle, leaving an opening for
turning. Trim excess fabric from
outer edge and notch curves. Turn
circle right side out. Stitch loop tape
close to one edge.

2. Bond the fusible web to the
wrong side of the yellow print scrap
fabric. Use the pattern to trace seven
petals onto the paper of the fusible
web.

3. Position petals and flower center
on one 9" x 10" "page" of the book.
Pin the petals then remove the center.
Fuse petals in place and put tear-
away stabilizer behind the fabric page.
Appliqué around the petals using a
blanket stitch; remove excess stabilizer.

4. Stitch the hook tape to the base
of one petal.

5. Match hook-and-loop tapes,
then pin center in place; appliqué
using a zigzag stitch.

FINISHING THE BOOK

1. Place each appliquéd page
wrong sides together with a plain one
and serge around all four edges using
a balanced 3-thread edge stitch.

2. Stitch two embroidered eyelets
along the left edge of each page,
about 2" from the upper and lower
edges. Note: Metal grommets or
buttonholes can be used if desired.

3. Thread ribbon through eyelets;
tie into a bow.

Lace a ribbon or shoe lace through the eyelets of each page to hold the book together.

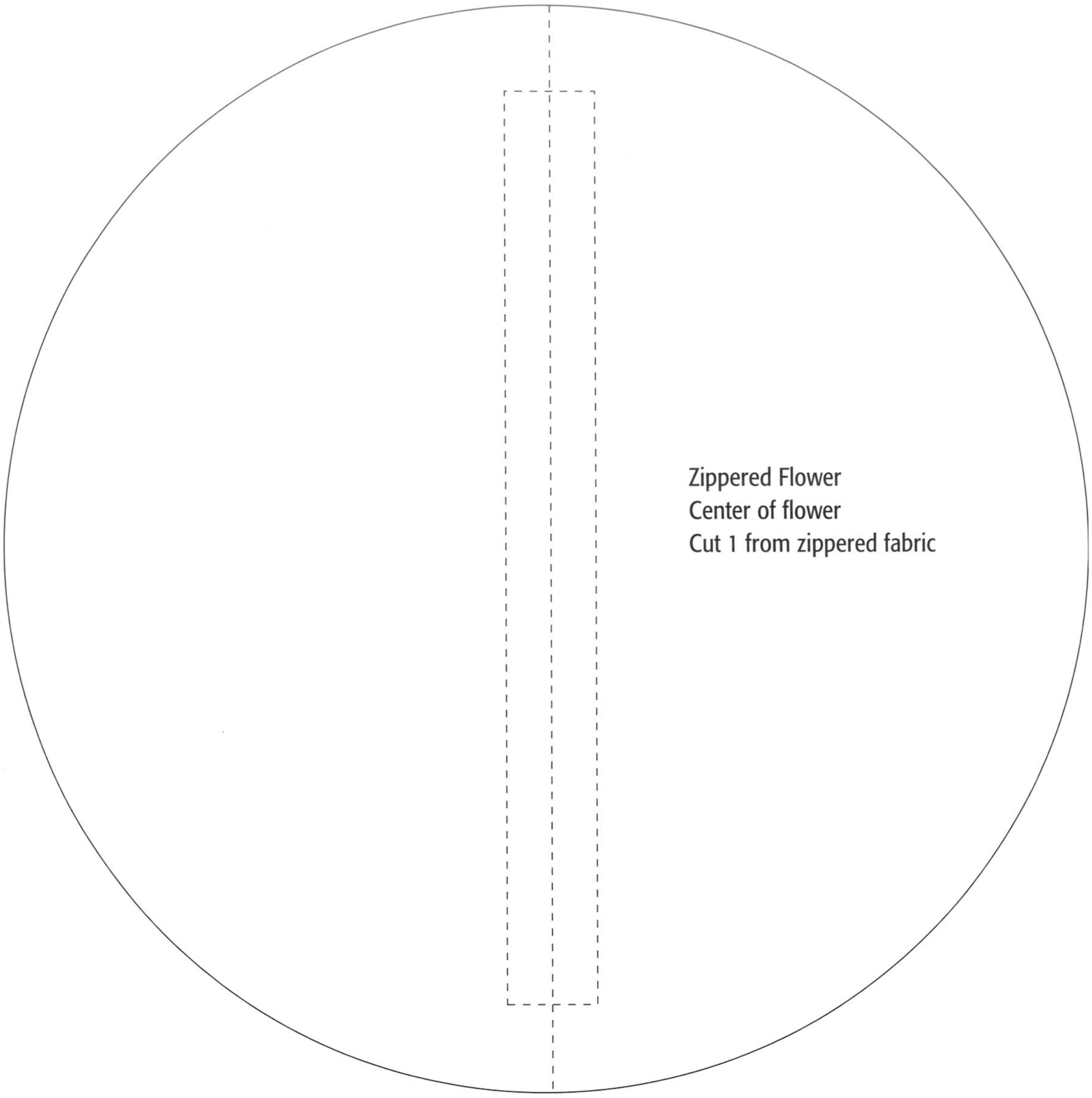

Zippered Flower
Center of flower
Cut 1 from zippered fabric

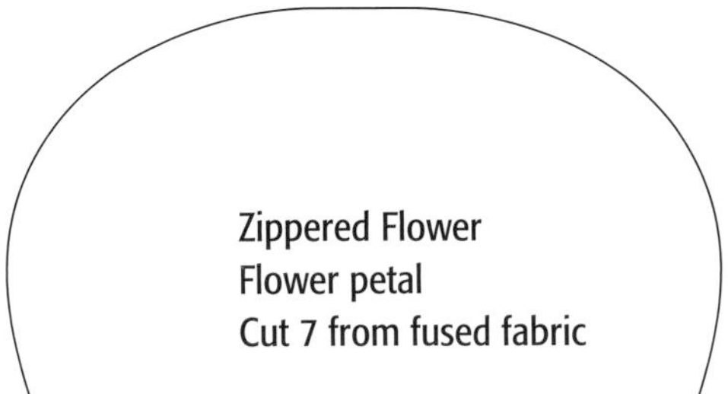

Zippered Flower
Flower petal
Cut 7 from fused fabric

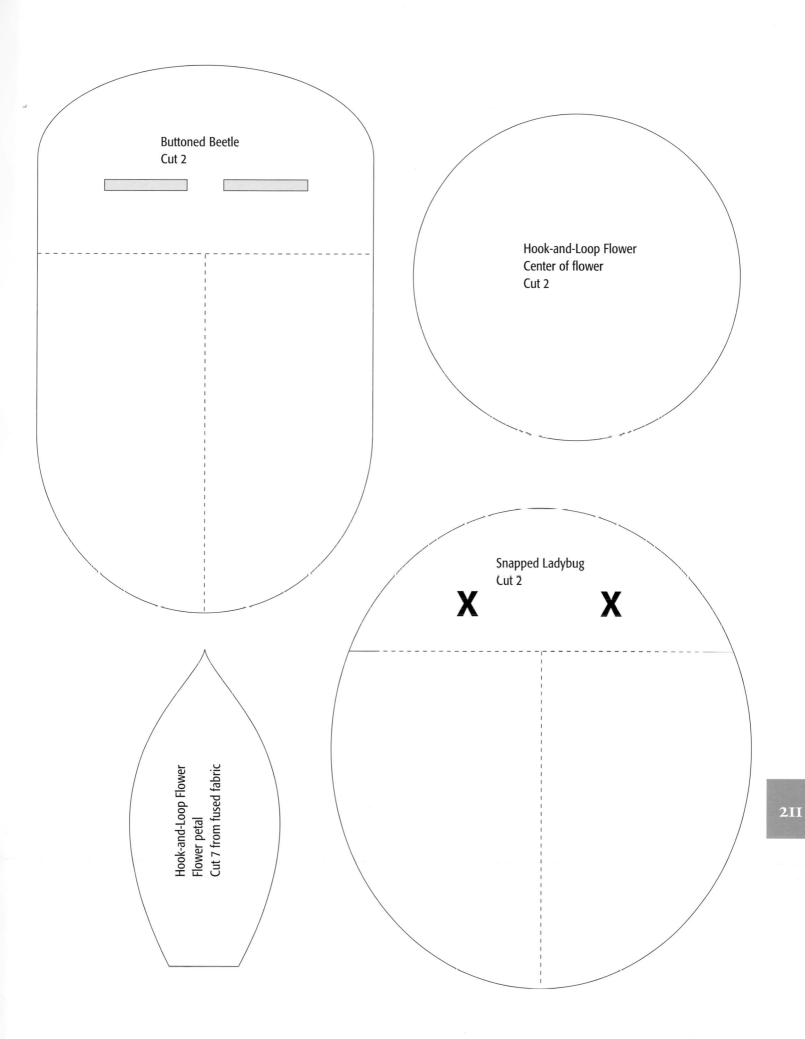

Buttoned Beetle
Cut 2

Hook-and-Loop Flower
Center of flower
Cut 2

Snapped Ladybug
Cut 2

X   X

Hook-and-Loop Flower
Flower petal
Cut 7 from fused fabric

let it rain yellow slicker

Make a fashionable splash in this colorful "one size fits most" rain poncho, perfect for keeping dry on those rainy days. Make it any length—a short poncho or an above-the-knee jacket. Add yellow or red galoshes to keep comfy and dry from head to toe.

DESIGNED AND MADE BY VICKI TRACY

Skill level: Intermediate

Finished size: Approximately 52½" x 64½"

Techniques: Sewing plastic, bound edges, simple pattern drafting, and simple construction

Seam allowances: ½"

MATERIALS

Yellow 100% cotton fabric 45" wide (see instructions for amount)

100% cotton fabric 45" wide for lining – can be the same as outer fabric (see instructions for amount)

Lightweight clear vinyl table covering – same amount as outer fabric (sold by the yard at full service fabric and home dec stores)

Optional: ½ yard contrast fabric for the inside of the hood

½ yard black and white stripe medium weight fabric for contrast binding

12 large black buttons

Teflon-coated presser foot for gliding over vinyl

24" separating zipper

Temporary spray adhesive

Construction thread

DETERMINING FABRIC

Decide the desired length of the finished slicker (measure from the shoulder down to the desired length). Double this amount for the outer fabric; purchase the same amount for the lining. Add ½ yard for the hood.

Example:

Finished desired length = 27" x 2 = 54" or 1½ yards outer fabric.

1½ yards outer fabric + 1½ yards lining fabric + ½ yard for hood = 3½ yards total.

CONSTRUCTING THE JACKET

1. Fold outer fabric in half across the width of the fabric. Find the center and cut the *upper layer only* up to the fold.

2. Use the templates on page 215 to create the neck opening as shown.

3. Shape the lower edges of the jacket as shown in the diagram. It should look like an exaggerated shirt tail hem.

4. Repeat for the lining fabric and clear vinyl.

5. Layer jacket and lining *wrong sides* together. Spray-baste the layers together to prevent shifting.

6. Beginning at the upper neck

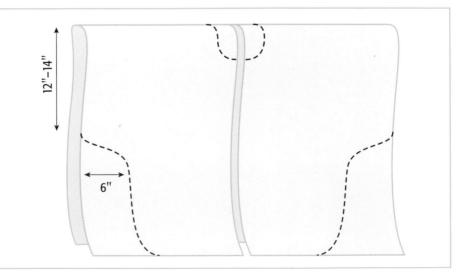

edge on the right-hand side of the jacket, bind around the cut opening and lower edge of the jacket, ending at the left neck edge.

CONSTRUCTING THE HOOD

1. Cut the hood, hood lining, and vinyl using the pattern on page 215.

2. Layer the hood pieces, wrong sides together and top with a layer of vinyl. Do this twice—one stack for each side of the hood.

3. Place the two stacks vinyl to vinyl and seam the curved edge of the hood. Finish the seam by covering it with bias binding and turn the hood right side

out with the vinyl on the outside.

4. Bind around the front edges of the hood, sewing through the fabric and the vinyl (refer to pages 128–129).

ASSEMBLING THE SLICKER

1. Add the vinyl over the outer fabric, matching neck edges. Use paper clips to hold it in place (do not use pins as they will create holes in the vinyl).

2. Sew the hood to the jacket, right sides together (vinyl to vinyl). Stitch using a ⅜" seam and bind the neckline seam.

3. Lay front bound edges over

zipper tape and stitch next to the binding through the zipper tape.

4. Position the vinyl over the outer fabric, placing the edges on the binding. Stitch vinyl next to bias binding at center front edges and straight sleeve edges (lower and underarm edges will be loose).

5. Lay jacket on table placing underarm edges together.

6. Sew buttons to front, layering another button on back and sewing through all layers. Groups of three buttons on each side will hold the jacket together under the arms to form sleeves.

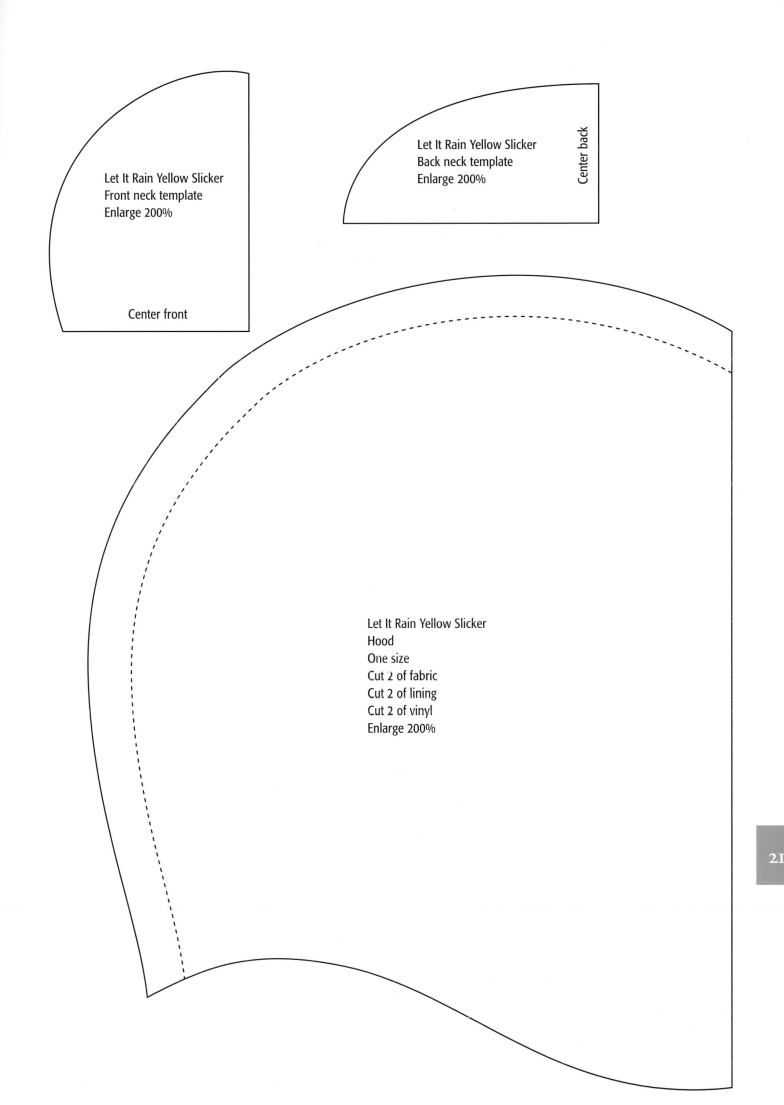

Let It Rain Yellow Slicker
Front neck template
Enlarge 200%

Center front

Let It Rain Yellow Slicker
Back neck template
Enlarge 200%

Center back

Let It Rain Yellow Slicker
Hood
One size
Cut 2 of fabric
Cut 2 of lining
Cut 2 of vinyl
Enlarge 200%

square yoke blouse

This softly gathered pullover has a square neckline that echoes the shape of the front and back yokes. Make the sleeveless version or add a short ruffled sleeve, if desired. Optional piping accents the gathered seam.

DESIGNED AND MADE BY SALLEY BOWMAN
Skill level: Intermediate
Finished size: Small (6–8), Medium (10–12), Large (14–16)
Techniques: Simple clothing construction, gathering, piped seam, and bias binding
Seam allowances: ½"

MATERIALS
1 yard light to medium weight fabric such
   as cotton, rayon, linen, etc.
1 yard cord to cover for piping
1½ yards 2" wide bias binding for armholes
1 bias strip, 1½" x 36" for piping
Construction thread

CUTTING AND PREPARATION
   1. Cut out two rectangles (front and back) as needed for the size blouse desired.

Small (6–8)	25½" x 22"
Med (10–12)	27" x 23"
Large (14–16)	29" x 24"

   2. Using the armhole template (see page 219), cut the upper corners of both the front and back rectangles as shown in the diagram.

   3. Using the pattern provided, cut one front yoke and one back yoke, placing the pattern pieces on the fold as indicated. Cut the same pieces for the yoke facings (total of 4 pieces).

   4. Mark the centers of the upper edges of the rectangles for gathering as indicated in the diagram.

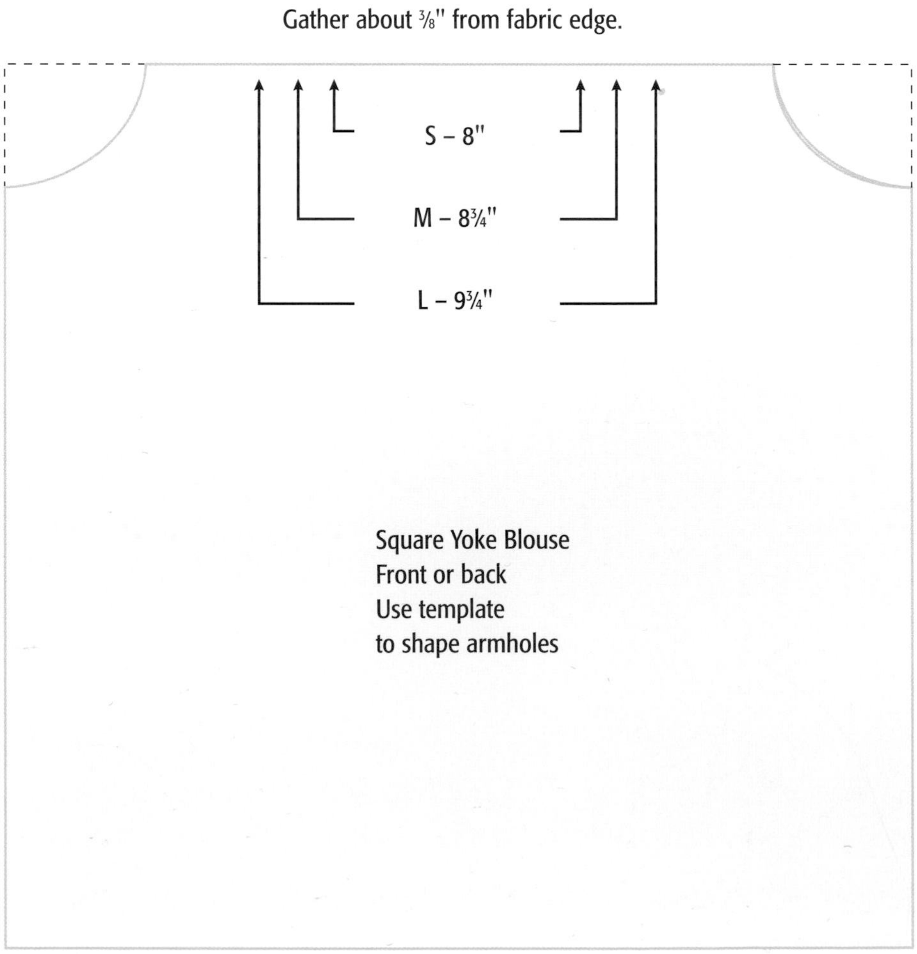

Gather about ⅜" from fabric edge.

S – 8"
M – 8¾"
L – 9¾"

Square Yoke Blouse
Front or back
Use template
to shape armholes

5. Optional piping: Cover 1 yard of cord with 1½" x 36" bias strip.

6. Ruffled Sleeve Version: Cut two ruffled sleeves, placing the pattern on the bias fold as indicated.

YOKE CONSTRUCTION

1. Stitch the yoke together at the shoulder seams. Repeat for yoke facing.

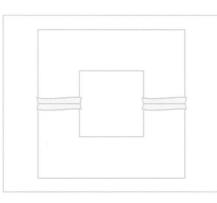

Stitching shoulder seams – Step 1

2. Place the yoke and the facing right sides together and stitch along the neck opening. Clip into the corners, turn the yoke right side out and press. Baste along the outer edges of the square and treat the faced yoke as one piece of fabric.

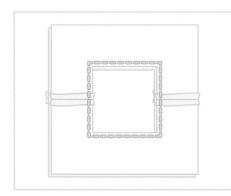

Sewing the neckline – Step 2

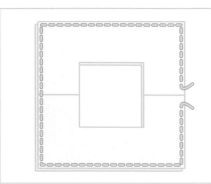

Basting lower edge of yoke – Step 2

3. Optional piping: Wrap the strip around the cord and, using a piping or zipper foot, sew next to the cord. Place the covered piping along each long edge of the yoke front and back; stitch in place over the previous stitching. (Refer to pages 134–137.)

ASSEMBLING THE BLOUSE

1. Gather the upper edge of the blouse front and back. Adjust the

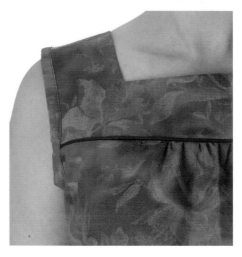

gathers to make the upper edges match the lower edges of the yoke, inserting the piping if desired. Repeat.

2. With right sides together, sew the gathered edge of the blouse front to the lower edge of the front yoke. Repeat for the back.

3. Serge or zigzag the seam allowances together and press them toward the yoke. Topstitch the seam through all layers if desired.

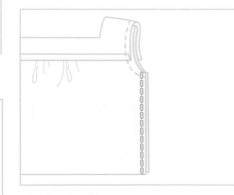

Stitching the side seam – Step 5

4. Optional ruffled sleeve: Hem the lower edge of the sleeve with a narrow hem. Gather the upper edge of the sleeve as indicated on the pattern. Pin the sleeve right sides together to the armhole. Adjust the gathers from each end until the sleeve fits the armhole. Starting at one underarm seam, stitch the sleeve in place, ending at the other underarm seam.

5. Turn the blouse wrong side out and align the front side seams to the back side seams. Stitch the side seams, starting at the underarm and ending at the lower edge of the blouse.

6. Bind the armholes using bias strips and following the directions for Single Binding on page 129.

7. Hem the lower edge of the blouse with a narrow or topstitched hem.

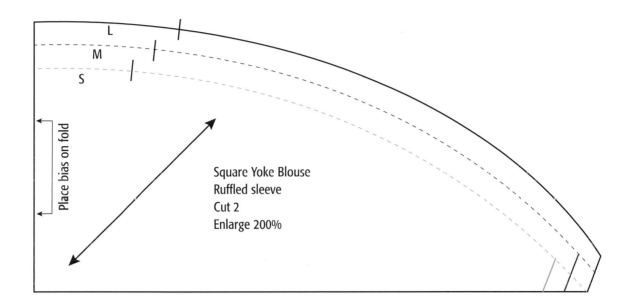

L

M

S

Place bias on fold

Square Yoke Blouse
Ruffled sleeve
Cut 2
Enlarge 200%

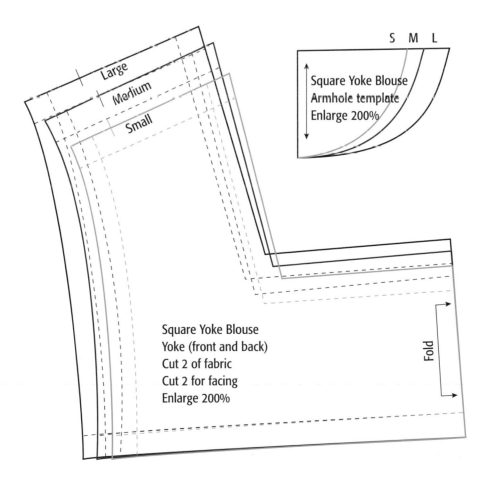

Large

Medium

Small

S M L

Square Yoke Blouse
Armhole template
Enlarge 200%

Square Yoke Blouse
Yoke (front and back)
Cut 2 of fabric
Cut 2 for facing
Enlarge 200%

Fold

ruffled wedge skirt

The vertical lines of this fun and flirty gored skirt make it a flattering addition to any wardrobe. The sample shown is made of lime-green linen fabric with colorful cotton batik ruffles. You'll love making (and wearing!) this skirt so much, you'll want to make it in several different fabric combinations.

DESIGNED AND MADE BY VICKI TRACY
Skill level: Intermediate
Finished size: Drafted to fit
Techniques: Simple pattern drafting, ruffles, and elastic waistline application
Seam allowances: ¼"

MATERIALS
10" x 24" piece of paper or stabilizer for
    creating pattern
Permanent ink marker for creating pattern
Medium weight fabric for skirt (amount
    determined after the pattern is created)
Light to medium weight fabric for ruffles
1½" wide elastic to fit snugly around waist
Construction thread

CREATING THE PATTERN
Draw a vertical line down the center of the paper. Measuring out from the drawn line, create a wedge, known as a gore, using the following diagram as a guide. Note: To make the skirt longer, follow the angles to the desired length.

DETERMINING THE NUMBER OF GORES
Measure your lower body at the widest point (usually the hip or high hip). Divide this number by

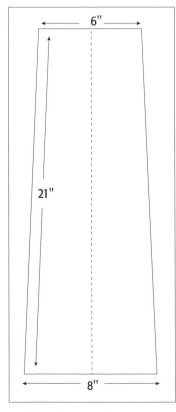

Drafting the skirt pattern

5½" (the width of each gore after seaming). Round up to the next whole number to determine how many gores are needed.

Example: Hip measurement 39" divided by 5.5 = 7.08; cut 8 gores for the complete skirt.

CUTTING AND PREPARATION
1. GORES: Cut out the number of gores needed according to the previous step. If the fabric selected has no nap or directional pattern, the orientation of the gores can be alternated as shown in the layout on page 223 and eight gores can be cut from one length. If the fabric requires a "with nap" layout, place the gores so they are all oriented in the same direction.

2. RUFFLES: Cut 1" bias strips for the ruffles (the sample shows ruffles made from a pink batik print). Note: Because ruffles are cut on the bias, the raw edges will not ravel or

VERSATILE PATTERN

Increase the length of each gore and use this garment as a strapless sundress. The elastic waistline becomes the upper edge of the dress. Add a colorful cordinating belt to finish the look. Follow the same directions as for the skirt adding 12" to 14" to the length of the gores as desired.

"fringe," so you do not need to finish the edge. You'll need one strip for each gore, pieced together to make a strip twice as long as the cut length of the gore. You'll also need about twice the circumference of the lower edge of 1" bias for the ruffled finish (piece as needed to make one long strip).

3. Using one of the methods shown on page 132, gather each bias strip ¼" from one long edge.

CONSTRUCTING THE SKIRT
GORES

1. Position a ruffle along the right edge of one gore (on right side of fabric) with raw edges even; pin or baste in place.

2. Position the left edge of the next gore right side down on the ruffle and seam the gores together with the ruffle sandwiched between.

3. Press the seam allowances to one side (the ruffle should face the opposite direction). Topstitch next to the seam through the seam allowances. Continue this with each gore until you have a complete circle.

Step 1

ELASTIC WAIST

1. Serge or clean-finish the raw edges at the waist. Measure the elastic for the waist; overlap edges to form a circle and stitch.

2. Divide elastic into four sections and mark. Pin the elastic to the right side of the skirt, matching the markings to the center back, center front, and side seams and overlapping the seam allowance about ⅜".

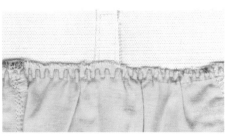

Step 2

3. Beginning at the center back, stitch from pin to pin, stretching the elastic as you sew. Turn the elastic to the inside. Tack at each gored seam to hold the elastic on the inside of the skirt.

Step 3

RUFFLED HEM

1. Position the ruffle along the lower edge of the skirt (on right side of fabric) with raw edges even; pin or baste in place.

2. Sew ruffle to the lower edge as pinned. Press the seam toward the skirt and topstitch close to the seam through the hem allowance.

Directional or "with nap" layout

Fabric saving layout

garden party lap quilt

The simple 4-patch design grows up with bordered blocks set on point. Double borders with a flange inserted between the narrow inner border and the pieced outer border finish off this delightful springtime quilt.

DESIGNED AND MADE BY APRIL OLIVEIRA-WARD

Skill level: Intermediate

Finished size: 52½" x 64½"

Techniques: Simple piecing, piecing bias edges, simple quilting, and bias bound edges

Seam allowances: ¼"

MATERIALS

Fabric:

- 7 coordinating pink prints – ¼ yard or fat quarter of each
- 7 coordinating light green prints – ¼ yard or fat quarter of each
- ¾ yard pink print with light background for 4-patch center blocks and for setting blocks
- ½ yard pink dots with light background for 1st inner border
- ⅓ yard pink and green stripe for 2nd inner border/flange
- 3 yards fabric for backing

Twin size batting (58" x 70")

Neutral color thread to blend with selected fabrics

Rotary cutter

Clear acrylic rulers: 6" x 12"; 10½" square

Cutting mat

Sticky notes

CUTTING

1. From each of the 7 coordinating pink fabrics cut 3 strips, 2½" x 42" across the width of the fabric (6 strips if you are cutting across the width of fat quarters).

2. Sub cut the strips into the following:

- 6 strips, 2½" x 8½"
- 6 strips, 2½" x 4½"

3. From each of the 7 coordinating green fabrics cut 4 strips, 2½" x 42" across the width of the fabric (8 strips if you are cutting across the width of fat quarters).

Sub cut the strips into the following:

- 4 strips, 2½" x 8½"
- 4 strips, 2½" x 4½"
- 1 strip, 2½" x 22"
- 3 strips, 2½" x 9"
- 3 strips, 2½" x 8"

4. From 4 of the 7 coordinating green fabrics, cut the following:

- 1 strip, 2½" x 10½"
- 8 strips 2½" x 21"

5. From the pink fabric with light background, cut the following:

- 4 strips, 2½" x the full width of the fabric

Sub cut these strips to make 8 strips, 2½" x 21"

1 strip, 5½" x the full width of the fabric + 1 strip, 5½" x 14"

Sub cut these strips into nine 5½" squares; cut each square diagonally to yield 18 triangles

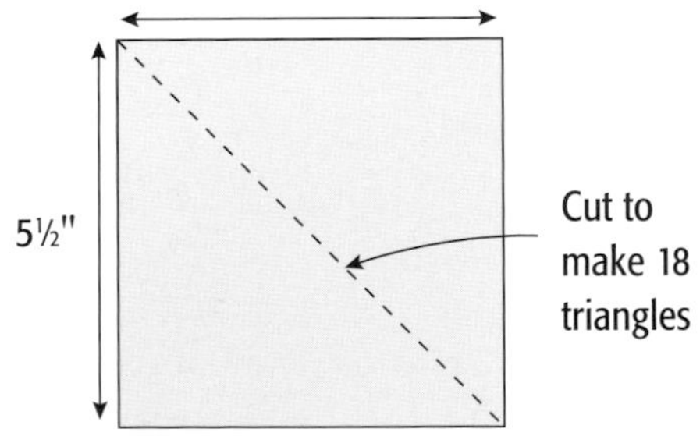

5½" Cut to make 18 triangles

6. From the pink dot fabric with light background cut the following:

- 3 strips, 2" x 42" across the width of the fabric
- 4 strips, 1¾" x 42" across the width of the fabric

7. From the green and pink striped fabric, cut the following:

- 8 strips 1" x 42" across the width of the fabric

PIECING

Blocks Required

8½" x 8½" blocks: 20 pink + 12 green = 32 total

Setting triangles for sides of quilt – 14 green

Setting triangles for corners of quilts – 4 green

8½" X 8½" BLOCKS

Constructing the center 4-patch:

1. Sew the 8 green strips (2½" x 21") to the 8 pink with light background strips (2½" x 21") to make a strip set of 4½" x 21". Press seam allowance to the green fabric. Cut apart at 2½" to get 8 units that measure 2½" x 4½" each.

Cut apart at 2½"

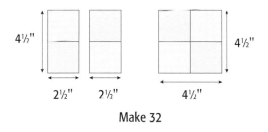

2. Join two of the 2½" x 4½" units together as shown to make 32 four-patch units. Press the seam to one side. Units should measure 4½" x 4½"; trim if needed.

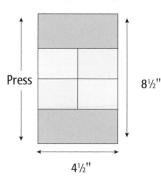

Make 32

3. Using the 2½" x 4½" pink and green strips, join to the 4-patch units as shown. Press seams toward the strips. Make 12 blocks with green strips and 20 blocks with pink strips.

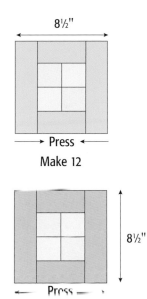

Press   **8½"**

4½"

4. Using the 2½" x 8½" pink and green strips, join to the opposite sides of the blocks as shown. Press the seams of the green blocks toward the 4-patch center and press the seams of the pink blocks toward the strips. Blocks should measure 8½" x 8½"; trim if needed.

8½"

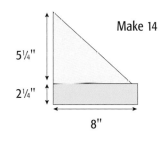

Press
Make 12

8½"

Press
Make 20

SIDE SETTING TRIANGLES

1. Sew the green 2½" x 8" strips to 14 of the pink and light background 5½" triangles along one of the right angle edges as shown. Press toward the green strip.

Make 14

5¼"

2¼"

8"

2. Sew the green 2½" x 9" strips to the other right angle edges of the triangle as shown. Press toward the green strip.

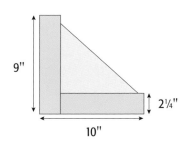

9"   **2¼"**

10"

CORNER SETTING TRIANGLES

1. Sew the green 2½" x 10½" strips to the bias edge of the remaining 4 pink and light background triangles, centering the triangle on the strip as shown. Press toward the green strip.

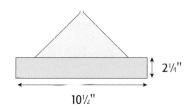

2¼"

10½"

ASSEMBLING THE BLOCKS

1. On the floor or using a design wall, arrange the 8½" x 8½" blocks and the setting blocks in a visually pleasing pattern. You will alternate pink and green blocks as shown in the block assembly diagram.

2. Once you have determined the arrangement of the blocks, label them using sticky notes to keep the order straight as you assemble the quilt top.

3. Sew the blocks together in rows; sew the rows together (see diagrams on pages 228–229). Note the arrows on the diagram for pressing directions.

Block assembly

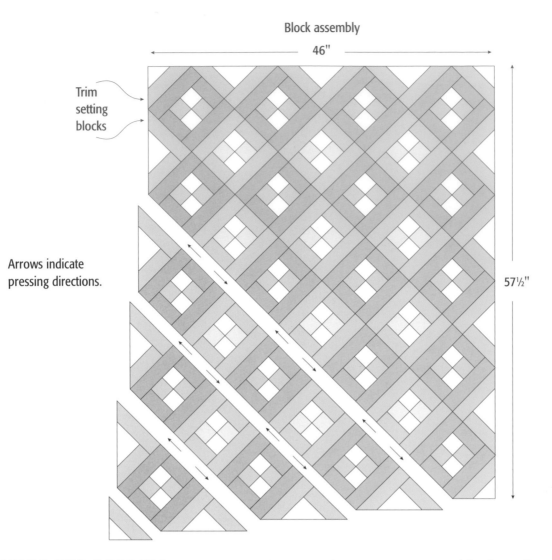

46"

Trim
setting
blocks

Arrows indicate
pressing directions.

57½"

STITCHING THE BORDERS

Before adding the borders, trim the side and corner blocks as shown in the block assembly diagram. Your quilt should now measure 46" x 57½".

FIRST BORDER: LIGHT BACKGROUND WITH PINK DOTS

1. Sew the 1¾" strips together and cut to equal 57½" for each longer side. Stitch to the long sides of the quilt.

2. Sew the 2" strips together and cut to equal 46" for each short side. Stitch to the short sides of the quilt. Your quilt should now measure 48½" x 60½".

SECOND BORDER/FLANGE: GREEN AND PINK STRIPE

3. Join all 8 strips to make one strip about 328" long. Press in half lengthwise with wrong sides together to make a ½" flange. Position the flange on the long sides of the quilt,

matching the raw edges; sew using a long stitch length. Repeat on the short sides of the quilt. Because you are sewing the flange on top of the first border the quilt size remains 48½" x 60½".

THIRD BORDER: MULTI PINK AND GREEN

4. Using the remaining 2½" strips of pink and green fabrics, cut 57 pink and 57 green 2½" squares. You may need to cut extra squares to get more variety from your 14 fabrics.

5. Sew squares together, alternating pink and green to make the four outer border strips. Use 30 squares for the long sides and 26 squares for the short sides.

6. Sew the border to the long sides first and add the short sides second. Your quilt should now measure 52½" x 64½".

FINISHING THE QUILT

1. Layer the quilt with the batting

and backing. Baste or pin the layers together.

2. Quilt the layers together as desired, stitching in the ditch along the seamlines or using an all-over free-motion design as desired.

3. Bind the quilt using a variety of the 14 pink and green fabrics. Cut 2" pieces of pink and green fabrics from the cross grain. For a scrappy look, cut a variety of lengths from 7"–11". Sew the lengths together, alternating pink and green to make one strip about 240" long. Press the binding in half lengthwise with wrong sides together; press.

4. Position the binding along the edge of the quilt front, matching the raw edges. Using a walking foot, sew the binding to the quilt using a ¼" seam allowance. After stitching, wrap the binding around the edge to the back of the quilt and stitch in place by hand using a hemming stitch and a neutral thread color.

Border Sewing

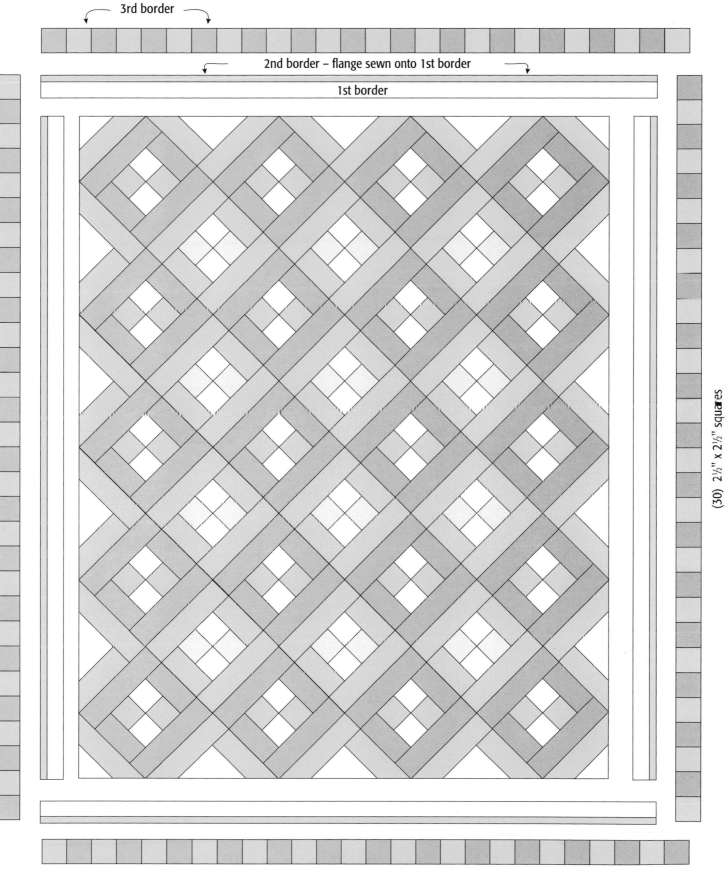

3rd border

2nd border – flange sewn onto 1st border

1st border

(30) 2½" x 2½" squares

(26) 2½" x 2½" squares

NOTES FOR THE HISTORY OF SEWING

1. Olive M. Elrich and Hazel L. Hunt, *The Secret of Sewing: Sewing Efficiency: Containing Concise and Definite Instructions for the Better Use of the Sewing Machine* (New Haven, Conn.: Greist Mfg. Co., 1914), [ii].

2. Catharine E. Beecher, *A Treatise on Domestic Economy: For the Use of Young Ladies at Home and at School* (New York: Harper & Brothers, 1856), 330.

3. Betty Ring, *Girlhood Embroidery: American Samplers and Pictorial Needlework, 1650-1850* (New York: A. A. Knopf, 1993), 16.

4. Ibid., 14.

5. Patricia T. Herr, *The Ornamental Branches: Needlework and Arts From Lititz Moravian Girls' School Between 1800 and 1965.* ([Lancaster, Pa.]: Heritage Center Museum of Lancaster County, 1996), 15.

6. John Burton, *Lectures on Female Education.* 3rd ed. (New York: Hugh Gaine, 1794), 64.

7. "Work Department, Fashionably Dressed Doll," *Godey's Lady's Book and Magazine*, 77 (1868): 72.

8. Catharine E. Beecher, *A Treatise on Domestic Economy: For the Use of Young Ladies at Home and at School*, 65.

9. Ibid.

10. Ibid.

11. Primary Documents in American History: Morrill Act. The Library of Congress. http://www.loc.gov/rr/program/bib/ourdocs/Morrill.html (accessed February 16, 2009).

12. Susan Strasser, *Never Done: A History of American Housework* (New York: Pantheon Books, 1982), 203.

13. Anne L. Jessup, ed., *The Sewing Book: Containing Complete Instructions in Sewing and Simple Garment-Making for Children in the Primary and Grammar Grades* (New York: Butterick Pub. Co., c1913), 1.

14. Ibid.

15. Ibid.

16. Susan Strasser, *Never Done: The History Of American Housework*, 126.

17. Rolla Milton Tryon, *Household Manufactures in the United States, 1640–1860* (Chicago: University of Chicago, 1917), 247.

18. Ibid., 248.

19. Ann L. McDonald, *Feminine Ingenuity: How Women Inventors Changed America* (New York: Ballantine Books, 1992), 77.

20. Ibid.

21. Ibid., 82.

22. United States Centennial Commission, *International Exhibition 1876, Official Catalogue, Part II* (Philadelphia: John R. Nagle & Co., 1876).

23. "Vocational Education." *The Columbia Encyclopedia*, 6th ed. (New York: Columbia University Press, 2001–07), www.bartleby.com/65/ (accessed February 16, 2009).

24. Susan Strasser, *Never Done: A History of American Housework*, 205.

25. Ibid., 41.

26. Barbara Burman, ed., *The Culture of Sewing: Gender, Consumption, and Home Dressmaking* (New York: Berg, 1999), 195.

27. Ibid., 197.

28. Ibid., 202.

29. Susan Strasser, *Never Done: A History of American Housework*, 4.

30. Catharine E. Beecher, *Miss Beecher's Housekeeper and Healthkeeper*, 364.

31. "Women's Institute of Domestic Arts and Sciences," *Needlecraft* 8 (1916): 19.

32. Frances Blondin, ed., *New Encyclopedia of Modern Sewing* (New York: Wm. H. Wise & Co., 1949), i.

33. Sylvia K. Mager, *A Complete Guide to Home Sewing* (New York: Pocket Books, 1952), ix.

34. Ladies' Depository (Philadelphia, Pa.), *The First Annual Report, of the Managers of the Ladies' Depository* (Philadelphia: Lydia R. Bailey, 1834), 1.

35. "Tracing Paper," *The Scientific American* 11 (1854): 163.

36. Ann L. McDonald, *Feminine Ingenuity: How Women Inventors Changed America* (New York: Ballantine Books, 1992), 33.

37. Margaret Walsh, "The Democratization of Fashion: The Emergence of the Women's Dress Pattern Industry," *Journal of American History* 66 (1979): 313.

38. "Tissue Paper Patterns," in Gordon, Sarah A. *"Make It Yourself": Home Sewing, Gender, and Culture, 1890–1930.* Columbia University Press, chapt. 4, 20. http://www.gutenberg-e.org/gordon/ (accessed March 1, 2009)

39. Ibid., chapt. 4, 20.

40. Mary Brooks Picken, *How to Make Dresses the Modern Singer Way* (New York: Singer Sewing Machine Co., 1930), 1.

41. Lydia Maria Child, *The Frugal Housewife*, 115.

42. *Eighty Years Progress of the United States: A Family Record of American Industry, Energy, and Enterprise* (Hartford, Conn.: L. Stebbins, 1867), 390.

43. Ibid.

44. Chauncey Mitchell Depew, *One Hundred Years of American Commerce* (New York: D.O. Haynes, 1895), 662.

45. "How is a Straight Pin Made?" Answers.com. http://www.answers.com/topic/straight-pin-2 (accessed March 1, 2009)

46. Ibid.

47. Horace Greeley, *The Great Industries of the United States* (Hartford: J.B. Burr & Hyde, 1872), 546.

48. *History of Coats and Clark.* http://www.coatsandclark.com/About+Coats/History/ (accessed March 1, 2009)

49. Simon Garfield, *Mauve: How One Man Invented a Color That Changed the World* (New York: Norton, 2001).

50. Catharine E. Beecher and Harriet Beecher Stowe, *The American Woman's Home, or, Principles of Domestic Science: Being a Guide to the Formation and Maintenance of Economical, Healthful, Beautiful, and Christian Home* (New York: J. B. Ford & Co., 1869), 354.

51. Mary Brooks Picken, *How to Make Dresses the Modern Singer Way*, 3.

52. Sylvia K. Mager, *A Complete Guide to Home Sewing*, 7.

53. Frances Blondin, ed., *New Encyclopedia of Modern Sewing*, [ii].

54. "Sewing Machines," *The Scientific American* 7 (1852): 349.

55. *Eighty Years Progress of the United States*, 413.

56. Ibid.

57. "Sewing Machines," *The Scientific American*, 349.

58. James Parton, "History of the Sewing Machine," *The Atlantic Monthly* (1867): 534.

59. Marguerite Connolly, "The Disappearance of the Domestic Sewing Machine, 1890–1925," *Winterthur Portfolio*, 32.

60. Susan Strasser, *Never Done: A History of American Housework*, 139.

61. Ibid.

62. "Sewing Machines," *The Scientific American*, 349.

63. Merritt Ierley, *The Comforts of Home: The American House and the Evolution of Modern Convenience* (New York: Clarkson Potter, 1999), 159.

64. Ruth Brandon, *Singer and the Sewing Machine: A Capitalist Romance* (Philadelphia: J.B. Lippincott Co., 1977), 73.

65. James Parton, "History of the Sewing Machine," 537.

66. James Parton, "History of the Sewing Machine," 538.

67. *Eighty Years Progress of the United States*, 420.

68. Susan Strasser, *Never Done: A History of American Housework*, 138.

69. Marguerite Connolly, "The Disappearance of the Domestic Sewing Machine, 1890–1925," 36.

70. David Lander, "The Buyable Past," *American Heritage Magazine*. http://www.americanheritage.com/articles/magazine/ah/2004/4/2004_4_11_print.shtml. (accessed February 2009)

71. *The History of the Sewing Machine* (Steckborn: Fritz Gegauf Ltd., [n.d.]), 13.

72. Ibid., 28.

73. Olive M. Elrich and Hazel L. Hunt, *The Secret of Sewing*, 3.

74. *Singer Company History*. http://singerco.com/company/history_pf.html (accessed 12/11/2008).

75. Merritt Ierley, *The Comforts of Home*, 193.

76. *How Sewing Machines Work*. http://home.howstuffworks.com/sewing-machine3.htm (accessed 3/1/09).

77. *Singer Company History*. http://singerco.com/company/history_pf.html (accessed 12/11/2008).

GENERAL BIBLIOGRAPHY

PRIMARY SOURCES

Beecher, Catharine E. *Miss Beecher's Housekeeper and Healthkeeper*. New York: Harper & Brothers, 1873.

Beecher, Catharine E. *A Treatise on Domestic Economy: For the Use of Young Ladies at Home and at School*. New York: Harper & Brothers, 1856.

Beecher, Catharine E. and Harriet Beecher Stowe. *The American Woman's Home, or, Principles of Domestic Science: Being a Guide to the Formation and Maintenance of Economical, Healthful, Beautiful, and Christian Home*. New York: J. B. Ford & Co., 1869.

Blondin, Frances, ed. *New Encyclopedia of Modern Sewing*. New York: Wm. H. Wise & Co., 1949.

Bryant, William Cullen, ed. *A New Library of Poetry and Song*. New York: J.B. Ford & Co., [1876].

Burton, John. *Lectures on Female Education*. 3rd ed. New York: Hugh Gaine, 1794.

Camp, Carole Ann. *The Complete Idiot's Guide to Sewing*. New York: The Penguin Group, 2005.

Child, Lydia Maria. *The Frugal Housewife*. Boston: Carter and Hendee, 1830.

Detrixhe, Sandra. *The Everything Sewing Book*. Avon, Mass.: Adams Media, 2004.

Depew, Chauncey Mitchell. *One Hundred Years of American Commerce*. New York: D.O. Haynes, 1895.

Dubicki, Elizabeth. *101 Ways to Use Your First Sewing Machine*. Iola, Wis.: Krause Publications, 2006.

Eighty Years Progress of the United States: A Family Record of American Industry, Energy, and Enterprise. Hartford, Conn.: L. Stebbins, 1867.

Elrich, Olive M. and Hazel L. Hunt. *The Secret of Sewing: Sewing Efficiency: Containing Concise and Definite Instructions for the Better Use of the Sewing Machine*. New Haven, Conn.: Greist Mfg. Co., 1914.

Gardiner, Wendy. *The Encyclopedia of Sewing Techniques*. Philadelphia: Quatro Publishing, London, 2003.

The Great Industrial Exhibition, in 1851. The Disastrous Consequences Which Are Likely to Arise to the Manufacturing Trade of This Country…by a Late Manufacturer. London, [1850].

Greeley, Horace. *The Great Industries of the United States*. Hartford: J.B. Burr & Hyde, 1872.

Jessup, Anne L., ed. *The Sewing Book: Containing Complete Instructions in Sewing and Simple Garment-Making for Children in the Primary and Grammar Grades*. New York: Butterick Pub. Co., c1913.

Knight, Lorna. *The Dressmaker's Technique Bible*. Iola: Krause Publications, 2008.

Knight, Lorna. *The Sewing, Stitch, & Textile Bible*. Iola: Krause Publications, 2007.

Ladies' Depository (Philadelphia, Pa.), *The First Annual Report, of the Managers of the Ladies' Depository*. Philadelphia: Lydia R. Bailey, 1834.

Maresh, Jan Saunders. *Sewing For Dummies*. Hoboken, N.J.: Wiley Publishing, Inc., 2004.

Mager, Sylvia K. *A Complete Guide to Home Sewing*. New York: Pocket Books, 1952.

New Complete Guide to Sewing. Pleasantville, N.Y.: Reader's Digest, 2002.

The New Sewing Essentials. Minneapolis: Creative Publishing International, 2008.

Picken, Mary Brooks. *How to Make Dresses the Modern Singer Way*. New York: Singer Sewing Machine Co., 1930.

Sandhurst, Phillip T. *The Great Centennial Exhibition, critically described and illustrated*. Philadelphia: P.W. Zeigler & Co., 1876.

The Sewing Machine: Its Origin, Introduction into General Use, Progress and Extent of Its Manufacture, A Great Machine-Shop Described. New York: Wheeler and Wilson Manufacturing Co., 1863.

The Story of the Sewing Machine. [S.1.]: Singer Manufacturing Co., 1897.

Tryon, Rolla Milton. *Household Manufactures in the United States, 1640–1860*. Chicago: University of Chicago, 1917.

United States Centennial Commission, *International Exhibition 1876, Official Catalogue, Part II*. Philadelphia: John R. Nagle & Co., 1876.

Wright's Polyester/Cotton Wide Bias Tape. West Warren, Mass.: Wm. E. Wright Co., 1979.

NINETEENTH-CENTURY PERIODICALS

"Sewing Machines," *The Scientific American* 7 (1852): 349

"Tracing Paper," *The Scientific American* 11 (1854): 163.

"Work Department, Fashionably Dressed Doll," *Godey's Lady's Book and Magazine*, 77 (1868): 72.

"Women's Institute of Domestic Arts and Sciences," *Needlecraft* 8 (1916): 19.

SECONDARY RESOURCES

Brandon, Ruth. *Singer and the Sewing Machine: A Capitalist Romance*. Philadelphia: J. B. Lippincott Co., 1977.

Burman, Barbara, ed., *The Culture of Sewing: Gender, Consumption, and Home Dressmaking*. New York: Berg, 1999.

Casper, Scott E., ed. *The Industrial Book, 1840-1880*. Chapel Hill: University of North Carolina Press, 2007.

Connolly, Marguerite. "The Disappearance of the Domestic Sewing Machine, 1890–1925," *Winterthur Portfolio*, 34 (1999): 40.

Garfield, Simon. *Mauve: How One Man Invented a Color That Changed the World*. New York: Norton, 2001.

Herr, Patricia T. *The Ornamental Branches: Needlework and Arts From Lititz Moravian Girls' School Between 1800 and 1965*. [Lancaster, Pa.]: Heritage Center Museum of Lancaster County, 1996.

The History of the Sewing Machine. Steckborn: Fritz Gegauf Ltd., [n.d.]).

Ierley, Merritt. *The Comforts of Home: The American House and the Evolution of Modern Convenience*. New York: Clarkson Potter, 1999.

McDonald, Ann L. *Feminine Ingenuity: How Women Inventors Changed America*. New York: Ballantine Books, 1992.

Ring, Betty. *Girlhood Embroidery: American Samplers and Pictorial Needlework, 1650-1850*. New York: A. A. Knopf, 1993.

Strasser, Susan. *Never Done: A History of American Housework*. New York: Pantheon Books, 1982.

Margaret Walsh, "The Democratization of Fashion: The Emergence of the Women's Dress Pattern Industry," *Journal of American History* 66 (1979): 313.

WEBSITES

History of Coats and Clark. http://www.coatsandclark.com/About+Coats/History/ (accessed March 1, 2009)

"How is a Straight Pin Made?" Answers.com. http://www.answers.com/topic/straight-pin-2 (accessed March 1, 2009)

How Sewing Machines Work. http://home.howstuffworks.com/sewing-machine3.htm (accessed 3/1/09).

David Lander, "The Buyable Past," *American Heritage Magazine*. http://www.americanheritage.com/articles/magazine/ah/2004/4/2004_4_11_print.shtml. (accessed February 2009)

Primary Documents in American History: Morrill Act. The Library of Congress. http://www.loc.gov/rr/program/bib/ourdocs/Morrill.html (accessed February 16, 2009).

Singer Company History. http://singerco.com/company/history_pf.html (accessed 12/11/2008).

"Tissue Paper Patterns," in Gordon, Sarah A. *"Make It Yourself": Home Sewing, Gender, and Culture, 1890–1930*. Columbia University Press, chapt. 4, 20. http://www.gutenberg-e.org/gordon/ (accessed March 1, 2009)

"Vocational Education." The Columbia Encyclopedia, 6th ed. (New York: Columbia University Press, 2001–07), www.bartleby.com/65/ (accessed February 16, 2009).

FURTHER READING

Boydston, Jeanne. *Home and Work: Housework, Wages, and the Ideology of Labor in the Early Republic*. New York: Oxford University Press, 1990.

Bushman, Richard L. *The Refinement of America*. New York: Alfred A. Knopf, 1992.

Carlson, Laurie. *Queen of Inventions: How the Sewing Machine Changed the World*. Brookfield, Conn.: The Millbrook Press, 2003.

Caulfeild, Sophia Frances Anne. *The Dictionary of Needlework, an Encyclopedia of Artistic, Plain, and Fancy Needlework*. New York: Arno Press; distributed by Crown Publishers, 1972. Reprint of the 1882 ed.

Cott, Nancy F. *The Bonds of Womanhood.* New Haven, Conn.: Yale University Press, 1977.

Deutsch, Davida Tenenbaum. "The Polite Lady: Portraits of American Schoolgirls and Their Accomplishments, 1725–1830." *The Magazine Antiques.* (March 1989) 743–753.

Ellen Carol DuBois and Lynn Dumenil. *Through Women's Eyes: An American History With Documents.* New York: Bedford/St. Martin's, 2005.

Forman-Brunell, Miriam, ed. *Girlhood in America: An Encyclopedia.* Santa Barbara: ABC-CLIO, 2001.

Graffam, Olive Blair. *"Youth is the Time for Progress": The Importance of American Schoolgirl Art, 1780–1860.* Washington, D.C.: DAR Museum, 1998.

Harbeson, Georgiana Brown. *American Needlework: The History of Decorative Stitchery and Embroidery from the Late Sixteenth to the Twentieth Century.* New York: Coward-McCann, Inc., 1938.

Mathews, Glenna. *"Just a Housewife": The Rise and Fall of Domesticity in America.* New York: Oxford University Press, 1987.

Mintz, Steven. *Domestic Revolutions: A Social History of American Family Life.* New York: The Free Press, 1988.

Osaki, Amy Boyce. *The Needle's Web: Sewing in One Early Nineteenth-Century American Home.* Master's thesis, University of Delaware, 1988.

Scalessa, Nicole. *The Hook and the Book: The Emergence of Crochet and Knitting in American Popular Culture, 1840–1876.* Philadelphia: The Library Company of Philadelphia, 2001.

Vincent, Margaret. *The Ladies' Work Table: Domestic Needlework in Nineteenth-century America.* Allentown, Pa.: Allentown Art Museum, 1988.

Waugh, Norah. *The Cut of Women's Clothes, 1600–1930.* New York: Theatre Arts Books, 1968.

Woloch, Nancy. *Women and the American Experience.* Boston: McGraw-Hill, 2000.

WEBSITES

A Servant in the House: A Brief History of the Sewing Machine. The Smithsonian Institution Libraries Digital Edition. http://www.sil.si.edu/digitalcollections/hst/lewton/ (accessed March 1, 2009)

Sewing Machines: Historical Trade Literature in the Smithsonian Institution Collections. The Smithsonian Institution Libraries. http://www.sil.si.edu/DigitalCollections/Trade-Literature/Sewing-Machines/ (accessed March 1, 2009)

Cooper, Grace Rogers. *The Sewing Machine: Its Invention and Development.* The Smithsonian Institution Libraries Digital Edition. http://www.sil.si.edu/DigitalCollections/HST/Cooper/ (accessed March 1, 2009)

History of Coats and Clark. http://www.coatsandclark.com/About+Coats/History/ (accessed March 1, 2009)

RESOURCES

The Sewing Machine Shop
www.sewingmachineshop.com
800 300-4739

Jane Foster Sewing Studio
www.janefosterdesign.com
925 939-2328

Diana McClun
From Me To You
www.dianaandlaura.com
925 934-1334

Sewing Machine Companies
Babylock
www.babylock.com

Bernina of America
www.berninausa.com

Brother
www.brother-usa.com/homesewing

Elna
www.elnausa.com

Janome
www.janome.com

Kenmore
www.kenmore.com

Pfaff
www.pfaffusa.com

Singer
www.singerco.com

Viking
www.husqvarnaviking.com/us

White
www.whitesewing.com

Pattern Companies
Burda
www.burdafashion.com
www.burdastyle.com

Butterick
www.butterick.com

Kwik Sew
www.kwiksew.com

McCalls
www.mccallpattern.com

New Look
www.newlookpatterns.com

Simplicity
www.simplicity.com

The Sewing Workshop
www.sewingworkshop.com

Vogue
www.voguepatterns.com

Thread Companies
American & Efird
www.amefird.com

Aurifil
www.aurifil.com

Coats and Clark
www.coatsandclark.com

Gutermann
www.gutermann-thread.com

Isacord
www.embroideryonline.com

Madeira
www.madeirausa.com

Superior
www.superiorthreads.com

Sulky
www.sulky.com

YLI Corporation
www.ylicorp.com

Notions
Bobbin Saver
www.blue-feather.com

Clover Mfg. Ltd.
www.clover-usa.com

Fasturn (fabric tube turner)
www.fasturn.net

Fiskars
www.fiskars.com

Floriani
www.rnkdistributing.com

Gingher
www.gingher.com

June Tailor, Inc.
www.junetailor.com

OESD
www.embroideryonline.com

Olfa
www.olfa.com

Prym-Dritz Corporation
www.dritz.com

Schmetz
www.schmetzneedles.com

Tiger Tape
www.oldmadequilts.com

Wrights
www.wrights.com

align – Matching two areas, usually raw edges.

alteration – Refers to changes made to pattern pieces or to a finished garment, usually to modify the fit or style.

apex – The highest point of the bust; the apex of the bust dart is where it tapers to a point.

appliqué – French, meaning "to apply", this technique involves stitching fabric shapes onto a background to form a design; can be stitched in a variety of ways, with a variety of threads as desired.

arrow – Symbol used on patterns to indicate grainlines, direction of stitching, and direction of folding for pleats and tucks.

awl – Pointed tool used to punch holes in leather and fabric.

backing – Fabric used to make the back of a quilt; also refers to stabilizers used on the wrong side of fabric for stitching and embroidery.

backstitching – Stitching in reverse; used at the beginning and end of a seam to secure the stitching. Also refers to a hand stitch used for seaming or embroidery.

ballpoint needle – Needle with a slightly rounded point designed to slide between the fibers of knit fabric to stitch it without snagging, pulling, or puckering.

bar tack – Made by machine or hand, this reinforcement stitch is used at stress points such as belt loops or pocket edges.

baste – To sew temporary seams or markings using a long stitch length, making the thread easy to remove.

batting – Middle layer of a quilt; made of cotton, polyester, wool or silk, this filler has insulating properties and gives varying degrees of "puffiness" to a quilt.

beading – Technique of attaching beads, either individually or as a strand, to the surface of fabric; can be machine or hand stitched.

between needle – Short hand-sewing needle with a fine point used for quilting and topstitching.

bias – Diagonal grain of fabric; true bias is a 45° diagonal.

bias tape – Folded strip of bias-cut fabric. Double-fold tape has both long edges folded to the wrong side, meeting in the center. Single-fold has one long edge folded to the wrong side.

binding – Strips of fabric used to cover raw edges.

blanket stitch – A stitch sewn by hand or machine that sews a straight line, taking a long horizontal stitch at regular intervals. Used to stitch appliqué shapes and secure bindings.

blind hem – A machine- or hand-stitched hem sewn mostly on the hem allowance with an occasional tiny stitch that picks up the garment. The machine-stitched version requires a machine equipped with a blindstitch and blind hem presser foot; excellent for draperies and some garments.

bobbin – A small spool-like item that holds thread to form the lower part of machine stitches.

bobbinwork – Decorative technique that uses heavy decorative threads and cords on the bobbin; project is turned upside down and sewn from the wrong side so the stitching is seen on the right side.

bodice – The upper portion of a ladies garment, covering the area from the shoulder to the waist.

bolt – Flat, cardboard "tube" that fabric is wrapped around for display and organization in a fabric store.

box pleats – Usually seen at center front and/or back, a box pleat has the folded fabric on the outside of the garment.

butt – Edges placed side-by-side for stitching.

buttonhole – An opening that fits around a button, the cut edges are sewn with satin stitching for strength and finish.

casing – A fabric "tunnel" created at waistlines or sleeve edges to hold elastic, drawing up the area to fit.

channel quilting – Parallel lines of stitching sewn through layers of fabric and batting.

chenille needle – Long, fat hand-sewing needle used for sewing with thick threads or yarns; may have blunt or sharp point.

clapper – Wooden pressing tool used to apply pressure to sewn fabric edges to flatten and smooth them.

clean finish – Edges that have been turned and stitched to prevent raveling and give a finished look; usually refers to seam allowances.

clip – Small snip into the edge of fabric meant to release the fabric to fit; often used on curved seams such as necklines and armholes so the fabric will turn smoothly to the right side.

collar stand – Attached to the neckline of a garment, the collar stand supports the collar. Some stands are extensions of the collar and others are separate pieces; flat collars do not have stands.

continuous lap – Strip of fabric used to bind the slit of a cuff opening.

continuous line – Type of free-motion quilting design that is stitched in one fluid motion from beginning to end without stopping.

cording – Decorative cord for edging pillows, jackets, etc.; may also be filler cord used to make piping by covering it with fabric.

couching – Stitching yarn, heavy threads, and cords to fabric surfaces to add color and/or texture as embellishment.

couture – Refers to high-end fashion often created with quality techniques and hand stitching.

crazypatch – A form of patchwork that seems to be pieced in a random fashion using odd-shaped patches of fabric. After piecing, the seamlines are heavily embellished with decorative stitching and added trims such as lace, buttons, charms, and trinkets.

cross grain – The horizontal grain of a piece of fabric; the cross grain has a small amount of "give," offering a bit more stretch than the lengthwise grain.

cutting line – The outer line of the paper pattern piece, this is usually a heavy black line that you follow when cutting out a project.

darn – A mending term that refers to covering a hole with stitches; may be a hand or machine technique.

dart – A tapered fold stitched into fabric to shape it to fit around the body, most commonly used in the bust, shoulder, and waist areas.

design ease – Fabric added to body measurements so clothing will fit in a certain way.

double needle tuck – A raised ridge of fabric created by stitching with a double needle and a straight stitch on light- to medium weight fabric; using a special grooved presser foot, usually called a pintuck foot, makes the tuck more pronounced.

drape – Refers to the way fabric yardage hangs or falls.

ease stitching – Similar to gathering, this type of stitching makes a longer piece of fabric smoothly match a shorter piece without puckers or pleats; most commonly used when setting in a sleeve.

echo quilting – Outline stitching that repeats the shape of a motif, patch or appliqué; usually stitched in concentric rows around the shape.

edgestitch – Straight stitching along a finished edge such as a collar, lapel or jacket opening; easily accomplished using an edgestitching foot that offers a guide for following the edge.

embellish – Add decorative elements such as embroidery, quilting, smocking, etc. to fabric or projects as you sew.

extended facing – A facing that is part of the main garment piece and both are cut as one. Usually seen along the front opening of a shirt or jacket, this is also referred to as a cut-on facing.

eyelet – An embroidered hole used as embellishment or for more practical uses such as on a belt or for lacing ties that serve as a closure.

facing – Fabric pieces used to finish edges such as necklines, armholes, and waistlines; facings are stitched to the outside of the garment and then turned to the inside to hide them.

fat quarter – A cut of fabric most often used by quilters where one yard of fabric is cut in half horizontally and then again vertically, making four quarters. This offers a larger piece of fabric for cutting patches than if the fabric is cut into four narrow strips across the width of the fabric.

feed dog – A series of moveable "teeth" on the bed of a sewing machine that carries the fabric to the back under the needle.

fiber content – Refers to the basic ingredient of fabric; fibers of silk, cotton, linen, etc. are woven into yardage.

finger pressing – Smoothing and sharpening a fabric edge or seam by applying pressure with your fingers or with a small wooden tool.

flat felled seam – A lapped seam finished on the inside of the garment and stitched with a double row of topstitching on the outside; often used on tailored shirts.

flounce – A circular ruffle that can be gathered or flat along the side attached to the garment or project edge.

free-motion stitching – Sewing machine stitching where the feed dog of the machine is covered or lowered; the stitcher moves the fabric, enabling the stitching of any pattern or motif in any direction.

French curve – A ruler with one curved side; used to redraw pattern lines when altering patterns.

French seam – An enclosed seam treatment used most often on sheer fabrics.

give – Refers to the amount of movement or stretch in a fabric; knit fabrics have the most "give."

gore – A tapered section of fabric used to make a gored skirt; the section repeats around the garment to make a complete skirt.

grading – Staggered trimming of seam allowances to reduce bulk and make seam flat; especially useful technique when using bulky fabrics such as wool.

grain – The direction of the fibers in woven fabric yardages; lengthwise grain is the most stable with no stretch; crosswise grain has a slight stretch; bias or diagonal grain has the most stretch.

grid quilting – Vertical and horizontal lines of stitching sewn through layers of fabric and batting.

hand – Refers to the drape and feel of fabric yardage.

hem – Turning fabric to the wrong side, then stitching it in place as a finish for raw edges of fabric; used at lower edge of garments and sleeves.

Hong Kong finish – A seam finish that binds the raw edges of seam allowances; often used on unlined garments to give the inside a more "finished" look.

hook & eye – A two-piece metal or plastic closure used at waistbands and necklines.

interfacing – Material made for adding support and shaping to fabric; often used at neckline, armholes, and garment openings.

interlining – Material used to add warmth to a garment.

inverted pleat - A pleat with the folded fabric on the inside of the garment.

knife pleat – A series of simple pleats that fold in the same direction.

knits – Fabrics that are created with a looped construction that enables the yardage to stretch; fabrics may have one-way, two-way, or all-way stretch, depending on how they are constructed.

lap quilt – A small quilt that does not measure more than 60 inches on any side.

lapel – Folded-back portion of a garment that is usually part of a facing sewn to a collar; found on jackets and shirts.

layout – Refers to the position of pattern pieces on fabric for cutting.

lengthwise grain – The vertical grain of a piece of fabric; the lengthwise grain is the most stable and has the least stretch.

lining – An inner construction component that adds structure and wearing comfort to a garment while covering the construction elements and protecting the fashion fabric.

loft – Refers to the thickness and softness of quilt batting; a batt with a full, soft loft works well for a comforter while lower-loft batts are often used for bed quilts.

marking – Transferring pattern symbols from the paper pattern pieces to the fabric; these symbols aid in positioning and alignment as the pattern pieces are stitched together.

miter – Fitting two pieces of fabric together with a diagonal seam or fold; used for the corners of a quilt, facing/hem edges, slit openings, etc.

muslin – Cotton fabric in bleached and unbleached versions often used as "practice" fabric; the term also refers to a trial garment made from muslin fabric to check fit and construction details before beginning the actual garment.

nap – Fabric that feels smooth in one direction and rough in the other; each direction reflects light differently, changing the look when turned in different directions. Examples of fabrics with nap are velvet, corduroy, and satin and require a one-direction layout.

needle – Made for both hand and machine sewing, these slender metal tools have a hole or "eye" in one pointed end that carries thread through the fabric.

needle punch – Sometimes called felting, this hand or machine technique uses sharp, barbed needles to push or punch fibers, yarns, and roving through a base fabric to add color and create designs.

notch – Symbol used on patterns, indicating an edge to be matched to another edge; the term also refers to cutting small pieces of fabric from seam allowances to enable fabric to turn smoothly to the right side.

notions – General term that indicates supplies needed to complete a sewing project along with the pattern and fabric; examples are zippers, buttons, twill tape, thread, etc.

overlock – Machine that trims, sews, and overcasts fabric edges in one operation; also called a serger.

overcasting – Stitching that forms around the raw edge of fabric.

patchwork – Piecing fabric to form patterns; commonly used for quilt tops.

pattern grading – Trimming and sizing of patterns to create different sizes of the same garment.

pattern repeat – The distance used to show one motif or pattern of a woven or print design of fabric.

piecing – Stitching patches of fabric together to form a pattern, pre-determined or random; most often used in making quilts.

pile – The surface of some fabrics made up of cut or uncut loops of fabric; examples are velvet, corduroy, and terrycloth.

pintuck – A raised ridge of fabric created by stitching with a double needle, a straight stitch and a pintuck foot to create texture on fabric; also sometimes used to refer to very narrow, delicate tucks stitched with a single needle.

pincushion – A small stuffed cushion designed to hold straight pins; modern pin "cushions" are magnetized dishes that hold pins.

pinking shears - Scissors with saw-toothed blades that cut fabric, leaving a zigzag pattern on the edge to help slow the raveling of the cut edge.

piping – Fabric covered cording used as a trim for seams and project edges.

pivot – Turning a corner when stitching, pivoting is done with the needle in the fabric.

pleats – Fabric manipulated to fold out fullness; skirts and draperies are common places for using pleats.

pre-treat – Launder or dry clean fabric in the same way you plan to care for the garment when it is finished.

press cloth – Fabric used to cover the surface of delicate or heat-sensitive fabric during pressing.

presser foot – Changeable component of a sewing machine that holds the fabric in place as it moves under the needle; an all-purpose presser foot works for most sewing and other presser feet are available for specialty techniques such as buttonholes, pintucks, appliqué, couching, etc.

pressing ham – Shaped like a ham, this useful pressing surface is for pressing shaped areas such as for darts, collars, sleeve caps, and curved seams.

quilting – Stitching through layers of fabric and batting.

raw edge – Unfinished or cut edge of fabric.

remnant – Small or leftover piece of fabric.

reverse sewing – Removing or ripping stitches that have been sewn incorrectly.

right side – The side of the fabric that will show on the outside of the garment or project being made.

roller foot – Presser foot with rollers on the bottom of the sole; used for sewing on plastic or leather.

rotary cutter – Tool with a circular blade resembling a pizza cutter used for cutting fabric; requires a special cutting mat to protect the layout surface.

RST – Stands for Right Sides Together and refers to the way most fabric is positioned for seaming.

ruffle – Gathered strip of fabric used as a trim for seamlines and project edges.

satin stitch – Zigzag stitch with a short length, giving a rich, full look to the stitch.

seam – Two pieces of fabric sewn together, usually right sides together.

seamline – Line where two pieces of fabric are sewn together, usually parallel to the cut edge of the fabric.

seam allowance – The amount of fabric between the seam line and the cut edge of the fabric.

seam ripper – Sharp tool used to cut threads when stitching needs to be removed.

selvage – Finished edge of fabric created in the manufacturing process.

serger – Machine that trims, sews, and overcasts fabric edges in one operation; also called an overlock machine.

shank button – Shaped button with a molded or attached loop on the back; these buttons are sewn on by hand, stitching through the loop (shank), and then the fabric.

shears – Large scissors for sewing and dressmaking.

silk ribbon embroidery – Hand or machine technique that creates embroidery stitches and designs using narrow silk ribbon instead of embroidery floss.

sizing – Special finish that makes fabric seem to have more body and weight; most sizing rinses out, leaving the fabric limp and lightweight.

stabilizer – Material used to support and reinforce fabric for decorative stitching and machine embroidery; most stabilizer is temporary and is removed once the stitching is complete.

stay stitching – Stitching sewn on a single layer of fabric to keep fabric edge from stretching or distorting; often used on curved edges like necklines.

stitch-in-the-ditch – Stitching in the well of a seam; often used when quilting a patchwork quilt. This technique is also used in garment making to secure facings to shoulder seams or to hold waistbands in place.

stiletto – Pointed tool used to punch holes in fabric or leather; also used to hold fabric as it goes under the needle when machine sewing.

tailor tacks – Loose hand-sewn stitches used to indicate construction and placement markings transferred from the pattern to fabric.

tape measure – Flexible ruler made of fiberglass or fabric.

tension – Amount of "pull" on the needle and bobbin threads of the sewing machine; proper tension settings are required for good stitch formation.

thimble – Used for hand sewing, a thimble is a protective covering worn on the second finger of your sewing hand; most thimbles are made of metal but can also be leather or plastic.

thread – Fiber used to sew fabric together whether sewing by hand or machine.

thread sketching – Free-motion machine technique that is the process of "drawing" on fabric using needle and thread.

trim – Cutting away excess fabric.

tuck – A stitched fold of fabric used as decoration; can also be used to shape fabric such as at a neckline or waistline.

true bias – The diagonal grain of the fabric at a 45° angle to the selvage.

topstitching – Lines of stitching sewn on the outside of a garment or project; usually decorative but can also reinforce or secure an edge.

twill tape – Stable tape used to reinforce seams, edges and roll lines.

underlining – Material used on the back of fashion fabric to add support; the two layers are treated as one in the construction process.

understitching – Sewing the seam allowances of a faced area to the facing to keep it from rolling to the outside.

universal needle – Most common type of sewing machine needle point, the universal point works for woven fabric and most knits.

wale – Raised line of corduroy fabric.

warp – Lengthwise threads of woven fabric.

wearing ease – Extra fabric added to body measurements so clothing will be comfortable and you can move around in it.

weft – Crosswise threads of woven fabric; also called woof threads.

wing needle – Sometimes called a hemstitch needle, this needle has flat extensions or "wings" on each side that work with decorative stitches to create embroidered holes.

wrong side – The underside of fabric that faces the inside of a garment or project.

WST – Stands for Wrong Sides Together and refers to the way some fabrics are positioned for specific techniques such as French seams.

INDEX

A

accessories, 48, 57, 81
advertisements, 17, 23
aid societies, 19
appliqué, 28, 29, 31, 33, 35, 48,
61, 71, 75-8, 127, 142-5,
148,162,
project – Singing Canary Pillow,
178–181
project – Bugs in the Garden
Baby Book, 206–211
apron, 14, 30, 138,
project – Deep Pocket Chef's
Apron, 188–93
attaching single beads, 147
attaching strands of beads, 146
attachments, 25, 28
needle punch, 89, 154

B

backstitch, 63, 93, 99, 129, 140,
166, 190
balanced 4-thread overlock stitch,
86
balanced thread tension, 72
ballpoint, 61, 72–4, 94, 164
bamboo, 36
basting, 23, 44, 51, 61–2, 64, 75,
84, 86, 106, 116, 118, 155, 184,
188, 190–91, 208, 218
common, 62
diagonal, 62
removing, 32
slip, 62
spray, 46, 83, 148, 155, 167,
178, 184, 194, 212
thread, 75
beading, 127, 142, 146–7, 152,
154, 202, 204
needle, 61
beads, 32, 35, 77, 113–4,
couching strands of, 146–7
single, 146–7
beeswax, 60-2, 65
beginner, 6, 42, 156
project – Berry Pie Pincushion,
202–5
project – Bohemian Bag, 174–7
project – Deep Pocket Chef's
Apron, 188–93
project – Tropical Table Runner,
198-201
Bell, Emily, 12
Best Thread for Sewing Machines,
20
Bethlehem Female Seminary in
Bethlehem, 11–12
bias, 39, 40, 44, 51, 93, 97, 111,
121, 134–6, 156, 224
continuous, 128
bias binding, 75, 79, 128–9, 220
project – Deep Pocket Chef's
Apron, 188–93
bias facing, 102–3
blanket stitch appliqué, 70, 142–43
project – Bugs in the Garden
Baby Book, 206-211
blindstitch, 65, 88, 145
bobbin, 24–5, 69–70, 72–6, 83,
130, 133, 135, 154
bobbin case, 70, 81, 148
bobbin thread, 69–70, 72, 76, 83,

147–8, 156, 159
bobbinwork, 148, 152, 159
bolt, 38–40
box pleats, 137
burn test, fiber, 38
buttonhole placement, 43, 113–4
buttonhole stitch, 64
buttonhole twist, 65, 140
buttonholes, 11, 59. 60, 63, 76–9,
84, 98, 110, 115, 206, 208–9
beautiful, 79, 114
corded, 114
cutter, 34
delicate, 113
finished, 114
keyhole, 113
pattern symbol, 43
standard, 113
stretch, 113
buttons, 112–13, 115

C

canvas interfacings, 44
casings, 34, 61, 126
elastic, 106–7
stitched, 107
chain stitch looper, 86
chair, 53–4, 57
charity, 18
charts
common pattern symbols, 43
clothing construction standards,
98
fabric and needle size compatibility, 73
fabric measurement conversion,
38
fabric types, 37
fiber burn test, 38
hand sewing needles, 61
International fabric care symbols,
39
multiple needles, 74
needle size equivalents, 73
skill level, 31
specialty needles, 74
standard needles, 73
chenille needles, 61
Civil War, 16, 18–20
clapper, 48
closures, 112, 114–16, 118
clothing construction standards, 98
collars
flat, 104
rolled, 105
standing, 104
color-coded thread paths, 86
computerized machine embroidery,
82
computerized machines, 25, 27, 71,
80, 89
construction techniques, 7
buttons, sewing on, 112
buttonholes, 113–4
collar, convertible, 105
collar, flat, 104
collar, rolled, 105
collar, standing, 104
cuffs, buttoned, 110
cuffs, French, 110
darts, 99
facing, bias, 103
facing, cut-on, 102
facing, shaped, 102

hem, double needle, 111
hem, faced, 111
hem, narrow, 111
hem, shirttail, 111
hooks, sewing on, 112
loops, 115
pocket, in-seam, 101
pocket, patch, 100
seam finishes, 97
seams, knit fabric, 94
seams, serged, 95
seams, specialty, 96
seams, woven fabric, 93
sleeves, eased, 109
sleeves, kimono, 109
sleeves, puffed, 108
sleeves, raglan, 109
sleeves, set-in, 108
snaps, sewing on, 112
tabs, 115
ties, 115
waistband, 106
waistline, elastic, 107
zipper, center, 117
zipper, exposed, 118
zipper, invisible, 119
zipper, lapped, 118
zipper, separating, 119
corner
mitered, 129
seam, 93
serged, 87–8
couching, 76–7, 146–7, 150–52,
154
cover stitch, 86
craft projects
Bohemian Bag, 174–7
Berry Pie Pincushion, 202–5
Bugs in the Garden Baby Book,
206–11
crewel needles, 61
cuffs, buttoned, 110
cuffs, French, 110
curved seams, 48, 50, 62, 93–4
curves, 98, 101, 103–5, 108, 109,
111

D

decorative cords, 77, 148
decorative details, 7
bound edges, 128–9
double and triple needle,
130–131
gathering, 132–133
piping, 134–136
pleats, 137
ruffles, circular, 139
ruffles, gathered, 138
topstitching, 140
tucks, single needle, 141
decorative stitches, 46, 70–1, 74,
78–9, 138, 142–3, 145, 148,
153, 159, 166
decorative stitching, 29, 31, 46,
75–6, 84, 148, 152–3
decorative threads, 70, 75–7, 148,
150, 160
design ease, 41
design wall, 55
designs, embroidered, 82–3
project – Scrappy Cottage Quilt,
182–187
double binding, 129
double eye needle, 74

double needle hem, 111
double needle tucks, 149
double welt seam, 96
double wing needle, 74
drape, 36–7, 39, 44, 54, 94
dress form, 23, 40, 55
dress patterns, 15, 19

E

ease, 41, 108–9, 111, 122
ease stitching, 106, 108–9
edges
bias, 93
binding, 128
collar, 48
corded, 135
cut, 33
cutting, 34
decorative, 64
gathered, 50, 202
knife, 30
overcasting, 78
raw, 31
rolled, 86, 138, 169
scalloped, 33
edgestitch, 77, 97, 100, 103, 110,
115, 158
edge stitcher, 26
edgestitching, 79, 104, 107, 140
edgestitching ribbon, 158
edging, 86, 88
elastic, 23, 34, 61, 73–5, 78, 133
elastic thread gathering, 133
electric sewing machines, 25
embellishing garments, 20
embellishments, 7
appliqué, fused, 142–3
appliqué, non-fused, 144–5
beading, 146–7
bobbinwork, 148
couching, 150–1
crazy patch, 152
decorative stitching, 153
double needle tucks, 149
needle punch, 154
quilting, 155–7
ribbonwork, 158
silk ribbon embroidery, 159
thread sketching, 160
wing needlework, 161
embroidered quilt design, 186
embroidery, 15, 25, 53, 61, 74–8, 82
embroidery designs, 45–6, 82–3,
154, 167, 186
silk ribbon, 159
embroidery machines, 53, 82–3, 186
multi-needle, 89
Emporium of Fashion, 20
equipment, specialty, 88–9
exposed zipper, 118
extended arm sewing machines, 88

F

fabric
atypical, 163
calculating, 42
dense, 61
distorted, 39
draping, 36, 40
fabulous, 36, 38
felted, 154
measuring, 33
napped, 38
plaid, 170

preparing, 39
ribbon, 158
scrap, 11, 35, 49, 73
silicone-treated, 48
specialty, 163
stretch, 73–4
types, 37
fabric choices, 39
fabric collage, 167
fabric marker, 32, 64, 99,137
fabric markings, 51
fabric matches, 170
fabric measurement conversion, 38
fabric off-grain, 39
fabric painting, 174
fabric weights, 34, 76, 80
fabric width, 38
faced hem, 111
facing
  bias, 103
  facing, cut-on, 102
  facing, shaped, 102
fasteners, 23, 98, 112
felled seams, 96
fiber content, 38, 60
fibers, 36–8, 72–5, 154
  burn test, 38
  natural, 32, 36, 161
filler cord, 134–5
fit, 31, 40–3, 48, 50–1, 55, 57,
  76–7, 92–3, 106–8
fitting, 53–4, 62
flange, 134, 224
flatlock stitch, 85–86
fleece, 7, 42, 64, 164
floss, 61, 63, 65, 81, 202
flounces, 23, 139
foot
  all-purpose, 76–7, 100, 114–5,
   152, 155, 164
  appliqué, 78, 143–8
  attaching, 77
  bare 147–8
  bottom of sole, 77
  button sew-on, 112
  buttonhole, 113–14
  clear, 144, 153
  cording, 135
  couching, 146
  edge, 140
  edgestitch, 76, 101, 103, 107,
   141, 158
  embroidery 78
  free-motion, 155, 174, 178
  gathering, 133
  generic, 77
  guides, 77, 92, 103, 107
  hemmer, 138–9
  inner toe, 143
  invisible zipper, 119
  lifter, 70
  piping, 135
  purpose, 76
  serger, 85–88, 115
  straight stitch, 140, 169
  Teflon, 174
  top of sole, 77
  up position, 81
  walking, 94, 155, 164–5, 170
  without, 74, 112, 146–7
  zipper, 76, 107, 117–19, 135
foot control, 48, 69–70, 147
foot pressure, 79, 164
form stitches, 76

formats, embroidery, 82
fray, 64, 144–5
frayed buttonholes, 63–4
fraying, 74
free-motion stitching, 31, 46,
  69–70, 74, 83, 154–7, 160
French seams, 96
functional stitches, 78
fur, 31, 79, 165
  fake, 165
  trims, 16
furniture, 36, 54, 80
fuse, 44, 64, 106, 143, 178, 206,
fusible interfacing, 44–45, 164
fusible web, paper-backed, 143,
  178, 206,
fusibles, 44–5, 48

G
garment, 6, 10–12, 28, 39–44,
  50–1, 54–5, 59, 62–5, 92–3, 95,
  91–119
  custom, 64
  custom-made, 79
  knit, 92
  men's, 113
  practice patterns, small-scale,
   120–124
  ready-made, 64, 83
  women's, 113
garment applications, 93
garment edge, 103
garment fabric, 91
garment front, 101
garment hang, 93
garment industry techniques, 88
garment patterns, 40–1
  commercial, 92, 99
garment pieces, 96
garment projects
  Gypsy Shrug, 194–7
  Let it Rain Yellow Slicker, 212–15
  Ruffled Wedge Skirt, 220–23
  Square Yoke Blouse, 216–19
garment seams, 45
gathering, 78, 85, 108, 132–3
gathers, 50, 98, 106–8, 132–3, 138,
  191, 202, 222
Gibbs Sewing Machine Company, 24
Godey's Lady's Book, 10–11, 13, 19
googly eyes, 207
  project – Bugs in the Garden
   Baby Book, 206–11
gores, 220, 222
  project – Ruffled Wedge Skirt,
   200–203
grade, 30, 94, 106, 110, 176
grain, 37, 39, 42–4, 85, 98, 106,
  120, 128, 134–5, 141, 156
grain lines, 39, 43
grid quilting, 155–6
Grover, 23–4
guard, presser foot/needle, 154
guide 11, 18, 35, 43, 61, 77, 84–5,
  92, 94, 100, 103, 131, 140, 143,
  149
guide sheets, 42–3
  folded, 43

H
ham, 48, 51
  tailor's, 48, 50, 93
hand sewn seams, 63
handwheel, 69, 85, 131

hankies, 194, 197
  project – Gypsy Shrug, 194–194
heavy darning needles, 61
hems
  hand stitched, 65
  machine stitched, 111
hemp, 36–7
high sheen thread, 75
history of sewing, 10–25
holes
  decorative, 161
  embroidered, 74, 161
  repairing, 63
home decor, 29
home dec projects
  Garden Party Lap Quilt, 224–29
  Scrappy Cottage Quilt, 182–7
  Singing Canary Pillow, 178–181
  Tropical Table Runner, 198–201
home embroidery machines, 82, 89
Homework Sampler, 11–12
hook system, 69–70, 81
hoop projects, 83
hooping, 82–3, 226
Howe, Elias, 21, 23–4

I
in-seam pockets, 101
Industrial Revolution, 15
interfacing
  fusible, 44–5
  non-woven, 44–5
  sew-in, 44–5
  tricot, 44–5
  woven, 44–5
inverted pleat, 137
invisible zipper, 116, 119
iron, 14, 23, 45, 47–50, 53–4, 75,
  103, 119, 143, 166
ironing, 47, 53
ironing board, 48, 50, 53, 103

J
jackets, 31, 37, 41, 44, 61, 63, 83,
  108, 113, 120, 137, 141, 154,
  159–60, 165
  project – Gypsy Shrug, 195–97
  project – Let it Rain Yellow
   Slicker, 212–15
  small-scale practice patterns,
   121–23
Jacquard fabric, 37
jeans double needle, 74

K
keyhole, 113
knife pleats, 137
knits, 31, 36–8, 44, 46, 61, 72–4,
  85–6, 94, 96, 111, 113–14, 164,
  171
knit hem, 111
knives, serger, 85
knot, 62, 64, 72, 87–8, 99, 132,
  166, 176

L
labels, 40, 42, 46, 57
lace fabrics, 44
large darning-needles, 22
layout, 42–3, 53, 220
  napped, 31, 42, 165–6, 170
  with nap, 220, 223
leather, 31, 33, 60, 74, 166
leather needles, 61, 166

leisure, 17–18, 23, 40
lengthwise grain, 37, 39, 43, 106,
  120, 128, 141
lettering, 82
letters, 40, 72, 83
Library Company of Philadelphia,
  10–13, 19, 21, 24
lightweight thread, 144
linen, 31, 36–7, 48
lingerie, 37, 76
lining, 16, 37, 40, 43, 62, 65, 91,
  98, 100, 174, 176, 212, 214
lint, 35, 70, 75, 81
lock stitch, 23, 63
  ingenious, 10
looper threader, 60
loopers, 25, 84, 86
loops, 37–8, 63, 70, 72–3, 85, 115
Lycra 73–4

M
machine
  basic, 76, 78
  blind hemming, 67
  blindstitch, 88
  combination, 82
  compact, 24
  companion 53
  computer-controlled, 25
  electric lock-stitch, 25
  electronic, 25
  heavy duty, 88
  hemstitching, 25
  household, 88
  knitting, 15
  longarm quilting, 88–9
  mechanical, 71
  multiple-needle, 54, 67
  needle punch, 67, 89
  perfect, 79
  single, 82
  specialized, 89
  specialty, 84
  top-of-the-line, 71
  unthreaded, 81
machine anatomy, 69
machine embroidery designs, 83,
  154
machine embroidery hoops, 83, 160
  wooden, 157
machine motor, 157
man-made fabrics, 36
markers, 27, 32, 57, 114, 137
markings, 32, 35, 43, 70, 92, 99,
  108, 114
McClun, Diana, 47, 52–5, 57
measurements, 41, 43, 55, 74, 92,
  106, 108
mercerized cotton thread, 60, 75
metal, 16, 33, 38, 57, 60, 75–6,
  85, 112, 117
metallic, 37, 72, 74, 80
metallic double needle, 74
metallic thread lightweight, 37
miter, 129
mitt, 48
monofilament thread, 31, 75, 135,
  143–5, 155–7, 165
multiple needle stitching, 130–31

N
nap, 37, 42, 49, 166, 223
narrow cord, 132, 134–6, 149
narrow flatlock stitch, 86

index

narrow hem, 111
narrow ribbon, 32, 35, 49, 131, 158–9
necklines, 44, 93, 98, 102–5
needle, 9–11, 22–3, 59–65, 69–70, 72–7, 79–81, 84–9, 92–4
  all-purpose, 73
  ballpoint, 164
  barbed, 89, 154
  bare, 146-7
  doll, 202, 204
  double, 74, 111, 130–1, 149, 158
  double/triple, 130–1
  hand, 34
  hand beading, 202, 204
  hand sewing, 60–1
  hand tapestry, 87
  hemstitch, 74
  large, 76
  large eye, 159
  left, 86
  long thin, 61
  multiple, 74, 86, 130–1
  right, 86
  specialty, 61, 74
  spring, 74, 160
  standard, 73–4
  stretch, 94
  strong, 73–4
  tapestry, 61
  thick, 61
  threaded, 9, 64
  titanium-coated, 74
  topstitching, 140, 168
  triple, 74, 78, 130, 140
  universal, 85
  wing, 74, 161
needle bar, 69
Needle Grabbers, 60
needle plate, 70
needle position, 69, 71, 79, 92, 135, 140, 143
  multiple, 79
needle,
  punch, 154
  punching, 154
needle size, 72–3
  compatibility, 73
  equivalents, 73
needle stop down, 93
needle tension, 70, 72, 83, 132, 149
  loosened, 75
needle threaders, 60
  automatic, 70
needle threading, 15, 62
Needlecraft, 14, 18
NeedleCraft Magazine, 16
needlework, 6, 13, 15, 20, 23
  decorative, 10
  ornamental, 11
  plain, 10–12
  sale of, 19
  wing, 161
needlework education, 11
  vocational, 13
Needlework Sampler, 10
new machine, 79–81
non-woven fabric, 37
notches, 43, 93, 94, 96, 108–9, 170
nylon, 36-7, 44, 75

O
off-grain, 39
oil, 36, 81

organdy, 37, 73, 167, 169
ornamental stitches, 78
outline quilt designs, 182, 186
  project – Scrappy Cottage Quilt, 182–7
overcast, 85–6
overcasting, 84
overlock seam, 94–5
overlock stitches, 78, 94
oversewn edges, 97

P
Peter Pan collar, 104
pants, 98, 106–7
paper patterns, 32–3, 43, 120
  tinted tissue, 20
  tissue, 20, 43
parallel, 43, 62, 96, 98140, 158
  stitched, 140
parallel rows, 92
parallel stitching, 74, 140
patch pockets, 98, 100
patches
  crazy, 152
  decorative, 171
patchwork quilt patterns, 92
patent, 20, 24
pattern companies, 40
  independent, 40
  large, 40
pattern envelope, 40–1, 43
pattern instructions, 57, 102, 110
pattern markings, 42
pattern pieces, 9, 30–2, 35, 42–3, 102, 120–5
  flat, 41
  tissue paper, 42, 168
pattern software, 43
pattern waistband, 106
patterns, 10–11, 19–20, 30–3, 38–40, 42–3, 62, 64
  all-over, 31, 37, 153, 226
  children's, 40
  commercial, 114
  decorative, 78, 159
  half, 71
  match, 170
  patchwork, 39, 153
  plaid, 170
  single, 20
  small-scale, 120-5
  versatile, 222
Peterson's Magazine, 11, 13, 19
piecing, 77, 152, 182, 198, 202, 224
piecing patchwork patterns, 74
pile, 15, 31, 37, 46, 49, 164
pin money, 21
pincushion, 14, 32, 60, 65
  project – Berry Pie Pincushion, 202–5
pins, 14, 21–3, 32–3, 43, 51, 54–5, 57, 60, 62–3, 93
  needleboard, 49
  safety, 65, 155
  spool, 130
  straight, 32, 60, 164–5
pintucks, 74, 149
piping, 77, 134 –6, 178–81
  corded, 134
  cordless, 134
  double, 136
placemats, 87, 128, 155, 200
placement lines, 137
placket, 98, 110, 113

plaids, 31, 39, 42, 98, 170
pleated skirt, practice pattern, 125
pleats
  box, 137
  inverted, 137
  knife, 137
pocket, 63, 98
  edgestitch, 100
  in-seam, 101
  patch, lined, 100
  patch, unlined, 100
  project – Deep Pocket Chef's Apron, 188–193
pocket edges, 100
pocket pieces, 101
pocket placement, 43, 188
point presser, 50
point presser/clapper, 48
polyester, 31–2, 36–7, 44, 60, 75
  coils, 117
  thread, 153, 158, 164, 168
press cloth, 48–9
pressing techniques, 49–51
presser foot, 24, 34, 127
  all-purpose, 76–7, 100, 114–5, 152, 155, 164
  appliqué, 78, 143–8
  attaching, 77
  bare, 147–8
  bottom of sole, 77
  button sew-on, 112
  buttonhole, 113–14
  clear, 144, 153
  cording, 135
  couching, 146
  edge, 140
  edgestitch, 76, 101, 103, 107, 141, 158
  embroidery, 78
  free-motion, 155, 174, 178
  gathering, 133
  generic, 77
  guides, 77, 92, 103, 107
  hemmer, 138–9
  inner toe, 143
  invisible zipper, 119
  lifter, 70
  piping, 135
  purpose, 76
  serger, 85–88, 115
  straight stitch, 140, 169
  Teflon, 174
  top of sole, 77
  up position, 81
  walking, 94, 155, 164–5, 170
  without, 74, 112, 146–7
  zipper, 76, 107, 117–19, 135
pressing ham, 48, 50–1, 99, 105, 108–9
pressure, 37, 45, 48–9, 62, 94, 169
  applying, 47
projects
  Berry Pie Pincushion, 202–5
  Bohemian Bag, 174–7
  Bugs in the Garden Baby Book, 206–11
  Deep Pocket Chef's Apron, 188–193
  Garden Party Lap Quilt, 224–29
  Gypsy Shrug, 194-7
  Let it Rain Yellow Slicker, 212–15
  Ruffled Wedge Skirt, 220–23
  Scrappy Cottage Quilt, 182–7
  Singing Canary Pillow, 178–181

  Square Yoke Blouse, 216–19
  Tropical Table Runner, 198-201
pull-on skirt, practice pattern, 125
pulled thread line, 39
punch, needle, 154

Q
Quaker City Sewing Machine, 24
quilting
  free-motion, 31, 46, 83, 156–7
  machine-fed, 155
quilting designs, 155–7
  outline, 182, 186
  project – Garden Party Lap Quilt, 224–29
  project – Scrappy Cottage Quilt, 182–7
quilting frame, 67, 88
quilting needle, 74

R
ribbon, 35, 49, 61, 77, 131, 158–9
ribbonwork, 158
rotary cutter, 27, 33
roving, 154
ruffles, 23, 30, 33, 220, 222
  double-edged, 132
  double layer, 132
  gathered, 132–3
rulers, 33
running stitch, 62, 65

S
samplers, 10–11
Scientific American, 19, 23–4
scissors, 14, 23, 32, 43, 65, 85, 126
seam allowances, 49–51, 92–7, 100–6, 108–11, 114–15, 118, 120, 126–7, 132–9, 164–6, 168–70
seam finishes, 92, 94, 96–7
seam gauge, 60–1
seam guide, 92, 140
seam roll, 48, 50–1, 109
seam sealant, 87, 112, 114
seams
  basted, 62, 118, 190
  common, 91
  corner, 93
  diagonal, 109, 128, 228
  enclosed, 50, 93, 96
  finishing, 50, 84, 97
  flat, 50
  flat-felled, 96
  flatten, 48
  gathered, 50
  narrow, 48, 95, 169
  neckline, 102–5
  permanent, 96
  plain, 96
  princess, 93
  serged, 86, 95
  shoulder, 103, 108–9
  specialty, 96
  stitched, 96
  strong, 95
  trimming, 23
  waistline, 99, 106–7, 170
selvages, 38–9, 42–4
separating zippers, 116–17, 119, 212
serged edges, 87, 97
  project – Bugs in the Garden Baby Book, 206–11
serged tube, 115

serger chain, 151
serger looper threader, 151
serger seams, 95
  basic, 95
serger stitches, 84–7, 95
  flat, 85
serger techniques, basic, 87
serger thread, 84, 206
serging, 53, 60, 67, 84–6, 94–5, 97, 115, 138, 151, 169
sew buttons, 112, 212
sew-in interfacing, 45
sewing bias-cut seams, 93
sewing computers, 71, 82
sewing fleece, 164
sewing fur, 165
sewing knits, 31, 36–8, 44, 46, 61, 72–4, 85–6, 94, 96, 111, 113–14, 164, 171
sewing leather, 166
Sewing Machine Combination, 24
sewing machine needles
  multiple, 73
  sizing, 72
  specialty, 73
  standard, 72
sewing machine technology, 25
sewing machines, 7, 10, 12–15, 17–20, 22–5, 46–7, 52–4, 59–61, 67–72, 74–6, 78–86, 89, 94, 151
  computerized, 54
  earliest, 16
  family, 23
  free arm, 107
  industrial, 88
  mechanical, 70
  semi-industrial, 88
sewing paper, 167
sewing plastic, 168
sewing room, 7, 35, 47, 52–5, 57
sewing sheer fabric, 169
sewing space, 54, 57
sewing supplies, 7, 32, 42, 57
shank, 64, 72, 74, 77, 112–3
sharp needle, 62
sharps, 22, 61
shears, 23, 32
sheer fabrics, 33, 44, 79, 95–6, 103, 111, 46, 86, 169
shirttail hem, 111
Shrimpton's Brass Pins, 22
shuttle, 24–5, 70
silk ribbon embroidery, 159
Singer Manufacturing Company, 20, 23–5
Singer Sewing Machines, 24
single ruffles, 138
sleeve
  kimono, 108–9
  puffed, 108
  raglan, 109
  set-in, 108-9, 120
  smooth eased, 108
sleeve cap, 108
slipstitch, 63
slit, 51, 64, 87
small-scale practice patterns
  blouse, 124
  jacket, 122-3
  kimono top, 121
  pleated skirt, 125
  pull-on skirt, 125
  raglan top, 121

smooth seams, 94
spools, 23–4, 57, 62, 65, 69, 75, 130–1, 151
square corners, 98
stabilizer, 44–6, 83, 114, 131, 142, 144–5, 148, 152–3, 158–60, 167–8
staystitching, 93, 137
stitch, 49–50, 61–5, 69–79, 82–8
  3-thread, 86, 95
  4-thread, 86, 95
  balanced, 72, 76, 97, 156
  open decorative, 167
  pintuck, 11
  stipple, 157
  satin, 78, 145
  serpentine, 78
  stretch, 78, 94
stitch and flip method, 152
stitch attributes, 79
stitch book, 78–9
stitch finger, 87
stitch formations, 72, 85
stitch-in-the-ditch, 102–3, 106, 155
stitch length, 69, 79, 85, 98
stitch regulator, 155
stitch width, 79
stitch-o-logy, 78
stitching
  blind, 79
  double needle, 86, 130–1
  free-motion, 31, 46, 69–70, 74, 83, 154–7, 160
  hand, 60–5
  saddle, 59
  satin, 144–5
  snaps, 112
  straight, 98, 140, 144–5
  triple needle, 86, 130–1
  utilitarian, 23
  wing needle, 161
straight seams, 49
  plain seams, 93
straight stitch, 70–2, 86, 92, 94–5, 135, 1430, 145, 150, 159, 160, 164, 166
  long, 132
  regular, 100–1, 111
straight stitch foot, 167
stray threads, removing, 35
stretch double needle, 74
supplies, 14, 23, 32-35, 57, 73
  hand sewing, 60–1
symbols, common pattern, 43
synthetics, 31, 36–7, 161

T
table, cutting, 14, 48, 52–3
tabs, 115
tape measures, 32, 60–1, 65
task lighting, 54
Teflon-coated presser foot
  project – Bohemian Bag, 174–7
  project – Let it Rain Yellow Slicker, 212–15
telescoping thread guide, 85
tension, 22, 24, 70, 72–3, 76, 80–1, 113, 131–2, 148–9
  serger, 84–6, 95
tension discs, upper thread, 81
thimbles, 14, 22, 60–1, 65
thread
  all-purpose, 75
  basting, 51

elastic, 75, 133
  fusible, 75
  invisible, 31, 75, 150
  long staple, 75
  looper, 86
  lower, 70, 72, 76
  metallic, 31, 74, 131, 153
  monofilament, 75, 145
  polyester embroidery, 75, 152, 160
  silk, 60
  single, 24
  specialty, 75
  spun, 15, 22
  topstitching, 64, 81, 140
  upper, 72
  variegated, 144
thread fibers, 60
thread guides, 25, 84–5
thread lines, 62
thread painting, 29, 31, 74
thread path, 128
thread selection, 75
thread shank, 64, 112
thread sketching, 160
  project – Singing Canary Pillow, 178–181
thread snips, 34, 60, 65
thread tails, 64–5, 87
thread topstitching, 140
thread weights, 76
threader, dental floss, 151
threading, 61–2, 74, 85
  couching foot, 151
  multiple needle, 130–1
  slotted, 70
tips
  beading, 146
  bobbinwork, 148
  button sew on, 112
  buttonholes, 114
  couching, 151
  decorative stitching, 153
  dart, 98
  facing, 103
  free motion stitching, 157
  fused appliqué, 144
  in-seam pocket, 101
  knit, 94
  know your machine, 70
  multiple needle, 131
  needle punch, 154
  non-fused appliqué, 144
  paper pattern, 43
  patch pocket, 101
  piecing, 182
  pintuck, 149
  piping, 136
  pressing, 51
  quilting, 156
  ribbonwork, 158
  rolled collar, 105
  seaming and finishing, 96
  serger learning, 86
  shopping, 80
  simple binding, 128
  single needle tuck, 141
  sleeve, 108
  stabilizer, 46
  threading, 62
  topstitching, 140
  waistband, 106
  wing needlework, 161
  zipper, 117
toppings, 45–6

topstitch, 65, 74, 96, 110–11, 140
topstitching, 63, 74–6, 80, 84, 92, 96, 100, 103, 106, 140, 164
touch screen, 25, 69–70
trade cards, 18, 21
transfer pattern markings, 64
triangular work pattern, 53
tube, 34–5, 115
tucks
  double needle, 149
  narrow, 141
  single needle, 141
tweezers, 34, 38, 62, 146–7, 159
twisted loop-stitch, 24

U
underarm, 98, 102, 108–9
underlap, 98, 106
understitch, 98, 102–5
universal double needle, 74
universal needle 73, 94, 164–5, 168
universal triple needle, 74
upholstery, 37–8, 61, 73
upper collar, 104–5

V
Victorian era, 150
vinyl, 61, 168

W
waistband, 44, 98, 106–7, 117
Wheeler, 20, 23–4
Wilcox and Gibbs Sewing Machine, 25
Wilson's Sewing Machines, 20
work triangle, 53
workbasket, 21–3
workspace, 53

Y
yarn darners, 61
yarns, 37, 77, 148, 150–1, 154

Z
zigzag, 25, 33, 70, 78, 94, 108–9, 112–3, 117, 132–3, 135, 145, 147, 158, 164–5, 172, 190–1, 197, 208, 210, 218
zigzag machine, 25
  electric free arm, 25
zipper
  zipper, center, 117
  zipper components, 117
  zipper, exposed, 118
  zipper foot, 76, 107, 117–19, 135
  zipper, invisible, 119
  zipper, lapped, 118
  zipper, separating, 119
  zipper types, 116

Index created with:
TExtract / www.Texyz.com

CONTRIBUTERS

Susan Beck
Susan has loved creating with fabric, needle and thread since she was a young child and holds a bachelor's degree in textiles and clothing and a master's degree in design. Susan has worked in the sewing industry as an educator, writer, and editor for a European sewing machine company for 22 years and is always planning her next sewing project.
sewspeak@gmail.com

Salley Bowman
Salley is a wife and mother of the "two silliest kids she's ever met." She loves to be creative and learned to sew in her early twenties.
salleygoose
http://salleygoose.blogspot.com/

Sarah Goodman
Sarah is a self-taught stitcher with a great eye for detail who's not afraid to try new techniques. A wife and mom of two, she loves to create and spends her spare time sewing projects for friends and family.
sarahjanegoodies.etsy.com

Jo Leichte
Jo has been sewing since she was 10 years old and enjoys all types of sewing including garment-making, quilting, crafts, and home dec. She is Education Editor for Bernina of America, Inc. where she edits *Through the Needle* magazine and blogs at www.berninaUSAblog.com. She lives in the North Carolina mountains.
jpleichte@netzero.com
Black Mountain, NC

April Oliveira-Ward
April started sewing in a 4-H sewing project in the sixth grade. A career in fashion design followed. Later, April fell in love with quilting and uses her precision sewing and great eye for color to create projects with unique fabric and print combinations.
april.ann.ward@gmail.com
Lafayette, CA

Vicki Tracy
Vicki graduated from Texas Tech University with a degree in Fashion Design and has owned the Bernina Sewing Studio in Lubbock, Texas since 1981. Vickitricks Design is a small division of her business featuring pattern and embroidery designing, freelance teaching, and writing. Vicki is always looking for off-beat and unusual sewing, embroidery, and embellishment techniques and teaching them is her passion.
vtracy@oesd.com
www.vickitricksdesign.com
2513 Purdue
Lubbock, Texas 79415

FEATURED PATTERNS

Pages 28, 108, 113, and 137: Zigzag Shirt, The Sewing Workshop, www.sewingworkshop.com

Pages 28 and 113: Mimosa Top, The Sewing Workshop, www.sewingworkshop.com

Page 29: Original design, Vicki Tracy

Pages 66–67: Original design, Vicki Tracy

Page 104: Liberty Shirt, The Sewing Workshop, www.sewingworkshop.com

Pages 105, 109, and 140: Bells and Whistles Shirt, The Sewing Workshop, www.sewingworkshop.com

Page 115: Original design, Vicki Tracy

Page 115: Veronica Pocketbook, Lazy Girl, www.lazygirldesigns.com

Pages 126–127: Original design, Vicki Tracy

Page 128: Get A Grip, Vickitricks Designs

Page 138: Flirty Skirty Apron, theapronlady@gmail.com, designed by Jan Lutz, made by Donna Lang

Page 142: Original design, Belinda Gibson

Page 147: Original design, Vicki Tracy

Page 171: Petal dress and hat pattern by Sewbaby, made by Donna Lang.
www.sewbaby.com